BANANA FALLOUT

CLASS, COLOR, AND
CULTURE AMONG WEST INDIANS
IN COSTA RICA

Afro-American Culture and Society Series

Volume 12

BANANA FALLOUT

CLASS, COLOR, AND
CULTURE AMONG WEST INDIANS
IN COSTA RICA

by

Trevor W. Purcell

foreword by R.S. Bryce-Laporte

Center for Afro-American Studies
University of California, Los Angeles

Library of Congress Cataloging-in-Publication Data

Purcell, Trevor W.
      Banana fallout : class, color, and culture among West Indians in
Costa Rica / Trevor W. Purcell.
            p. cm. -- (Afro-American culture and society, ISSN 0882-5297 ; v.
12)
            Includes bibliographical references and index.
            ISBN 0-934934-37-1 (pbk.)
1. West Indians--Costa Rica--Limón (Province)--Social conditions.
2. Blacks--Costa Rica--Limón (Province)--Social conditions.
3. Limón (Costa Rica : Province)--Race relations.
I. Title
II. Series
F1549.L55P87 1993   93-18874
972.86'1--dc20   CIP

Center for Afro-American Studies Publications
University of California, Los Angeles 90024

©1993 by The Regents of the University of California.

Library of Congress Catalog Card Number:
ISBN: 0-934934-37-1 (pbk)
ISSN: 0882:5297

Cover art by Franceska Schiffrin
Cover design by Westwork Design
Text typography by Ross D. Steiner

To my mother, who never graduated elementary

school but who intuitively behaves

as if she is a college graduate;

and to my father, a brilliant man whose illiteracy

is testimony of our collective struggle.

—T.W.P.

CONTENTS

TABLES

ILLUSTRATIONS

FOREWORD

BY R. S. BRYCE-LAPORTE

he purpose of this introductory comment is to invite the reader to participate in a vicarious journey to a subregion and its people, both too little studied and very little understood until lately. It is an invitation to share the personal meaning that the book holds for me, a person with roots in the region and one of the earliest insiders to speak in social scientific terms about its reality. It is an attempt to share the enthusiasm I feel as a senior colleague who has collaborated quite closely in the past with this younger author—a brother—as I witness the culmination of his efforts as represented in the pages of *Banana Fallout*, a new benchmark toward the fuller understanding of West Indian sociocultural complexity in Costa Rica, Central America.

The geographer, James Parsons, speaks of a configuration of countries, and in some cases really parts of countries, as the Western Caribbean. It is comprised of the offshore islands located west of the Greater Antilles and the Caribbean rimland of the Middle American area, including some extensions into the interior, across the mainland, and onto the Pacific coast. At first either abandoned or sparsely inhabited by the indigenous population; never settled seriously or extensively by its colonial peoples; and, even in recent times, home to very limited numbers of Europeans and Asians, the area has been characterized since post-Columbian times by the unusual demographic and cultural presence of Black settlements of non-Hispanic origins in the midst of essentially Spanish-American countries.

As part of the expeditions pursued by the Spanish conquistadors in their efforts to establish early colonial settlements in lower Central America from its Pacific Coast, some Africans did enter the isthmus as part of the slave trade via Mexico or after crossing Honduras or Panama. Today traces of their presence continue to be recognized in such places as Guanacaste on the western coast of Costa Rica, among people of mixed ancestry and significant Hispanic acculturation. However, the Black concentrations in Central America are more heavily pronounced along its Atlantic Coast and tend to involve people of non-Hispanic tradition and direct or indirect Caribbean origins, including those coming from the offshore islands of Colombia, Nicaragua, and Honduras. Hence, while the combined number of colonial Blacks and mulattoes totaled less than 10,000 at the beginning of the nineteenth century in Costa Rica, "Jamaicans" alone numbered over 17,000 in the 1920s.

This group of overseas West Indians, which constitutes the principal focus of *Banana Fallout*, is referred to in the anthropological literature as Afro-Antillean Blacks, thereby distinguishing them from the other groups of Blacks mentioned above, as well as the occasional and limited (U.S.) Afro-American presence in the larger subregion. Purcell's focus on the Afro-Antillean segment of the Costa Rican Black population is significant for many reasons, some of them quite timely to share with the reader in introducing his text.

To begin, together with those countries comprising the southernmost coast of South America (i.e., Argentina, Chile, and Uruguay), modern Costa Rica has been publicly regarded as a "white" country, in contrast to the rest of Latin America. Its general demographics and predominant culture reinforce the image of Costa Rica as not only European but more particularly as the most Caucasian, Castilian, and Catholic country in Central America. From that perspective, not only does its Black population in general constitute a historical and demographic minority, but the Atlantic Coast home of that subpopulation's West Indian core represents a cultural anomaly among Costa Rican provinces.

Yet, in terms of my own personal experience, Black Costa Ricans were not unusual. As a child growing up in one of the West Indian barrios of Panama City, my earliest acquaintances with and images of Costa Ricans involved not whites or *mestizos* but Blacks. For all purposes, my earliest impression was that Costa Ricans were another group of Black West Indian people who had come to Panama—like St. Lucians, Dominicans, Jamaicans, or Barbadians—but who could speak some Spanish mixed with English or a lot of English mixed with some Spanish, yet they spoke in a "funny" way (meaning differently) compared to most of us on the Pacific side of Panama. When I was that age, in the 1930s, Costa Rica was for me some country near Panama that Black Panamanian West Indian people visited.

During World War II, thousands of Central American and West Indian men came to Panama to provide labor for the building and maintenance of the canal and to update the country's military installations. These workers were housed in special quarters in the nonwhite communities of the Zone, commmunities such as ours. Among them were Costa Ricans, some of whom were Black, spoke English, and were mostly Protestants; many others were "Spanish"— meaning white or mestizo, Hispanicized, and mostly Catholics. There seemed to be few Costa Ricans who reflected mixtures between the two groups, nor did the two groups seem to mix socially in Panama. To us, at the time, it almost seemed as if there were two types of Costa Ricans or people from two different parts of Costa Rica or two different Costa Ricas.

I later discussed my emerging interest in the comparative history of Central America with one of my professors at the University of Nebraska in the early 1960s, and he introduced me to an emergent graduate program in Caribbean Studies for Latin American students at the University of Puerto Rico. There it became clear through my studies that our situation in Panama, and the situation of Panama itself, were not so unique compared to other societies of the Caribbean rimland, such as Costa Rica, as we tended to believe. Rather, we were all part of a secondary Black diaspora, this time from islands to isthmus, as free immigrant labor rather than slaves, and in the service of Americans not Europeans—but, whatever, still Blacks under whites. And our nations, whether "independent" or "colonial," were minor, subordinate, and often dependent components of a larger regional arena controlled and coveted by powerful metropolitan states, which have been competing with each other for successive domination of the region for five hundred years.

I would conclude, therefore, that notwithstanding peculiar differences among us, we West Indians of Panama, Central America, and the archipelago, were culturally and historically one basic people—one "fambily" in creole parlance. But, as a consequence of the particular fragmentation and transplantation suffered since the middle of the past century, we have been experiencing an array of sociocultural dislocations, discontinuities, and destructions, all associated with prolonged massive migration and sustained foreign domination; and also an array of relocations, continuities, and reconstructions as part of our resettlement and readjustment history. So I began to ask of myself questions—as an insider—about commonalities, continuities, change, and linkages among us as a people and about the future of our place and role within (and beyond) the subregion. Armed with the anthropological concepts of the Caribbean cultural area or sphere by Mintz and Wagley, respectively, and the geographical writings of Augelli, West, and Parsons, I came to visualize Limón, then, not so much as an anomaly among Costa Rican provinces but as a normal component of the Caribbean littoral of the Middle American mainland. Most specifically, it was Parson's observation (1954, 13) that "a feeling of kinship and community of interest which still stretches from Belice and Kingston to Bocas del Toro and Colon" which would provide me with the most compelling reason to study Limón, Costa Rica. And it was the fortuituous influence of his colleague, James Blaut, as the director of the program, which would lead me to choose New Sligoville, "the most Jamaican village in Limón, Costa Rica" according to him, as an appropriate site for my field study and thesis preparation.

As late as the 1960s, no intensive, much less comprehensive, social scientific work had been done on the Limón province and its Black people or villages—even by an insider. Hence, even while I was completing my thesis, I already saw quite clearly that in the New Sligoville study I had struck upon a crucial area for consideration in any comprehensive appreciation of the larger Black Diaspora and the postslavery history of our domination, transplantation, and reconstruction as Afro-Caribbean people in Central America. Given the blatant dearth of other than secondary materials or indirect historical comments at the time on West Indian presence in the general Central American rimland area and specifically Costa Rica, my thesis, "Social Relations and Cultural Persistence (or Change) Among Jamaicans in a Rural Area of Costa Rica," has come to serve, even though unpublished in its entirety, as a seminal piece on the study of West Indians in Limón, Costa Rica (Bryce-Laporte 1962; Bryce-Laporte 1973, 65–94; see also Bozolli de Wille 1972, 215–31 and Duncan 1972, 230–31). I was convinced that I should return there to conduct further research for a doctoral dissertation or postdoctoral publications. For several reasons, neither was done, but the idea, the sense of calling, was never dismissed. Rather it was postponed, projected, and pursued in other roles, situations, and forms—in a way exemplary of the "pragmatic flexibility" that Purcell and his classmate, Val Carnegie (1983), have discussed as a prevailing feature of West Indian immigrant culture and socialization. Hence, when I founded the Research Institute on Immigration and Ethnic Studies at the Smithsonian in the early 1970s, I decided that among its quieter objectives would be to seek out and support trained Central American- or West Indian-born students residing in the United States to further the kind of research I had started on the study of the rimland area and our people, who by then were beginning to figure among the new waves of immigrants entering the United States.

After some unsuccessful earlier efforts, I was fortunate to be invited by Professor Sidney Mintz, by then of Johns Hopkins University, to help prepare Trevor Purcell, our author, for fieldwork in Central America. Purcell was young, bright, and well-trained; he shared with me mentors and colleagues of an earlier day and, in fact, at one point would become my neighbor. But also, Purcell was a Black Jamaican of rural background—a brother, an insider! Thus, I hoped and felt he would bring with him to the task a special insight, identification, and inspiration, to couple with his ethnographic training.

We began to work together, including readings of my work and other pieces on Costa Rica and Central America, but my hopes that I would accompany him to the field were not fulfilled. Nevertheless, aside from supporting directly or indirectly his subsequent fieldwork and taking part in his dissertation defense, I was later able to draw upon his expertise in a collaboration on a comparative-historical-sociological paper for the African Diaspora Studies Institute held at Howard University in Washington, D.C. That paper, entitled "A Lesser-Known Chapter of the African Diaspora: West Indians in Costa Rica, Central America" (Bryce-Laporte and Purcell 1982) constitutes a much-referred-to chapter of Joseph E. Harris's *Global Dimensions of the African Diaspora.*

Intended as a whole to specify the fate of Black labor following the abandonment of the plantation system by U.S. capital in Limón, the paper includes a section on the incorporation of Afro-Costa Ricans into the national society, which was Purcell's particular contribution. There, in analyzing the historically important 1978 conference held in San José on the situation of Blacks in Costa Rica, he wrote:

Clearly the two strata of blacks view the problem and its solution in distinct ways, based on the aspect that seems to affect them most. The black elite, though positing the problem as one pertaining to all blacks, and seeking support accordingly, have conceptualized in a manner which highlights those aspects affecting their lives: identity and discriminatory stereotypes. Exposure to dominant values and social mobility have rendered these aspects of racial discrimination more problematic for them. Poor blacks, on the other hand, not yet exposed to the collision of consciousness inherent in the discrepancies and conflict in social mobility, and the frustration arising from unrealized expectations, see their plight as resting on the absence of the concrete means to satisfy their daily needs as blacks in a white-dominated society. Examination of the Costa Rican core suggests the emergence of a new form of race relations intimately tied to the nature of development as well as the structure of the society as a whole. With the destruction of the old plantation structure which managed to sustain racial separation while providing basic conomic support, Afro-Costa Ricans have become dependent on the main structure of a society wherein their life chances rest on competition, not just with other blacks, but also with Hispanics. Two related problems have surfaced: first, Limón, the traditionally black region, has become an economic frontier for Hispanics seeking jobs, land and other economic opportunities, thereby heightening latent hostilities long hidden by the structure of racial and economic paration. Second, blacks who have attempted mobility have discovered that instead of their expectations and aspirations being met, they are confronted with new forms of racism and value conflicts generated by selective competition of each higher level of mobility. Both these problems may be attributed to the emphasis on social mobility as a solution to racial and economic ills in a structure ill-prepared for mobility of such magnitude and complexity. The stipulation of mobility within an equal opportunity structure was intended not as a vehicle to facilitate thnic integration but as the ideal principle for the society as a whole. Its society therefore lacks any provision for resolving the conflicts inherent in such selective competition as occurs in the context of racial plurality.

The above quotation makes many statements. To begin, it represents a basic thesis and major concern that the author addresses and amplifies in *Banana Fallout*, where we learn that the Black population of Costa Rica is neither monolithic, static, nor unified. Now, more than during the period when "Social Relations" was written, Blacks are living in substantial numbers in different parts of the Costa Rican mainland, including the capital city and highlands; they now are located in various sectors, occupations, and classes in its socioeconomic structure; and the differences among them are manifested in subcultural, ideological, intraethnic, and class interest-oriented activities.*Banana Fallout* goes beyond a holistic study of a single local community. Rather, it covers a wider selection and range of communities within what may be considered an almost urban-rural continuum or typology of Costa Rican Black settlements.

Banana Fallout further debunks the image of Costa Rica as a Caucasian, Castilian, or Catholic country. It does so by going beyond an emphasis on the concentration of a Black, English-speaking, Protestant population principally in Limón province. Rather, it discusses the internal migration pursued by both Blacks to the Meseta Central and mestizos to the coast, exposing signs of ideological overlays about the political culture of the nation that were being shared at least by the Black middle class and the rest of the country. We learn about the concern of the emergent Black middle or professional class with the limits imposed on its chances for full integration and empowerment within the reality of Costa Rican politics and economics. Alongside this, *Banana Fallout* emphasizes the continued economic disenfranchisement felt by a larger and still-segregated Black working class and peasant population. These people seem to have been abandoned, unrepresented, and even snubbed by the more mobile sectors of the race.

But while migration and race relations in Costa Rica were not simply locally bounded affairs in my incipient observations of the province, now, according to *Banana Fallout*, the impact of the internalizations of these prophecies have become manifest more fully throughout Costa Rica and even in New Sligoville in terms of modifications of roles and status, land ownership, household and economic activities, aspirations of Blacks versus mestizos, culture, language, and the like. Hence, not only New Sligoville but the Puerto Limón that Purcell encountered years after my study appears to be significantly different. This raises questions about whether such differences reflect methodology or material, whether they represent change rather than continuity, or whether they simply reflect the limitations of single synchronic studies in understanding human conditions and behavior.

Purcell must be credited for the ethnographic attention he pays to the roles and plights of Black women, in various historical periods and sociocultural milieus in Costa Rica. He acquaints us with women in a range of roles, from higglers—like his own mother in Jamaica, for a time—to scholars such as Kathleen Sawyers Royal, whom he cites repeatedly as subject and source in his work.

But we also know from the emerging literature that Black Costa Rican women's views are being increasingly asserted in the literary, scholarly, and political domains. With respect to the question of ethnic and national identification, we can read the writings of such young scholars as Kathleen Sawyers Royal (1972, 203–4) and also Ruth Simms Hamilton and Lorein Powell-Bernard (1990, 1–2). However, their activism is perhaps most dramatically voiced by poet Eulalia Bernard. In her *Ritmoheroe,* she writes, but in Spanish:

> No!! West Indians
> You are foolish if you prefer
> To bury your ethnicity
> Your eyes, your heart, you
> In essence are
> West Indians.

Her dedication reads:

> To my ancestors or their
> descendants who have
> contributed to the forging
> of our beloved Fatherland.

The point is that beyond the communal and domestic domains, activist and professional Black women do exist and exert themselves in Costa Rica. Their political participation is evident, active and felt, and merits attention and study as such.

Since my thesis, a number of dissertations and publications have been completed on West Indians in rural Limón. In fact, compared to the epoch in which "Social Relations" was written, Purcell's dissertation and even moreso his *Fallout,* were written in a period of heightened interest among scholars and a blooming of statistical reports, documentation, and publications on West Indian Blacks in Central America, not only Costa Rica. Many of these works—not all, to be sure—may be the products of outsiders with temporary career interests or ulterior motives for studying this presently important region of Central American "banana republics." Further, as Bourgois (1989) has informed us, as a white American scholar he was privileged to obtain contacts, data, and commentaries unavailable to or different from those which might be obtained by Black insiders (or even outsiders). In a similar manner, the work of Purcell benefitted from not only privileged insight, intimacy, and confidence, but empathetic identification on his part with a range of Costa Rican Blacks. Clearly, his language and argument at times reveal both passion and pensiveness. But overall his analytic effort proves that insiders can speak interpretively for themselves as scholars, informants, and fellow subjects of the very studies they pursue. Obviously, the complementary contributions of these two bodies of scholars make for a richer literature, and, at some point, their future collaboration would lead to a more reflexive and sensitive methodology.

This work by Purcell will carry special meaning for many of us in both a personal and professional sense. He is symbolic of a new generation of torch bearers, which has been arising in our midst. Hence, for me personally, *Banana Fallout* not only advances knowledge and injects new thinking into the study of the reality of Black people in Costa Rica, but it evokes a kind of fraternal and poetic sense of fulfillment. As such, it brings new life to "Social Relations," a pioneering study done thirty years ago, and it will shed new light on the struggle of the people and region about which it speaks. Professionally, then, for its readers and those generally interested in its topics, theses, and treatments, *Banana Fallout* widens the scope of information and freshens our insight on color, class, and culture in an area, among a people, and about an experience yet too little known and appreciated. In that sense, it holds real potential as a contribution to the further advancement of theoretical issues having to do with inter-and intra-ethnic relations, mobility, stratification, culture, and development in Third World countries, particularly those that share a pluralistic legacy that comes from a colonial or neocolonial plantation past. It also suggests the broadened variety of techniques and concepts that modern social anthropology must begin to develop if it seeks to lift its level of grounded analysis and the validity of its theoretical generalizations and therefore confront more effectively the historical and ongoing processes and postmodern structures of the moment.

Trevor Purcell deserves our honest congratulations for this kind of benchmark contribution which was long in coming. And UCLA's Center for Afro-American Studies must be commended once more for publishing yet another critical work on an unfamiliar aspect of the Black Experience. For the opportunity to have associated with them both, I am proud; for the opportunity to introduce Purcell's *Banana Fallout*, I am pleased.

R.S. BRYCE-LAPORTE
John D. and Katherine T. MacArthur Professor of Sociology
Director of Africana and Latin American Studies
Colgate University

PREFACE

In 1977, I went to Costa Rica with the intention of conducting a straight-forward ethnohistorical study of the social and economic adjustment of West Indian immigrants in Limón. However, I felt impelled to change my focus, after issues raised in an earlier field trip came up again during the first few weeks.

Observations in 1976 had led me to wonder why, after the decline of the United Fruit Company plantation on which they had worked, most Blacks aspired almost exclusively to wage labor. After all, there was relatively easy access to cultivable land—compared to the more limited access in places like Jamaica, Trinidad, or Barbados. Initially, I thought that the long experience in a closed plantation society (Wolf 1957), preceded by a period of about one generation out of slavery, had conditioned their perception of alternatives and their ability to exercise independent initiatives in their new political and economic circumstances. Unfortunately, substantiating this hypothesis was a task far more demanding than I could handle in the time I had left in the field. Nevertheless, the question of why these immigrants and their descendants overwhelmingly chose wage employment over farming and other independent ventures—alternatives that might have produced a greater measure of economic, if not political, independence—continued to nag at my imagination.

Early in my second visit to Limón, it became clear that these old questions were complicated by other factors. The Afro-Costa Rican reality rebuffed my naive expectation of ethnic unity and nationalist consciousness. In spite of their common origin, geographic concentration, and position as a dis-criminated minority, the group displayed status differences. Some Blacks insisted on the superiority of Spanish while others clung self-consciously to "the Queen's English." Some spoke in nostalgic tones of Marcus Garvey's visit to Costa Rica and bemoaned the dwindling of the nationalism he implanted, while others insisted that success for Blacks lies in becoming more like whites. Although a Black headed the local branch of the Commu-nist party, a growing number of Blacks were shifting support from the liberal National Liberation party (which facilitated their citizenship, begin-ning in the early 1950s) to the conservative National Unity Party. Clearly, the group recognized itself as an ethnic entity, yet there were glaring cleavages in almost every aspect and opinion.

Living from the late 1960s through the late 1970s in the United States had led me to expect that ideological diversity among Blacks would be outweighed by nationalist consciousness and a relatively unified front vis-à-vis the white majority. In Costa Rica, however, Blacks seemed to comprise a graded diversity that crudely melded ideologically, culturally, and even racially into the dominant white majority.

The literature on Blacks in South America treats extensively the notion of a social continuum between Blacks and whites, but for the most part, those studies describe Black populations established during the colonial period, and in different political-economic contexts. To complicate matters, everything I knew about Blacks in the Americas suggested that one should expect racism wherever Blacks and whites share social, economic, and political space. Yet, in contrast to the United States or even places like Jamaica, more than a few Afro-Costa Ricans protested any suggestion that there was racism in their adopted country. Intriguingly, shades of color difference—if not the political debate about them—were of greater social importance in Costa Rica at a time when the issue had retreated to the background in the Anglophone Caribbean from which Afro-Costa Ricans had emigrated—and long after the nationalist wave of the 1960s and 1970s that swept the United States and the Caribbean.

On the surface, theories of economic and racial inequality suggested some explanations. But no simple theory of racial and class discrimination would do; for one, the most vocal protesters of racial discrimination were largely from the same class as those who insisted there was no racial problem. At the same time, some of the most ardent supporters of Costa Rican nationalism were among the most economically deprived. "Improving one's lot" was, however, a dominant theme in conversations, energizing not only discussions of the position of Blacks relative to whites in Costa Rica but also of the relative positions of individuals within the Black community. Taking this preoccupation as my methodological cue, I decided to train my sights on the strategies involved in negotiating the class, culture, and color hierarchy, as well as the historical and ideological conditions that necessitated those strategies. The idea was to get at the strategies by observing the way people actualized (or attempted to actualize) their strivings.

My research was conducted over a total of eighteen months and encompassed five communities. I lived for various lengths of time in three of these: New Sligoville, Point Cove, and Los Corales, a barrio in Puerto Limón. I also lived for about nine weeks in another barrio, Pueblo Nuevo, although it was not one of the systematically studied communities. I have chosen to use pseudonyms in this study in order to protect the privacy of the people who, directly or indirectly, collaborated in it. For the same reason, I use real place names only where, in my judgment, the risks are minimal.

It is only fair to say that my own background as a mobile West Indian has sensitized me to the issues I found in Costa Rica. I share with Afro-Costa Ricans the experience of secondary emigration, and I can empathize with the fire of ambition and the consuming frustration that marked their life moves. As a result, the line between ethnographer and subject was never and could never be clearly drawn; my cultural and psychological closeness prevented my being the "objective" anthropologist, filtering cold facts through the mythical clarity of studied theories. When I looked at a Black woman selling ground provisions in the Limón market, I was instantly reminded of my own mother doing the same thing in Jamaica's Linstead market—before she joined the throng of economic defectors to Great Britain in the early 1960s.

In a very real sense, observing social inequality was partly observing my own journey along the pitted path of upward mobility. In effect, culture and experience had blurred the subject-object divide that is so characteristic of social science methodology.

This situation typifies both the problem posed and the privilege offered by what Dr. Bryce-LaPorte calls "insider" ethnography. It is a problem because scholars investigating cultures in which they have roots themselves cannot achieve the posture of the dispassionate, objective outsider—assuming that there is any real merit to that posture, given our place in the political economy of today's world. It is a privilege, however, because such scholars bring to their work an understanding born of experience and hence a historical and existential connectedness that can be achieved no other way. Feeling and knowing are unified as an ethnographic source.

The methodology is, therefore, necessarily collaborative, and the objective of the study cannot be separated from the aspirations or frustrations of those studied. Indeed, when, in 1976, Dr. Bryce-LaPorte pointed me in the direction of Puerto Limon for my initial study, he already knew this. Today, it is my firm opinion that we are both the better for being insiders.

TREVOR W. PURCELL

Acknowledgments

All anthropological fieldwork is a collaboration (sometimes reluctant) between the observer and the observed. I am deeply grateful to all those who participated—knowingly and unknowingly—especially those who did not simply participate but who offered personal and professional guidance and comfort: Enrique March, Kathleen and Joyce Sawyers, Delroy Barton, Quince Duncan, Mrs. Linda Senior and her granddaughter, Mirna Henry, the late Irod Clark, Delano Reid, Miss Julia Simmons, Tancred Senior, and countless others.

The initial fieldwork on which this book is based was funded by three grants: a Johns Hopkins University Department of Anthropology summer fieldwork grant; a Ford Foundation research award for the movement of Caribbean peoples; and an Organization of American States fellowship. My sincere gratitude to all of these.

Thanks to Dra. Mariá E. Bozzoli de Wille for facilitating my affiliation with the University of Costa Rica during my research; and to Marjorie Smith and Gloria Porter for their invaluable assistance in completing surveys.

I am eternally grateful to professors Sidney Mintz, Roy Bryce–Laporte, Franklin Knight, and the faculty of the Johns Hopkins anthropology department for their generous support. I am also indebted to my former student, Sarah Hautzinger, for her painstaking reading of the manuscript when it was still in its most boring state.

The efforts of Center for Afro-American Studies managing editor Toyomi Igus and copy editor Jacqueline A. Tasch have made a significant difference in presentation. I am grateful for their efforts, and for having had the opportunity to be exposed to their skill and charm.

Finally, this work would not have been available to the public without the emotional, editorial, and typing support of my dear wife, Dorothy Parker.

AFRO-COSTA RICANS:
RACE, CULTURE, AND INEQUALITY

In most of South America and the Caribbean, the major African-American populations have been in place since the establishment of colonial plantations. Not so with Costa Rica; its African-American population, for the most part, is the product of a secondary, postcolonial immigration. Yet the historical current that brought this dark-skinned group to Costa Rica's Atlantic shores in the late nineteenth century is merely a structural and temporal extension of the same historical trajectory that earlier brought Africans to other American territories.

It is not surprising, therefore, that although they were latecomers, their relationship to the dominant group in their new home has taken on some of the same characteristics that exist elsewhere in the region. In contrast, however, the Costa Rican ethnic "cauldron" (to borrow Nash's [1989] apt terminology) has been spiced by the fact that most Blacks arrived with a different Western language (English) and with the confidence of British imperial citizenship. They arrived, mainly from the then-British West Indies, to labor on the construction of Costa Rica's Atlantic railroad and later in the banana plantations of that germinator of banana republics, the United Fruit Company. These factors were to play a pivotal role in how Blacks adapted to their new mainland home.

This book is essentially about the adjustment of Afro-Costa Ricans, from their arrival as recruited migrant labor to their present position as an integral, but only partially accepted, ethnic minority. Seen on a wider canvas, this work points up the need to integrate studies of Central America's Atlantic littoral with such Caribbeanwide concerns as cultural domination and prospects for the full integration of African-Americans into the sociopolitical life of the region. From Belize in the north to Panama in the south, much of Central America has long been Caribbeanized by secondary migration, yet few studies of the region give more than passing acknowledgment to this fact—instead, scholars such as James Parsons (1954) view the heterogeneity as an anomaly. A more fitting population could hardly be

1

found to begin to make that link than the one studied here. In this introductory chapter, a framework for examining the life of Afro-Costa Ricans is constructed, first, by taking a brief look at the history of Africans in the region, then by recalling the primary social science theories used to explain the pervasive process of domination and inequality there, and finally by adopting a strategy for this work in analyzing such forces.

AFRICANS IN COSTA RICA: THE FIRST PHASE

It is almost two decades since Colin Palmer (1976) lamented the lack of knowledge about Blacks in Central America, but his complaint applies with only slightly diminished force today. We tend to think of African immigrants during this period as slaves, and to think of slavery as encompassing South America (mainly Brazil), North America, and the Caribbean. Neither of these suppositions is true.

Indeed, the Atlantic littoral was touched by Africans long before slavery as an institution brought large migrations to the region. According to Melendez (1977, 24), a few Blacks were present "step by step" alongside the likes of Nunez del Balboa and Gil Gonzalez in the conquest and settlement of the territory—that is, as early as 1522.

With the establishment of slavery, of course, the number of Africans increased substantially. About 50 percent of the slaves that came to the New World between 1521 and 1639—about 111,000 by Palmer's (1976, 28) estimate—came to Mexico. Although Central America's slave plantation economy would never have the magnitude and intensity of the institution in the Caribbean or Brazil, at one point or another African slaves were imported throughout the region (Palmer 1976, 29).

Costa Rica had one of the smallest slave populations; at Emancipation in 1824, only eighty-nine persons were accounted for (Melendez 1977, 48). Nevertheless, the movement of Africans as items of commerce, not only among the mainland countries but also between the islands and the mainland, was to define the region in terms of race, culture, and class domination. Interestingly, most slaves in Central America were purchased from the English in Jamaica, suggesting the probability of a strong West Indian link among the earliest Blacks in the region. However, West Indian Blacks also came to the region as peddlers in the 1820s, arriving in fishing and trading schooners and then traveling overland on mules to trade with the Guaymi Indians—eventually teaching the Indians to speak English and converting them to Protestantism (Conniff 1985, 16). Others worked on the Vanderbilt steamship and stageline in Nicaragua (Conniff 1985, 17).

In addition to the original slave population, the character of which was radically transformed through assimilation, another group of Blacks inhabited the area during this early period. These were the so-called Black Caribs or Garifuna—a biological and cultural mixture of Africans and native Caribs who came to the area after the initial migration but before the nineteenth century migration that is the subject of this work.

The Garifuna were forcibly shipped from St. Vincent to the island of Roatán in 1797. From there, most Garifuna were transported to Trujillo on the mainland, where they spread along the Atlantic Coast from what was then British Honduras south to Nicaragua. The Trujillo area still has the largest concentration of Garifuna. Overall, more than 74,000 are now in the region (Gonzalez 1988; Wilk and Chapin 1990, 24).

AFRICANS IN COSTA RICA: THE SECOND PHASE

The second grand movement of Blacks into Central America began in the early nineteenth century, increasing during the British lumber period in Nicaragua and what was then British Honduras, during railroad and canal construction in Panama, and during railroad construction and the banana plantation period in Costa Rica. This was the period of the largest immigration of West Indians. Panama alone received more than 100,000 (Conniff 1985, 3).

Chapters 2 and 3 provide a more detailed history of the arrival of West Indian Blacks—primarily from Jamaica but also from other parts of the Caribbean—to work on the banana plantations in the steamy lowlands of Costa Rica's Atlantic coast and to build a railroad connecting that coast with the central plateau where most Hispanics lived. As increasing numbers of Blacks were brought into the economy of Central America's Atlantic Coast during the early twentieth century, Hispanics came to deplore the Africanization of the region (Helms 1977, 164). In Costa Rica as in Panama, West Indian Blacks were first viewed as a necessary inconvenience, and when competition for jobs increased (in the 1920s in Panama and the 1930s in Costa Rica), campaigns to deport them began. West Indian immigration to Costa Rica tapered off by the 1930s.

With the completion of Costa Rica's railroad and the subsequent demise of its new style, postcolonial plantation system, most Black workers—even those who had once practiced farming while working on the plantation—joined the development trend in Central American by turning to nonagricultural endeavors. Along the coast, many Garifuna who had, by and large, not been plantation laborers, remained small cultivators. But overall, for reasons which form a major theme of the ensuing chapters, full-time agricultural activity is a dying occupation among Afro-Costa Ricans.

THE DYNAMICS OF DOMINATION AND INEQUALITY

The Caribbean, including the Atlantic coast of Central America, is a virtual crucible of political, cultural, and ethnic conflicts and compromises, a crucible molded out of domination, continuously concocting a mix of inequality and twisted values that enriches some, impoverishes others, and poisons the souls of most.

And yet, armed with all the insight of modern social science, anthropologists have given more attention to real and imagined mating patterns than they have given to the process and product of domination. There are some inspiring exceptions: Among pioneers in Caribbean studies, Sidney Mintz and Eric Wolf immediately come to mind as anthropologists who have from the very beginning seen inequality and domination as central to Caribbean culture. In 1971, Mintz published a review article in which he argued—using the example of the rise of the *gens de couleur* in Haiti—that material conditions and civil status go further to explain race relations than postulated categories such as Harry Hoetink's somatic norm image and somatic distance (1971, 437–50), concepts based on skin color. Hoetink (1973) and M.G. Smith (1965a, 1984), on the other hand, are reluctant to grant the material conditions of life any real significance in determining how individuals and groups treat one another across racial and ethnic boundaries. In addressing inequality, the typical perspective has been to assume that the major lines of cleavage in these societies correspond to cultural and racial distinctions. The tone was set early by Henriques (1953), who used the phrase "colour-class system" to define Caribbean stratification. But the writer most responsible for turning this view of society into a theory is sociologist M. G. Smith (1965a, 1969). Others have already expertly exposed the strengths and the weaknesses of the plural society theory. I will, therefore, say only enough to set this work within the context of relevant works on the region.

M. G. Smith's definition of the plural society is well-known: It is one characterized by different and incompatible forms of cultural institutions, by different ethnic sections of the population (1965a, 62; 1984, 32). He is explicit in his view that the study of social stratification cannot adequately explain the major cleavages in West Indian society. The reason is that in plural societies, the plurality forms a discontinuous status order; cultural differences and social stratification are said to vary independently (M. G. Smith 1965a, 83). This is an implicit argument against class determination, a point made clear in Smith's (1984, 140–41) statement, paraphrased here, that the decisive determinant of social structure is the distribution of power among and within culturally distinct groups. Class and social stratification are subordinated to culture and political power. Class determinism has never adequately explained inequality in the Caribbean. And so, in looking at the swirling complexity that is the Caribbean, it is quite plausible to assume that in certain social contexts and at certain periods of history, cultural or political considerations may assume a decisive role. It is quite another thing, however, to argue that this is the driving force of Caribbean history, the creator of its institutions, and the preeminent motive for social action.

The invention of the plural perspective was, by and large, a response to the Parsonian notion of value consensus, popular in the Caribbean in the 1960s. In his classic work on Guyana, R. T. Smith (1956) took the position that the colonial period created an indigenous elite with a legitimizing ideology that became the integrative force in Guyana, as elsewhere in the Anglophone Caribbean. This position finds strong support in the early work of Lloyd Braithwaite (1960), who believes that the emphasis on European-derived values serves as an integrative force—a sort of ideal. R. T. Smith (1982) was later to recognize a far more complex integrative process in which class works to reform values, where individuals exercise responsibility in adjusting against the odds, and where dominance and submission coexist. And M. G. Smith (1984), too, while not abandoning his plural society view, later gave greater recognition to the material side of class relations.

The problems encountered in the study of inequality in the Anglophone Caribbean are not unique to the region. They form part of a more general shortcoming in the social sciences: the absence of a unified theory of stratification (Cancian 1976; Elster 1985; Parkin 1979). The chasm between the ideal and the material approaches must be bridged, and the sentient actor must be both product and creator of structure. As the sociologist Jon Elster (1985, 266) has observed, the contradiction between the forces of production and the relations of production does not tell the whole story of how individuals decide to accept their situation or change it.

The tendency has been to think in terms of a linear, somewhat rigid relationship, in which either class or color dominates, and in which the upper echelon maintains power while the relationship among the other strata remains immutable—except in cases of gradual elimination or assimilation. But the winds of history tend to rock the crucible from assimilation to cultural nationalism, from denigrating an ethnic group today to esteeming the same group tomorrow.

West Indian laborers in the United Fruit Company plantations initially esteemed their white North American employers and spurned their white Hispanic co-workers, a distinction in which class was more important than color. When the plantation abandoned them and they came under the control of a Hispanic-dominated society, Afro-Costa Ricans began to appreciate those they had despised.

In the Caribbean, ethnic conflict coexists with and becomes an instrument of class domination, but what values or cultural features are employed at a particular historical juncture is a question to be answered by research.

CULTURE AND INEQUALITY

In a sense, there is nothing unusual about inequality in itself; it is inherent to culture. Culture evaluates and classifies its natural and social environment, creating a hierarchized systemic whole. It also evaluates and classifies itself vis-à-vis another culture. From this intrinsic discriminatory aspect of culture, Rousseau's "moral inequality" is derived.

Likewise, each culture is a complex of cause-and-effect relations with the natural and social environment; each is unique and must, like a species, protect its survival. A threat to a culture's survival may also mean a threat to the survival of its carriers—as is evident among Native Americans. Without major catastrophe or coercion, each cultural group seems likely to operate best on its own cultural resources. As Levi-Strauss (1985) has observed, cultures "borrow from one another on occasion, but, in order not to perish, they must, in other connections, remain somewhat impermeable toward one another" (xv). Thus, the tendency toward self-preservation, combined with the necessity of cultural values, underlies social inequality and nationalism as well.

If inequality is inherent in cultures, why then is it problematic, and why do social scientists numb their fingers writing about its pathogenic aspects? Inequality—particularly, as in the case at hand, where class inequality is combined with racial and color discrimination—threatens the continued existence of a culture when it becomes the mechanism for denying a group self-determination in accordance with its own cultural knowledge. If the threat is actualized, the effect is the social equivalent of the extinction of a species—the reduction of the diversity of knowledge about the world and thereby our understanding of it.

In Costa Rica, as in other parts of South America and the Caribbean where Blacks form significant components of the population, a process of cultural co-optation is built into the system of inequality: Deprived non-Caucasians are forced (moreso than in Anglophone America) to relinquish important components of their culture in order to be accepted—and at times merely to survive. The emergence and persistence of this process of co-optation—both cause and product of inequality—is at the heart of Black social, economic, and political adjustment in Costa Rica.

COLONIALISM AND CLASS

In a seminal article published in 1957, anthropologists Eric Wolf and Sidney Mintz analyzed the social formations of the Caribbean basin based on the two economic institutions—the plantation and the hacienda—that were dominant during the colonial period and set the tone for social processes long afterward. These economic institutions are treated as two forms of social systems, each designed around the control and use of land, labor, and capital. The plantation system was typical of what geographer John Augelli (1962) has called the "EuroAfrican Caribbean Rimland," which includes the Caribbean islands, and the hacienda system flourished on the "Euro-Indian Mainland."

Both systems were created by Europeans, based on the exploitation of large expanses of land appropriated from the indigenous peoples and worked by coerced labor; both were organized into classes; both produced for the world market; both were based on capital accumulation; and both evolved politico-legal systems that operated in the interest of the dominant class, at the expense of labor and native inhabitants. Differences between the two systems focus on geography and the degree of exploitation that was involved. Haciendas emerged in the more temperate upland regions of Central America, where Hispanic settlers found themselves physically more comfortable. Plantations, colonial and postcolonial, were established in flatlands where industrial-scale crop production was more efficient. The less hospitable climate was irrelevant, for Europeans did not undertake the back-breaking work—slaves did.

Thus, when Costa Ricans established cacao plantations on the Atlantic coast in the seventeenth century, the owners stayed in the cool Meseta Central, while the slaves worked, largely unsupervised, on the steamy Atlantic coast. Not surprisingly, the slaves kept running away, some to join the Miskitu Indians. And later, in the nineteenth century, Hispanic labor refused to build a railroad through that inhospitable territory, forcing Costa Rica to let railroad contractors import West Indian laborers, who were already used to working in tropical lowlands.

The social organization of the old-style slave plantation was also in sharp contrast with the hacienda. While the hacienda was a hierarchy based on coerced labor, appropriated land, and capital accumulation, its raison d'être was maintaining social status rather than accumulating profit, and the link between labor and owners was permeated with mutual social obligations (Mintz and Wolf 1950; Wolf and Mintz 1957). In short, the hacienda closely resembled a feudal society.

The plantation social formation, on the other hand, was organized mainly for profits; its class relations were, therefore, not only more impersonal but also more efficiently exploitative (Wolf and Mintz 1957). In contrast to the "settler" nature of the upland hacienda or the plantations of the American South, the lowland plantation was a strictly exploitative form of social organization, with all that implies for those who willingly or unwillingly came to live there (Knight 1974, 59–68).

It has been argued convincingly that the rate of exploitation of plantation slaves has been a far stronger determinant of race relations during and after slavery than the legalities regarding the slave's social recognition as a human being (see, for example, Genovese 1969, 238–55; Mintz 1969, 27–37; Knight 1974). The case of Cuba is exemplary in this regard; the deterioriation of the treatment of slaves, and race relations in general, has been linked to the intensification of sugar production as Cuba took advantage of decreasing French and British production, on the one hand, and the technological benefits of the industrial revolution on the other (see Knight 1970). Race relations in the plantation colonies depended on much more than rate of exploitation, but overall, it is not out of line to speculate that the rate of exploitation—particularly if exploitation is seen as the denial of "the prerogatives of the human condition, as defined by the culture" (Mintz 1969, 37)—along with its ideological rationalization—was not only a strong determinant of race relations but perhaps the most enduring.

As Blacks moved from slavery to free labor on the postemancipation industrial plantations of the region, including the banana plantations of Costa Rica, these structural and ideological conditions relating to class changed little. Their impact on race relations remained.

COLONIALISM AND SKIN COLOR

Class and culture were traditional tools of measuring value; colonialism, with its need to rationalize brutality, complicated the process by adding skin color. No group of societies better demonstrates this than those where transported Blacks are found today. From survival on the slave plantation to upward mobility in the nations rising from the ruins of those plantations, from assuaging an irate master to applying for a job, from deciding allegiance between community and country to choosing whom to marry, Blacks in the Americas have never been allowed the luxury of ignoring the color of their skin—nor the culture of those who made skin color important.

Palmer's statement that "the possession of black skin was not considered an asset in early colonial Mexico" is a gentle understatement—particularly with regard to *bozales* (Africans) who were considered "naturally evil" and a "bad caste"; more tellingly, given the language construction, "being a slave was a `vile person'" (Palmer 1976, 42). Blacks were the lowest in the ethnic hierarchy, with Hispanics on top and the Indians, rescued from slavery by Bishop Barthalome de las Casas, in the low middle. Each ethnic group was stratified as well, based on relative assimilation, occupation, and color.

The same process occurred throughout the region. In British, French, and Dutch dominated territories, the line between whites and Blacks was clear and hard; the subjugated were left to struggle over the line between the various shades produced by miscegenation. In Spanish-dominated territories, the lines were blurred in ideology but quite clear in terms of political and economic power.

The situation resulted in one pervasive and intractable problem: an insistence on treating people according to their race, with no objective definition of who belongs to which race. As with many obstacles to a moral community created by colonialism, Blacks had to manipulate this, too, into an advantage: the lack of a standard allows for ambiguity, and ambiguity is fertile ground for negotiation. The problem is one exacerbated by the incredible variety of terms used to describe people whose appearance might be quite similar: Black, Afro-American, Creole, Mulatto, Garifuna, Black-Indian, Black Carib, Antillean Negro, Moreno, *pardo, negre, preto*—the list is extensive.

Because of its obvious significance and relevance to social status, skin color has also become a key feature of rationales explaining social structures. While Mintz and others view race relations in the Caribbean as the complex outcome of plantation and hacienda societies, categories based on economic conditions, some scholars, such as the sociologist Harry Hoetink (1967, 1973) analyze race relations in terms of two variants grounded in skin color. These are the Anglo or West European variant, typical of former British and Dutch territories, and the Latin American or Iberian variant, sometimes called the Latin-Arab variant.

Unlike the North Europeans, Hoetink argues, the Iberians benefited from a cultural familiarity with dark-skinned North Africans, prior experience with slavery, and most important, a religion that, in collaboration with the state, saw to the preservation of the moral personality of slaves and freemen. These factors, Hoetink believes, made for mild slavery, frequent manumission, and tolerant postslavery race relations, resulting in what Hoetink calls a color continuum. More recently Hoetink (1973) put forward a demographic theory of race relations, centering on the need of whites for physical and economic security.

Hoetink (1973, 98) is partly right when he comments that the sociological peculiarity of the Caribbean is not to be found in its socioeconomic structures but in the importance of somatic traits, such as skin color, to one's position and chances in life. He is only partly right—in the opinion of this writer—because somatic traits are important precisely because of the socioeconomic structure and not vice versa. Be that as it may, it is the human rainbow of the Caribbean landscape and its place in the socioeconomic structure that make the sociology of the area so potent. Race relations in Costa Rica add another twist to this ceaselessly engaging story.

Costa Rica shares the Iberian historical heritage, but race relations there do not fit neatly into that variant; for reasons of history, economy, and politics, Costa Rica is a variation on a variant. Colonial Costa Rica had all the features necessary for a color continuum except one: a sufficiently large slave plantation system. Although Costa Rica experienced its own period of plantation slavery—not sugar, but cacao—the magnitude never compared to such colonies as Cuba, Santo Domingo, or its northern neighbors. There were never more than about two hundred slaves at any one time, and these were located, not in the main white settlement in the highlands, but on the Atlantic coast and with minimal supervision. Evidently, their numbers were far too small to darken the complexion of the country. The absence of a large slave population (and a large freed population) as well as the isolation of Blacks from white settlers/owners, meant that whites had no reason to feel threatened physically or economically. There was no intermediate colored population for Blacks to join as allies. Therefore, there was no real continuum.

When a large number of Black West Indians finally arrived in Costa Rica toward the end of the nineteenth century, they were again removed from the main population in every respect except that they, along with their employer, the United Fruit Company, were the backbone, brain, and bank in the country's effort to achieve economic development. By this time, however, in spite of the presence of native Americans in their midst, Costa Ricans' perception of their country as racially homogeneous was firmly rooted (in fact, even today, Costa Ricans see themselves as very European).

These new immigrants were neither Catholics nor Spanish-speakers. There was, therefore, little room for the development of a continuum: In spite of the oft-touted Spanish heritage of racial tolerance, and in spite of the essential role that West Indians played in the modernization of Costa Rica's medieval economy, Blacks came to be perceived, at least up to the mid-1940s, as a threat to the economic and cultural security of the white population. Here were the economic and psychological conditions for a continuum, but not the demographic. For all practical purposes, race relations seemed closer to the Anglo version than to the Iberian.

With the dismantling of the United Fruit plantations in the 1950s, and with deliberate, if instrumental, efforts by one political party to mold West Indians into Costa Ricans, white Costa Ricans no longer insisted on keeping the nation homogeneous. In spite of increasing Black nationalism, the past three decades have produced enough mixed-race offspring to suggest a limited softening of the color contrast. Today Spanish is the first language among many Blacks, and their numbers are growing in Catholic congregations.

While race relations in Costa Rica may not have resembled the Iberian variant in the beginning, they seem to have gradually acquired some of its distinctive features. Though in decreasing numbers, Costa Ricans readily deny the existence of racial discrimination, even while they continue to treat African cultural traits as at best exotic and entertaining and at worst uncivilized and inherently inferior. Add to this denial a widely accepted ideology of equal opportunity and equal political participation, and Costa Rica begins to resemble Brazil or the Dominican Republic far more than it resembles any racially plural Anglophone society. Even so, Costa Rica most closely resembles the Latin model in its ideology of race relations, rather than in their practice.

STRATEGIES OF ADJUSTMENT TO SOCIAL INEQUALITY

If a colonial society is stratified by class, color, and culture, it is quite logical, in terms of social process, that individuals would use class, color, and culture as instrumental symbols of struggle, even after colonialism. In short, Blacks had to escape, and escape took many forms, mental and physical.

Blanqueamiento (or whitening), the pervasive practice of biological and cultural assimilation to Hispanic norms, is only one example of the effort to escape oppression. A less questionable form of escape was the process of marronage, the formation of autonomous communities by escaped slaves who often had to fight for their freedom. And accounts of bloody rebellions are at least as numerous as descriptions of compliant house slaves—the same slaves who sometimes poisoned the master. One thing was certain, Blacks never accepted their own bondage—though individual free Blacks, even maroons, throughout the region did become slave owners (Campbell 1992; Gordon 1987, 136).

Ultimately, escape has been achieved through self-definition and the persistent struggle for meaning. In the English, French, and Dutch territories, identity was created in a framework of cultural, biological, and ideological exclusion. In the Hispanic territories, identity has been affirmed within the framework of a condescending ideology of relative inclusion, largely frustrated by political and economic exclusion.

To survive, Blacks have occasionally had to appropriate the heritage of powerful others in deciding how to act, even as they struggle to define themselves in the image of their own cultural legacy. In the Central American lowlands, they have been influenced during the nineteenth century by a rigid and severely dehumanizing North American form of exclusion. This practice of cultural, class, and color domination persisted through this century. When the opportunity has presented itself, Blacks have themselves formed hierarchies in which race and color were symbols of demarcation. They have been willing, at least ideologically, to ally themselves with their white oppressors while discriminating against other non-white groups.

Nicaraguan Creoles, for example, have perceived themselves as superior vis à vis the Garifuna and the native Miskitu. They have exercised economic, political, and social control of the Mosquitia, only to lose power to U.S. interests (including the Moravian Church) in the 1880s and to the Nicaraguan government with reincorporation in 1984. Nicaraguan Blacks—like many insular West Indians well into the postcolonial period and like Blacks in Costa Rica even more recently—have expressed pride in their association with British culture and later with their North American employers.

During the early decades of United Fruit Company employment, West Indians in Costa Rica saw their Hispanic class-equals as their inferiors. This reflects a distinct tendency among Blacks in the Hispanic region to extol British culture, even during periods of anticolonialism on the Caribbean islands. In a world where the standard of acceptability—or even humanity—was established by Anglo-European culture, Blacks found it more useful to flaunt their Britishness in the face of Hispanic denigration, rather than to flaunt their Africanness, the font of inferiority in the eyes of the "civilized" world.

Moreover, the Spanish colonial concept of corporate society, combined with the hegemonic Hispanic culture's pressure to gain acceptance through assimilation, led to more stratification in Black communities than occurred in Black-dominated states, with cultural and economic assimilation as the standard of success. Quite consistent with this process is the present tendency for Blacks in Central America to identify with the national ideology of their respective states—even when these same people are protesting racial discrimination (Gordon 1987; Purcell and Sawyers 1993).

That Blacks should become hyper-class and -color sensitive is not at all surprising. Social inequality increasingly captures the collective consciousness, penetrating every aspect of social life and encompassing class and race at the same time it transcends them. The hierarchical division in the region between Caucasians and non-Caucasians is well-known, the ideology of racial democracy in Hispanic-dominated territories notwithstanding. Less well known—or at least less often analyzed in the literature—are the extent of inter- as well as intraethnic division among Blacks, the extent of intra-ethnic divisions based on shades of skin, education, or even personal comportment, and the extent of Black-Native American divisions. In all this, the common denominator is the dialectic of domination and hence the unyielding pressure toward varying degrees of assimilation.

CULTURAL DUALITY: PRODUCT OF DOMINATION

Another way to describe the process of social adjustment, common to just about all attempts to define Caribbean culture, is the notion of duality of value orientation. Perhaps the first important mention of duality can be credited to Herskovits (1937). In *Life in a Haitian Valley*, he advanced the idea that Haitian culture is comprised of two sets of counterposed behavioral alternatives. The notion of behavioral alternatives suggests a useful social function, but it also implies socialized ambivalence, which hints at pathological behavior.

Later the concept would appear in the works of M. G. Smith (1953), R. T. Smith (1956), Bourguignon (1952), and others. It was Madeline Kerr ([1952]1963), however, who elaborated the idea of cultural duality as pathological. Speaking of the Jamaican personality, Kerr remarks that "most of the psychological and sociological problems arise out of two culture patterns with ideologies which conflict in important aspects leaving the individual bewildered and insecure" (165). Further on, she observes that "when a man moves from peasant to middle class he steps from one culture pattern to another" (194). Other scholars, among them Reisman (1970), Price (1970), and Nettleford (1978), have been kinder, viewing cultural duality as a creative response to cultural oppression.

Caribbean culture is part African, part European, and wholly Caribbean. As Mintz (1974) points out, "it is wholly acceptable that the identity of Caribbean peoples should emerge in good part out of the linkage, real or symbolic, between colony or erstwhile colony and metropolis" (258). In fact, cultural duality is always present in immigrant territory, inside and outside the Caribbean; it is as much part of the adjustment of Germans, Jews, or Italians in New York as it is of West Indians in Limón.

Cultural duality is also an inherent part of class relations. Peter Wilson's fieldwork (1969, 1973) on the Colombian island of Providencia is of particular relevance to my own analysis, because Providencia bears some historical and cultural resemblance to Limón, and also because Wilson extends his analysis to the Anglophone Caribbean as a whole.

He defines Caribbean culture in terms of two dialectically related principles, reputation and respectability, which characterize opposing forms of behavior, ideology, and value orientation displayed by individuals and groups in accordance with class background and gender. *Reputation,* the culture of camaraderie and performance, is a lower-class response to colonial dependency, while *respectability,* the culture of etiquette and conformity, is embraced by those in the upper strata and represents implanted colonial elite values. The dialectics between these principles produce crab antics, the attempt by those below to pull down individuals who try to achieve upward mobility. For Wilson, reputation embodies a sui generis egalitarian resistance to colonially imposed respectability, and it is therefore an appropriate model for decolonization of Caribbean societies.

One need not accept Wilson's decolonization project (nor would I want to define the Caribbean in terms of a duality) to agree that reputation, respectability, and the dialectic of crab antics are important ingredients of the Caribbean crucible. But while the components are evident among West Indians in Costa Rica, the following chapters will show that they do not define Black culture; rather, they appear as ingredients in a broader ideological and cultural field of symbolic behavior that is enmeshed with class/ productive relations. From this field individuals select, reject, and manipulate ingredients as they negotiate their way in a society where their color and culture are liabilities. Cultural duality is both an asset and a liability: It becomes part of a strategy to penetrate class, color, and cultural barriers; but it is also a source of self-denigration among those who, for whatever reason, take the values of the dominant culture too seriously.

A Strategy for This Work

Except for the plural society theorists, social scientists working in the Caribbean—from the functionalists like R. T. Smith and Lloyd Braithwaite to the dependency theorists like Best and Beckford and the historical materialists like Mintz—have recognized an encompassing dominant ideology supporting class stratification alongside an amalgam of folk ideas and values that either accommodate or implicitly resist domination. There has been no satisfactory explanation, however, of the dialectical synthesis between the two sets of ideas in a particular mode of production—a problem that is rooted in the tendency to see cultures as bounded both ideationally and geographically, and that is instructively critiqued by the anthropologist Eric Wolf (1982, 3–23, 379–91).

Caribbean scholars of all theoretical persuasions agree that culture, color/race, and ideology are made to serve domination: There is agreement that (1) race, culture, and material conditions in one way or another determine social relations; and (2) that these three factors are functionally intertwined. The disagreement arises over how the process works; which factor is the primary determinant of the texture of society.

In analyzing the Costa Rican material, I do not concern myself with which factor has primary explanatory power. Instead, I focus on three sets of questions that shed light on class, color, culture, and migrant status as cofunctional variables in the creation of inequality and dependency:

1. Under what specific material, social, and political conditions do racial and cultural identities take priority, if indeed they do?

2. How do such identities function and change within broader historical contexts?

3. Most importantly, how does this process affect the ability of the subjects of this secondary diaspora to determine their own life conditions?

I also honor the present limitations of analysis in understanding how the individual operates within society. While our understanding of structure has indeed advanced, our understanding of the more intricate relationship between structure and the individual is stunted. Individual experience and motivation get lost in grand structural friction, aspects of culture lose their full explanatory potential, and ambiguity forfeits its subtle reality to the elegance of abstract logic.

And yet, when a Jamaican man with near-white skin wears dreadlocks, when an Afro-Costa Rican insists on speaking English creole in San José, or when a Black shopkeeper places greater value on his place in his community than on the prosperity of his business, these are individual choices that, on a sufficiently large scale, have important implications for structure. And again, when the overemphasis on structure is transported to the world of real politics, we end up with situations like the one in Jamaica in the late 1970s: When the ambiguous position of the petit bourgeoisie was not recognized, many potential allies of democratic socialism were branded as the enemy in the zeal to see all through undigested dichotomous class lenses.

In my own mind, the basic problem in the study of social inequality turns on (1) how different sets of symbols (cultural values, beliefs, ideologies) are pressed into the service of classifying individuals according to the structural demands of the social system, thereby creating and reproducing relations of power; and (2) how individuals and groups respond to such relations of power. Whether the set of symbols constitutes an ideology of caste, equal opportunity (i.e., equity), or apartheid, we are still concerned with how a society defines who and what is valuable in particular historical contexts.

To describe the way people cope with this situation, I have adapted the term *transaction* from the anthropologist Fredrik Barth (1966). Thus, I view individuals as negotiating or manipulating values, ideas, and symbols—both from the dominant sector and from their own cultural group—according to the demands of their social and historical environment, including the power relations they encounter. Some values will be forfeited to gain other values, which are, in the individual's opinion, greater. Thus, to use a simple example, in the 1970s a teen-age boy might forgo an "Afro" hairstyle to win the approval of a new set of peers.

I call *intrinsic values* those deep-seated, traditional cultural features that are not easily shed in transacting toward adjustment. Intrinsic values are at the ontological level of what Heidegger (1962, 213) calls the undifferentiated mode of being, that from which the individual has no "possibility of extrication." These values may, however, become sublimated as folklore and eventually lose their efficacy in day-to-day life. *Extrinsic values,* such as vocabulary or dress style, are more easily discarded; they become strategic currency (consciously or unconsciously) in the process of transaction.

In reality, no absolute distinction can be established between intrinsic and extrinsic; Nash's (1989, 115) onion metaphor (in his discussion of identity) would perhaps be a more realistic illustration—aside from the core and the skin, what is intrinsic or extrinsic is relative. The point is that as new values are formed through intercultural-interclass transaction, the individual retains some of the more deep-seated values, thereby maintaining a degree of cultural rootedness and psychological stability.

There is one key difference between Barth's theory and my adaptation. Barth saw freedom of choice as central to transaction; I believe power relations have greater significance in the lives of Blacks in Costa Rica—and Blacks in all plural societies. Choice exists but it is not free: it is the choice between cooperating with domination or taking the responsibility of resisting it. I use transaction to describe how individuals, constrained by structures of domination—which in Costa Rica are wrapped in the seductive ideology of equal opportunity and racial democracy—unwittingly participate in the reproduction of those structures; in the process they become part of what they struggle against.

My use of the transactional framework in analyzing social process is not meant to suggest that individual actions or strategies are paramount or prior to collective processes, such as class or hegemonic relations of domination. Individuals are inextricably embedded in the values of the place where they are born and socialized, and those values are forged not just by their culture but most certainly by class relations. Each decision is consciously or subconsciously informed by cultural as well as social values. In this sense, the Weberian notion (Weber 1978, 3–74) of purposive social action informed by social value has merit, with the exception, of course, that all this may not occur at the conscious intentional level that Weberians suppose.

The element of *ambition* (see Chapter 5), a driving force in transaction, derives less from individual values or original culture than from the ideology that legitimizes class structure. Elements of this ideology have been syncretized with Black culture and ideology and internalized as a necessary social tool for confronting—though often in a compliant manner—class domination and cultural hegemony. Ambition, then, arises out of the interpretation of class constraints; like pain medication, it is an addictive antidote that perpetuates the very structure that made it necessary.

The point is well-known: The reproduction of class is achieved through the action of individuals—individuals who are each the ensemble of social relations (Marx and Engels 1970, 122). The point is, however, often neglected in the fervor for a more direct cause-effect structural determination, as Eric Wolf (1975) noted a while back: "In the truly structuralist manner, human aspirations are . . . purged from the structures by which, in which, and through which men shape their fate."

This attempt to highlight the role of individuals should not be viewed in the Weberian sense of the utilitarian, purposive (intentional) individual. Weber (and later North American functionalists) places the individual at center stage, without the balancing effect of an individual-structure dialectic—except to the extent that individual social action by definition is based on cognizance of institutional values that legitimize such action (Weber 1978, 3–26). For Weber the institutional order takes the place of structure, and his view of individual action must be viewed against his broader historical perspective: Individualism arises with the increasing rationalization of society, which like Durkheim's historical march from mechanical to organic solidarity, uproots people from their moral foundation but liberates the rational individual. In an increasingly rational but amoral order, this becomes overwhelming utilitarian purposive-rational action. No critical stance is taken against the institutional order, and there is no room for politically responsible man. "This type," Habermas (1984) notes in a critique of Weber, "can include only action orientations of an ethic of conviction and not an ethic of responsibility."

For Blacks in a multiracial class society, color and culture, which define their morality, are in constant conflict with ever-increasing utilitarianism under the guise of rationality, a utilitarianism that fuels both class and racial domination. To be completely utilitarian would be to submit to the structure of domination as a legitimate order. It would also mean transcendence of the morality of their own culture, a morality, as indicated by the monist orientation of their culture, which is quite distinct from that of the capitalist structure they must negotiate. Transaction, then, may be viewed as a strategy that mediates this conflict in the interest of psychic and social—even economic—survival.

The nature of unequal relations of power between Blacks and whites and among Blacks themselves suggests that Black strategies of adjustment cannot gain them socioeconomic parity or social acceptance without radical transformation of their ancestral knowledge. Some would argue that this is a small price to pay. However, color plays a central role in ethnic domination; thus, changing one's cultural beliefs, even if this is accompanied by economic gains, is not likely to produce parity or social acceptance without biological assimilation—or without transformation of the conscience of the dominant majority. There is continuing movement in all of these directions, but the very strategies that produce this movement bring with them the countervailing forces of cultural nationalism and racism, which retard assimilation.

Because Blacks came to Costa Rica as immigrant labor, proud of their British citizenship and speaking a foreign language, their early struggles and strategies of adjustment may seem at times to diverge somewhat from what the literature suggests for Blacks elsewhere in South and Central America. As time goes by, however, they come ever closer to the typical Latin pattern. And by and large, even though many have moved into the middle class, Afro-Costa Ricans seem to have been no more successful in gaining parity and acceptance than Blacks in other Latin countries (such as Brazil, Cuba, or the Dominican Republic, to name a few). Their long-established numerical strength on the Atlantic coast has decreased from an estimated 40 percent in the 1970s to an estimated 29 percent in 1983 (Headley Mullings 1983, 185). Yet in their struggle for acceptance and cultural integrity, they have etched an indelible mark on Costa Rica's political culture, transforming in the process its very image of itself.

Two

FROM PLANTATION COLONY TO NATIONAL ENCLAVE: RACE AND INEQUALITY

When West Indian laborers first came to Costa Rica in the nineteenth century, they arrived by sea in the province of Limón, which stretches the length of the Atlantic coast. It took over seven decades before they and their descendants began to wind their way freely up the mountain to the capital of San José, perched on the Meseta Central—the central plateau or central valley—and the center of population since the country was colonized.

There were no infrastructural connections between the capital and the coast when the West Indians arrived. In fact, many of them were brought to Costa Rica to build the railroad that provided the first link, a seven- to eight-hour trip covering about a hundred miles. In the mid 1970s, a highway was completed, and today the less affluent majority can make the trip in three hours in relatively comfortable buses.

Widely used into the 1980s, the railroad offered a breathtaking panorama of the Costa Rican countryside as it wound down the central mountains. Travelers by way of Cartago—the old capital, east of San José—watched as healthy-looking fields of vegetables and cozy red-roofed farmhouses gave way to coffee plantations, and farther on, to wide expanses of sugarcane fields once owned by the Lindo brothers of Jamaica, large independent farmers during the United Fruit Company days. Not far down the road was a sugar factory.

Occasional coffee plantations, sugarcane fields, and grazing pastures punctuated the rest of the route to Turrialba, the little town that symbolically divides the Atlantic coast region from the Meseta Central. Here, during the United Fruit Company days, trains going to San José switched their Black crew for whites as if changing soiled clothes at the end of a day.

Rich, subtropical vegetation and mixed cultivation—bananas, sugar cane, plantain, coffee, and some citrus—filled the view as the route generally followed the banks of the Reventazon River from Turrialba to Siquirres, the first major town inside the province of Limón (see Map 1). The steamy

MAP 1
Costa Rica

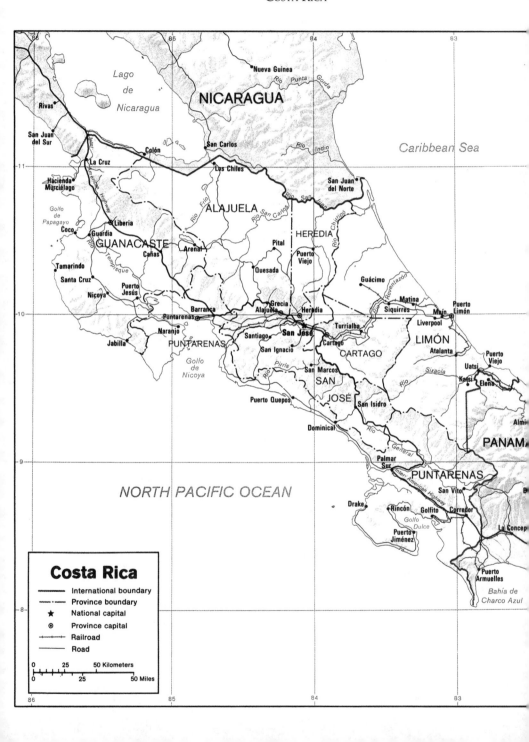

lowlands begin here, sugarcane and coffee replaced by coconut, cacao, and banana fields. Traveling by rail revealed one of the characteristic features of the province: Residential and commercial subcenters adjoin the tracks at intervals. These centers sprang up as labor villages and camps during the railroad construction period in the late nineteenth century.

Travelers leaving the train station in Puerto Limón were quickly engulfed in the daily activities of the town: the hustle of workers at the port and the inordinate number of bars bustling with activity, no matter what time of day. With a 1984 population of just under 59,000, Puerto Limón had more than two hundred bars, or about one bar for every 295 persons—all within an area of about nine by seven blocks (see Map 2).

Limón, with its busy port and railway, is above all a transportation town, with a hardy working-class population still distinguished by rural cordiality and conviviality. As in most small towns in the region, only a small area is occupied exclusively by businesses. The rest of the central area accommodates a seemingly comfortable mix of one- and two-story dwellings and small, mom-and-pop *pulperias* (small grocery stores). Many two-story buildings house a business on the ground floor and a dwelling above.

Moving out from the center of town, the number of businesses decreases in relation to the number of dwellings. Here there is a telltale mixture of old wooden structures alongside newer, modern concrete buildings. Most are imposingly colorful, in bright reds, greens, yellows, and various shades of blue and brown. There is hardly a dwelling without a veranda, an architectural signpost that has an indispensable place in the life of people on the Atlantic because of the steamy weather.

Although it is one of the last areas of the country to be inhabited by non-natives, the province of Limón is one of Costa Rica's most important economic regions. In the 1970s it produced 66 percent of Costa Rica's bananas and 83 percent of its cacao—the principal agricultural exports. The region supplied 28 percent of the national export income between 1970 and 1974. Limón province also includes the country's main commercial port, which handles about twice the tonnage of both the Puntarenas and Golfito ports on the Pacific coast. The economic mainstay of the region is agriculture and transportation, although petroleum processing also takes place.

Ironically, in comparison to other provinces, Limón is poor and sparsely populated. According to the 1973 census, only 1.1 percent of Limónese were in the highest salary scale, compared to 1.9 percent for the nation and 2.4 percent for the Central Valley. There are approximately 168,000 inhabitants including Blacks, Hispanics, Amerindians, and Chinese (see Table 1 for distribution of population by counties). Costa Rica does not use ethnic categories in its national statistics. However, according to a 1973 estimate, the ethnic proportions were : 49 percent Hispanic, 46 percent Black, 3

MAP 2
Puerto Limón

N

CARIBBEAN SEA

PIUTA

BARRIO
TRINIDAD

BARRIO
SANTA
EDUVIEGES

BARRIO
LOS CORALES

BARRIO
CARIARI

ZONA
HANANERA

BARRIO
ROOSEVELT

PUEBLO
NUEVO

BARRIO
BELLA VISTA

To San José

BARRIO
SAN JUAN

Río Chocolate

Estrella

Dock

Río Limoncito

BARRIO
CIENEGUITA

Río Cieneguita

PUERTO LIMÓN

| 0 | 1/8 | 1/4 |

miles

‒ ‒ ‒ ‒ Railroad line

· · · · · · Unpaved road

percent Amerindian, and 2 percent Chinese, with the proportion of Hispanics rising at a rapid rate (OFIPLAN 1977, 6). More than a decade later, perhaps due largely to immigration of poor Hispanics from the highlands, Blacks are said to constitute less than 25 percent of the total population (Bourgois 1986, 149).

Some would argue that it is precisely because of its racial composition that the province has remained poor. Travel between San José and Limón is still mostly one way. For the services typical of a capital city, as well as some forms of employment, people from Limón must still travel up the mountain. For the past five or six decades, Limón has attracted some surplus labor and land hunters, and once a year thousands of Josefinos descend the mountain to revel at the Limón carnival. But few Josefinos need travel regularly to Limón.

The contrast is significant because it suggests, in spatial terms, some of the dynamics of West Indian integration into Costa Rican society, dynamics that are of central importance in understanding the nature of change in the society, and that have no known close parallels in the West Indies.

COLONIZATION OF THE ATLANTIC COAST

Until the early 1870s, the province of Limón remained a virtual jungle, penetrable by and hospitable to only the few scattered groups of native Americans (the Bribri and the Cabecares) who inhabited its southern reaches. But the coastal area boasted one special geographic feature that was to make the region essential to the country's economy: a naturally propitious docking area for large oceangoing vessels, protected by a projecting bay and coral formations. In 1502, Christopher Columbus was the first European to use this port, then called Cariari.

The harsh climatic and ecological conditions of the lowland tropical jungle prevented colonization of the Atlantic zone until the mid-eighteenth century, when the promise of profits from cacao (*Theobroma L.*) cultivation made what is now called the Matina Valley seem attractive. Here Costa Rica developed perhaps the purest form of absentee slave plantation; cacao cultivators manned their plantations with slaves[1] while they themselves resided in the cooler climate of Cartago. It did not work: The plantations were frequently sacked, and the slaves often opted to join the pirates and Zambo Moskito pillagers. The plantations were ultimately abandoned.

But Limón was destined to play a key role in the struggle to set this poorest of Central American republics on the road to economic development. By 1865 Puerto Limón had been declared the principal port of the nation. The driving force, main agricultural product, and economic mainstay was coffee. Coffee entered the export market—to Great Britain and

TABLE 1

POPULATION OF LIMÓN PROVINCE DISTRIBUTED BY COUNTY (1984)

COUNTY	TOTAL	MALE	FEMALE	RATIO
Limón (City and Vicinity)	59,487	30,657	28,830	1.06:1
Pococi	57,197	29,945	27,252	1.10:1
Siquirres	28,367	14,935	13,432	1.11:1
Talamanca	11,029	5,830	5,199	1.12:1
Matina	14,751	7,843	6,908	1.14:1
Guacimo	16,724	8,504	7,722	1.10:1

Source: Ministerio de Economia Industria y Comercio, Direccion General de Estadistica, 1984.

Chile—in the early 1830s, but there were some snags: It was grown on the slopes of the eastern highlands, but the main port of exit then was on the Pacific coast. There was no motorized transportation, no serviceable roads, and there was a shortage of labor. Under the circumstances, building an Atlantic port with transportation connecting it to the fields was just plain good economics.

Yet it took the government a surprisingly long time to decide that a railroad from the Meseta Central to the Atlantic would be the answer. Costa Rica, of course, lacked the technology and, being so poor, the necessary funds to launch such a project. The alternative was to import the necessary technology and skill.

After several false starts, a contract was negotiated in 1871 between the government under Tomás Guardia and a North American, Henry Meiggs. The execution of the contract later fell into the hands of Minor C. Keith, Meiggs's nephew, who would later become one of the architects of the United Fruit Company and its man in Costa Rica.

Construction of the railroad linking the port with the capital faced dire financial difficulties from its inception, difficulties that resulted in the notorious Soto-Keith contract of 1884, which shortsightedly granted Keith a ninety-nine-year lease on the railroad, an expanse of 323,760 hectares (about 800,000 acres) of public land, a number of import and tax concessions, and in sum, unprecedented influence over the nation's affairs (Jones 1935, 86–87; Stewart 1964, 53–55). Most important here is that this contract set the basic conditions for the establishment of a banana plantation colony on the Atlantic seaboard and for the import and settlement of West Indian migrant labor.

Costa Ricans were willing to work on the uplands section of the railroad but not on the *tierra caliente* or "hotlands" section. Many who attempted to brave conditions in the hotlands had to flee back to the highlands or risk malaria, yellow fever, dysentery, and other tropical diseases, as well as scandalously unsafe working conditions—even by nineteenth century standards. As the human misery mounted, the government was forced to withdraw "all Costa Rican peones on the Atlantic" for health reasons, according to the *Gaceta Oficial* for December 11, 1872. The other logical source of labor was the local Amerindian population, but they had long ago retreated to the southern mountains and insisted on staying there. Once again the effort developed an international angle; Keith was forced to import West Indians, Chinese, and for a brief period, Italians.[2]

West Indians were well suited for this venture as a result of prior exposure to similar weather, work, and diseased conditions. Except for oral accounts of frequent suicides, the Chinese, too, appear to have managed quite well in spite of the inhuman conditions, but the Italians soon rebelled.

Not as disposed to labor under the prevailing conditions as were the West Indians and the Chinese, they soon asked to be released from their contract; the government and the United Fruit Company obliged (Stewart 1964, 67). A few Black North Americans were also recruited in the early stages of construction, but most soon left for the more attractive Panama Canal project south of the border.

A few West Indians came from Barbados, St. Lucia, and St. Kitts, but the bulk came from Jamaica. Jamaica not only had a larger population than the other supplying islands, but it was at the time experiencing a depression in the sugar industry, the backbone of its economy. It might have been cheaper to have a single source of labor, but during later work stoppages, the Company used island differences among laborers to its advantage. The first group arrived in 1872, and by 1874 there were anywhere from 766 to 1,000 (see Table 2).

Twenty years after the first arrival, the population seems to have decreased by more than 30 percent, apparently due to the competitive positions in which the railroad project and the emerging banana plantation found themselves vis-à-vis the Panama Canal project. In any case, workers moved back and forth with the ebb and flow of opportunities and salaries, and by 1927 the census showed more than 19,000 "Jamaicans" in Costa Rica (in the census all West Indians were referred to as Jamaicans).

Conditions did not improve with the foreign labor force. It is estimated that the first twenty miles of rail out of Puerto Limón claimed four thousand lives (Stewart 1964, 43). Today, West Indians who survived do not give casualty figures; they simply sum up the conditions thus: "Under every one of those pole*en* [railroad tie] is the body of a colored man."

FROM CONSTRUCTION TO CULTIVATION

Although their labor was unquestionably vital to the construction of the railroad, the economic role of West Indians in Costa Rica matured with the cultivation of bananas and cacao, not with railroad construction. No other group played a comparable role in the development of the plantation, for by the time the railroad was completed in 1889, the remaining Chinese were established in business for themselves.

Hispanic Costa Ricans—who were derogatorily referred to by Jamaicans as *Paña*—ventured into the area for the second time only about 1912, when conditions had been greatly improved and plantation development was already approaching its peak. Hispanics were for the most part confined to hard manual labor, digging drains, and building access railway tracks and roads. By the 1920s their numbers were increasing, no doubt due to the drop in coffee prices in the highlands and the resulting rise in unemployment.

TABLE 2
Distribution of West Indians in Costa Rica by Province, 1874–1984[a]

YEAR	TOTAL	LIMÓN	SAN JOSÉ	CARTAGO	HEREDIA	ALAJUELA	GUANACASTE	PUNTARENAS
1874	766	—	—	—	—	—	—	—
1882	902	—	—	—	—	—	—	—
1888	839	—	—	—	—	—	—	—
1892	634	541	63	16	5	6	1	—
1927	19,136	18,003	431	309	1	24	64	—
1950	15,118	13,749	694	146	22	46	20	41
1963	35,250[b]	—	—	—	—	—	—	—
1973	54,090[b]	—	—	—	—	—	—	—
1974	55,442[b]	—	—	—	—	—	—	—
1963	69,822[c]	—	—	—	—	—	—	—

Sources: Melendez and Duncan, 1974; Ministerio de Economia, Industria y Comercio, Direccion General de Estadistica, 1963, 1973, 1974, 1984.

[a] These figures must be taken with caution for the following reasons: The pre-1892 figures were derived from shipping records. However, it is well known that many Jamaicans and other West Indians arrived in Costa Rica by unknown routes, and therefore were unlikely to have had their presence recorded. The *Gaceta Oficial* of April 11, 1874, for example, cites a railroad official who states that 1,00 of the 2,500 workers were Jamaican. For this reason also it is very likely that the 1882, 1927, and 1950 census figures grossly underrepresent the population. After 1950, no ethnic distinctions were made in the census, and the ethnic mix continues to change with migration and differential natural growth.

[b] Estimates calculated from census data.

[c] Ana Maria Headley Mullings (1983) estimates Blacks to be 29.2% of Limón city population.

The growing scarcity of arable land in the highlands may have contributed as well. *Latifundismo* (the establishment of large estates) was becoming a baneful problem in Costa Rica, a country with a proud tradition of *minifundismo* (small farming). As coffee's value on the export market made its cultivation more attractive, small-scale farmers were increasingly squeezed out of their holdings (Stone 1975, 90–96 and cf. Biesanz 1945).

Once Blacks settled on the plantation, cheap wages, company-owned commissary debt practices, as well as social and racial discrimination made them completely dependent on it. The Company determined (or influenced) and supplied practically all their needs: housing, health care, living arrangements, travel. Benefits and services provided to workers were the barest minimum necessary to keep them working. At times the Company used the workers' alien status to deny them benefits, threatening deportation of vocal malcontents (see Bourgois 1985, 185). Furthermore, unlike the Hispanic laborers, Blacks in the 1930s were forbidden by law to seek employment outside of the Atlantic zone (Biesanz et al. 1982, 66).

In acquiescence to the demands of the plantation colony, Limón became a potpourri of national groups of varying sizes: East Indians, all of whom came via Jamaica, arrived on the scene; Syrians and Germans filled certain commercial niches; a few English engineers are mentioned; and manual laborers were attracted from various Central American countries. North American whites, however, sat atop the hierarchy. English was the operative language, and those who did not speak it remained at a distinct disadvantage. Blacks, being primarily from the Anglophone islands, could communicate with their Anglo-American supervisors, who typically never bothered to learn Spanish. Therefore, they were favored among the laborers, and this had important implications for social relations from the late 1920s onward.

INDUSTRIAL-SCALE PLANTATION

Before the rails of the newly constructed railroad began to rust, Minor C. Keith had the revelation that its use as a mere transporter of coffee from the highlands to the newly constructed Atlantic port could not keep it profitable. The answer: augmenting railroad activity with commercial cultivation of bananas, using the same loyal—and soon to be expanded—labor force. The type of productive regime that evolved gradually from the reluctantly tamed tropical forest was industrial-scale plantation—an expanded and now highly capitalized postemancipation version of the larger slave plantation.

According to Mintz (1959), the characteristic distinctions between the slave plantation (based on Gray's [1941] definition) and the modern large-scale plantation are: (1) labor is not enslaved, and (2) the modern agro-social form (e.g., the United Fruit Company) represents a much-magnified scale and intensity of capitalistic development. Other features include a vast increase in capital investment and the freeing of capital tied up in owned labor (Mintz, 1959, 43–44). The more specific nature of such plantations depends on the type and scale of the productive forces and the way in which they are combined in the particular ecological setting (Wolf and Mintz 1957). In Costa Rica, land was granted by the government as a concession— a policy the government had used on other occasions to cancel public debts (Hill 1964, 41)—and the importation of labor was made possible by relaxing restrictions on the immigration of non-whites (Melendez and Duncan 1977, 87). In addition, the government gave the Company a free hand in the disposition of labor and land, facilitating this with legislative authority.

The historical links between the West Indies and the colonizing countries were significant in the movement of labor then as they are today. At the time that migrants were being recruited for plantation labor and railroad construction, the erstwhile slave plantation economies of the West Indian territories were declining. People were out of work everywhere. In addition, most ex-slaves and their descendants had developed cultural and nationalistic ties with their colonizer, in this case Great Britain, and this fact was grasped and used by some labor recruiters. According to the account of some first-generation migrants, American labor recruiters operating in Jamaica at the time spoke from church pulpits, explaining to prospective workers that if they went to work for the United Fruit Company they would be serving Her Majesty's cause.

The internationalization of the Costa Rican effort continued. The United Fruit Company was incorporated by 1899 with capital stock of $20 million, most of it from Great Britain (Kepner 1936, 22). Like plantations in other areas of the Caribbean (Jamaica, Cuba, Puerto Rico) and Central America (Nicaragua, Honduras, Guatemala, and Panama)—most owned by the United Fruit Company—the Costa Rican plantation was largely a monocrop endeavor, and its product was destined for the markets of the developed world. Other products such as cacao, hemp, and lumber were introduced later, but only on a small scale and only when banana production began to decline.

By 1908, bananas held first place in exports from Costa Rica, more than twice the value of coffee exported (International Bureau of American Republics 1909, 13).[3] The Limón port, built and controlled by Keith, handled 75 percent of the country's exports. This meant foreign control of the export economy. Furthermore, monopoly of the transportation system, control over use of land, labor supply, and the provision of various infrastructures meant that the Company could and did control competition in production, as well as marketing.[4]

Costa Rica's emerging infrastructure appeared to reflect the assumption that "what's good for the Company is good for the country." Keith managed to acquire other government contracts; he established electrification, sewage, and water systems in the Meseta Central; he built markets, and even established his own banks in San José and Limón (Stewart 1964, 136–43).

The government also provided all political and legal sanctions. It broke de facto national rules in order to import West Indians into what Hispanic Costa Ricans mistakenly regarded as a racially homogeneous population; it initially allowed United Fruit to police its own workers, and later, when the national police were introduced in the region, their salary was paid in full or augmented by the Company. Puerto Limón was unmistakably a prototypical company town, aided and abetted by the state (see Kepner and Soothill 1935, 215–16). This comfortable relationship was not to last, however. By the 1930s the government itself, pressed by newly organized plantation laborers, was making public its disagreement with the Company's policies. But a colony within a society had been created, and the elements of its organization were not intended to fulfill the needs of an emergent society but those of a monopolistic corporation. Conflict was inevitable.

NEED AND GREED: SOCIAL ORGANIZATION AND CULTURAL MANIPULATION

As the United Fruit Company molded the Atlantic landscape, it also molded the social organization of those within its grasp, and by doing so it helped to shape their ideas, even in the face of continued resistance.

In considering the social organization of the plantation, there are three factors of immediate importance to the central theme of inequality and social transformation: (1) the organization of the productive forces; (2) the code of relations among the racial groups, viewed as a function of the organization of labor; and (3) the role of distinctive cultural symbols in the interaction (or noninteraction) of those groups within the context of the plantation. The preeminent symbol of the plantation class structure was the exclusive gold or silver payroll, for Anglos and non-Anglos respectively. In true apartheid fashion, Anglos were paid more than non-Anglos regardless of task and skill.

Both the plantation owners and their West Indian laborers manipulated cultural distinctions in concert, toward different but mutually supportive ends. The Company engaged in cultural manipulation in order to maximize its profits; the West Indian laborers engaged in it as an instrument of competition in the struggle for position with Hispanics. Other than their physical strength, cultural symbols were the only edge West Indians had over Hispanics: They, like their employers, shared a version of British culture. The collusion of interest arising out of the need for jobs among West Indians and the Company's perceived need for ever-increasing profits lubricated the wheels of exploitation. But the use of foreign labor, at first an ecological necessity, led to a major contradiction between national interest and plantation development, contributing to the decline of the Atlantic coast economy. Culture and ethnic relations, then, were ultimately key elements in the organization of the relations of production, and therefore in their transformation.

In general outline, the role of culture and color in the organization of Costa Rican plantations was not very different from the slave and postslavery plantations in the Caribbean, particularly where two ethnic labor groups competed—Asians and Blacks, for example, in Guyana and Trinidad. What was different on United Fruit plantations was the complex six-directional competition and conflict involving Anglos, Hispanics, and Blacks.

By the beginning of this century, the banana plantation had spread along most of the Atlantic coast, and the distribution of population clusters, with Puerto Limón as the administrative center, corresponded to the layout requirements of the plantation and the transportation system. The personnel concerned with the day-to-day activities on a particular section of the plantation lived nearby in what were referred to as "camps—much like army camps," according to McCann (1976, 140), a former public relations officer for the Company. From the standpoint of daily production, each camp was semiautonomous.

An Anglo (usually American) supervisor headed each section. His dwelling was easily distinguished from all others by size, structure, environs, and general appearance. Next in order were the foremen and timekeepers, some of whom were Jamaican Coloreds, with an occasional dark-skinned Black. In size, comfort, and appearance, their dwellings matched their status. The laborers, at the bottom of the scale, were housed in large, barracklike structures, with partitioned rooms or compartments shared by several men at a time. Sanitary facilities were rudimentary and at times nonexistent; overcrowding was common, and proper health care little more than a wish. In the latter stage of plantation development, however, dwellings for laborers were improved, in some cases to enable entire families to cohabit—even if uncomfortably. Most were two-story, two-family structures with detached toilets. Elevated on stilts, living quarters consisted of four upper-floor rooms (two for each family), with cement-floored, partially enclosed cooking facilities on the lower level.

In dwellings as well as working arrangements, Hispanic laborers were effectively separated from Blacks. Hispanic laborers were employed directly by an Hispanic subcontractor, while Blacks were for the most part employed and supervised directly by Company personnel. The relationship between both ethnic groups was like water and oil in a bottle: close but no mixing.

As is true throughout the Caribbean plantation system, ethnic/national divisions were manipulated along with class divisions as a means of social and economic control. J. L. Williams, a United Fruit overseer in eastern Guatemala, observed that "whites could bank on the support of the American Negroes . . . [who] forewarned the whites of any Jamaican plot" (Kepner 1936, 170). There are numerous oral accounts of West Indians spying on their Hispanic countrymen in Costa Rica, and Bourgois (1985, 212) cites numerous press reports stating that during the 1934 strike, the Company formed an all-Black West Indian organization called the Sojourners' Committee to denounce West Indian support for the strikers. In fact, the Company imported laborers from different West Indian islands to avoid labor solidarity. Exploiting deep seated Black-Hispanic divisions required little effort. When Blacks went on strike, the Company used Hispanic strike breakers and vice versa. Also, "it was the company's policy to avoid as much as possible putting [Costa Rican] nationals in high positions because of their divided allegiance in disputes with the national government" (Kepner 1936, 177). To make matters worse, the Company often paid Blacks more than Hispanics for the same type of work.

Between North Americans and West Indians, social closure was not confined to residential and occupational arrangements. Blacks had to lift their hats and give right-of-way to a white person. Leisure activities also ensured separation, although on occasion there was racial mingling at the frequent baseball games. Yet, the fact that middle-level Colored employees established their own club—called variously the Black-white or the Brown Man's Club—and a separate tennis court, suggests that mingling was confined primarily to one sport, baseball.

It was apparently the intent of white Americans to impart that one aspect of American culture to the plantation worker, not for the latter's benefit but for the enjoyment of the Americans themselves. If they could revel in the entertainment of the north while accumulating the profits of the south, why not? That much they accomplished in Cuba, Nicaragua, and the Dominican Republic. This was cultural imperialism at its most subtle. But the dominated have a tendency to bloom where they are planted: A few Blacks became living legends among their own in the sport of baseball. Yet, it is a testimony to the West Indians' hold on a culture they regarded as superior that throughout the plantation heyday cricket continued to be the sport of the Black man in Limón.

To a small degree, the social chasm between North American whites and West Indians was bridged in the workplace. Many positions such as accountant, clerk, telegraph operator, foreman, and timekeeper were held by Coloreds—"educated" Jamaicans—and even the famous Marcus Garvey, the blackest of Blacks, was for a brief period a timekeeper. But attempts to stem the decline in production and accompanying rising costs in the 1930s saw race/color once again used as an instrument of profit. According to Ezequiel Gutierrez, treasurer of the municipality of Limón, some positions held by Coloreds and whites were downgraded and filled by "Negroes" (Kepner and Soothill 1935, 92–93). The United Fruit Company was not alone in this respect; the reverberations of the Depression caused planters in other parts of the world to do likewise (Jain 1970, 222).

A HIERARCHY BASED ON RACE

Gradations in its structure helped to make the inherent contradictions of the plantation system less apparent than if the structure had been strictly dichotomous (see Figure 1). Lower-level workers found tenuous hope in seeing people of their own color or ethnic group in higher positions. It affirmed, at least in their own minds, the possibility of mobility which the dominant social ideology of the time promised, if not for themselves, for their children. It also afforded the development of some personal relationship between worker and supervisor—outside of the workplace. Through such relationships, time sheets could be padded, absences ignored, and products stolen and sold, all to the mutual benefit of the worker and supervisor.

In spite of sharp racial differences, then, the social organization of the plantation formed a single, integrated system based largely on overlapping class and cultural differences. The class cleavage was softened by those who filled positions between management and labor, such as the foremen and the piece-job bosses. On the one hand, these individuals represented (at least ostensibly) the interest of the Company and dealt directly with the managerial class; on the other hand, off the job they were socially a part of the laboring population, perhaps of a higher social status than the common laborer but nevertheless a part of the ethnic group. In effect, they were social brokers who stood at the gate to upward mobility (see Jain 1970, Trouillot 1984).

The strict hierarchy made upward mobility a rare and valued opportunity. Those above had immeasurable power over their subordinates; a simple whisper in the appropriate ear above could profoundly alter a life below. Blacks and Coloreds in intermediate positions of authority responded, out of insecurity and ambition, by driving their Black subordinates just a bit harder and thereby preserving their own positions.

The structure of the plantation system may be conceptualized, at one level, as a two-tiered class hierarchy consisting of white owners of the

FIGURE 1
Pre-1930 Plantation Organizational Hierarchy

W = White Anglo
C = Colored
H = Hispanic/Creole
B = Black

FOREIGN

LOCAL

Division Manager (W)

Superintendents (of transportation, agriculture, commissary, etc.) (W)

Professional Staff (construction, maintenance, agriculture) (W)

Section Overseers (W)

Large independent planters (W&C)[a]

Accounting and Bookkeeping Staff

(limit of mobility for Blacks) ————————————————————————

Clerks (commissary, administrative) (B&C)

Locomotive Operators (B&C)   Construction and Maintenance Foreman (B&C)

Station Masters, Conductors, Piece-Job Foremen, Timekeepers (B, C&H)

(limit of intra-generational on-the-job mobility) — — — — — — — — — — — — — — — — — — —

Semi-skilled (brakemen, mechanics, line repair, etc.—B&C)

Unskilled (planters, cutters, carriers, loaders—B&C; drain diggers, road and rail repair—H)

[a]Racial designations in parenthesis represent the majority—though not all—of the individuals in those categories.

means of production with their loyal white cadre on top, and Black and Hispanic labor at the bottom. But at another level, we have the underclass of Hispanics and Blacks displaying an intraclass hierarchy animated by race/culture, status/prestige, and occupational criteria of separation. This conceptualization is similar to that posed by Jain (1970) for the social organization of the rubber plantation he studied in Malaya. He notes that the overall social stratification manifests itself in class divisions between the foreign owners at the top, the Asian (Indians and Ceylonese) white-collar staff and supervisory element in the middle, and the Indian workers below. But the Indian laborers themselves are stratified, part of a larger pattern of social stratification imposed by the occupational hierarchy of the estate. Personal interaction between Indian laborer and Asian cadre seems to parallel that between the Black and Colored cadre in Limón; but occupational lines of distinction between Indians and Asians appear to be much more rigid. Jain notes that even after acquiring the necessary education, Indians were not given the types of jobs held by Asians. Thus, it seems that in Malaya, more than in Costa Rica, traditional occupational differentiation served to maintain cultural differentiation rather than the other way around.

Objectively, Hispanics in Costa Rica shared a lower-level structural position with Blacks, but Blacks evaluated Hispanics collectively as culturally, racially, and in some cases, occupationally inferior. Blacks, on the other hand, were differentiated primarily on the basis of color gradations and occupational ranking. The various levels were not as monolithic as they seem on the surface, however. There were instances of dark-skinned individuals in positions normally held by Coloreds. And Coloreds did not fill these positions primarily because of the color of their skin; there were educational requirements. As it happened, however, most educated West Indians were, by reason of the history of class-color relations in the Caribbean, people of lighter skin color. Nor was the lower-level dark-skinned group monolithic outside of the occupational setting; their low position on the job did not prevent a respectable and influential standing in social and religious contexts.

Regardless of the specific intricacies of the objective cultural, social, racial, and economic hierarchy, individuals within each group formed their own mental model based on their perception and self-interest at particular moments in the history of the region. Whether or not their mental models coincided with the objective reality at any point is of interest primarily in that it communicated information about how each group manipulated or transacted social and cultural values in its own interest.

THE POLITICAL ECONOMY OF PERCEPTION

In spite of the structural equality between Blacks and Hispanics, Blacks regarded themselves as superior to Hispanics. Four sets of factors are of significance in explaining this:

1. Being largely of Anglophone provenance, most Blacks identified themselves with the existing British ideology of cultural and national superiority. To them, anyone who did not share this identity in any form could be viewed as inferior.

2. Lacking objective knowledge of life in other areas of Costa Rica, West Indians saw the country through the window of the plantation, and, compared to their idealized image of Jamaica, it was primitive.

3. Costa Ricans working in the plantation zone were drawn from the growing group of recently disenfranchised, uneducated peasantry, representing the lowest socioeconomic stratum of Costa Rican society. West Indians perceived this stratum as representative of the whole.

4. West Indians, unlike Costa Ricans, spoke a common language with their employers.

5. West Indians perceived themselves as physically stronger than Costa Ricans; they survived working conditions when Costa Ricans succumbed.

If there was one factor responsible for the position of Hispanic Costa Ricans at the bottom of the social hierarchy, it was that they could not speak the language of their employers. Many Blacks, such as drain diggers and unskilled field hands, were in identical occupational positions. Language was the single most important criterion of status allocation, as it was of image formation. The attitude is encapsulated in this greeting from an elderly friend in Limón: "Lord, Mr. T, I can't tell you how glad I am to see you . . . it is always a God-given pleasure to see someone you can speak the Queen's language with." To this man, who had worked for the United Fruit Company for more than forty years, English was more than just an instrument of communication; it was the most telling symbol of British culture in a country where nationals spoke only the contemptuous "bird language"— as the immigrants condescendingly referred to Spanish.

The perceived superiority of English, and hence of those who mastered it, is expressed in a passage by Quince Duncan, a Costa Rican writer of Jamaican descent: "To belong to the British Empire means not only to be a member of a multinational and 'super-developed' state . . . but that the ideal of the imperial is in itself a type of religion that developed in the individual such a concept of loyalty toward the crown, toward English values, that he becomes incapable of identifying with any other culture" (Melendez and Duncan [1974] 1977, 101).

In the minds of many of the first-generation migrants, Great Britain was

"Gran Britania" in the most majestic, sublime, and noble sense: "Britons never, never shall be slaves." The presence of a British consulate in Limón gave them an added sense of sovereign superiority, and many thought—even in the face of evidence to the contrary—that they were serving the interest of Great Britain in Costa Rica. *El Limónense* on November 1, 1914, reports that concerned individuals convened a meeting at the outbreak of World War I "to invite contribution to the English War Relief Fund," noting that "this is the time that Britishers should show their loyalty to the flag."

It is reasonable to assume that the West Indian sense of pride (if not superiority) did not derive only from British citizenship. By the 1920s, the torch of nationalism, flickering though it was, had been lit among Blacks in the Diaspora. The torch carrier was Marcus Garvey. The condition of West Indian laborers, not only in Costa Rica but in other Central American territories and in South America, fueled his campaign for racial pride and dignity, leading to the establishment in Limón of one of the few still-active branches of the Universal Negro Improvement Association (UNIA). UNIA became an organ for labor demands, but its potential was blunted by Garvey's own stance against unions and, apparently, eventual support of United Fruit (see Bourgois 1985, 185–216). The racial dignity Garvey evoked was a lasting source of strength for West Indians, but it helped to set them apart from Hispanics, ultimately becoming a wedge against class alliance and effective participation with Hispanics in the 1934 strike against United Fruit.[5]

SUPERIORITY AND STEREOTYPES

The ideology of superiority involved more than attitudes toward language, citizenship, and nationalism. Attributes such as body odor and cultural practices such as eating patterns, personal and domestic hygiene, and attire all became a part of the ideology. Blacks built their houses on stilts, dyed and polished their floors, and ate with knife and fork seated at a table. In contrast, they complained, Hispanics spit on their floors, ate wherever and however they thought convenient, and allowed their domestic animals to share their houses. Mrs. Lewin, a field hand who began working for the Company as early as 1910, spoke of Hispanics in these terms: "Dey looks to me like dey were barbarians, like dey would kill an' eat people . . . . Dese people were illiterate an' ignorant an' we was always afraid of dem. If you going along de street an' you see dem, you walk on de other side. Dey always carry dere cutlass wid dem." On special occasions, Jamaicans dressed in their "Sunday best." For males this meant a suit, tie, and hat; for "ladies" it meant a specially tailored dress, hat, and gloves. The fact that the local Hispanics paid no such attention to their attire was testimony enough to their incivility.

Not surprisingly, Hispanics nurtured their own stereotypes of Blacks. In his celebrated novel about his experiences working for the United Fruit Company, Carlos Fallas gives us a glimpse:They [Blacks] would argue at each other horrifyingly, gesticulating like devils; you would think that they were trying to kill each other.... On payday they would get drunk and make merry with rum. . . . They sang wild and monotonous songs, formed themselves in a circle clapping their hands and rhythmically stomping their feet. . . . The fiesta would then end with them lying like tree trunks on the ground, a mountain of sweaty flesh snoring noisily" (1975, 134). Referring to his own group he wrote: "We also became intoxicated once in a while, and almost always we were inclined to be sentimental and romantic with rum" (136).

The main stereotype Hispanics held (and to some extent still hold) was that Blacks were inherently inferior and pitifully primitive; that they had a tailbone was biological proof of their primitive origin. A Hispanic education official confided: "When I was growing up, there were three things that my parents used to scare me; one was the Devil, the second I can't remember, and the third was the Negro." And apparently the saying *Negro Chumeco, panza de muñeco* (roughly: "doll-belly Jamaicans") goes back to plantation days, a derogatory reference to the stereotype of Black children playing with cloth dolls whose bellies were in disrepair. In an atmosphere of bemusement on both sides, Hispanics saw Blacks as obstreperous, pugnacious, carefree, and, yes, inherently inferior, while Blacks saw Hispanics as uncivilized, ignorant, dangerous, and unclean. Some West Indians went so far as to prevent their children from associating with local Hispanics. (Today, many of those children, now adults, complain that the prejudice of their parents prevented them from learning Spanish.) The separation was not difficult to maintain because Company operations and policy supported it.

The enfeebling hierarchy of life on the plantation was cognitively congruent with the colonial conception of society inherited by Blacks. There were a few significant differences between the colonial and the new-style plantation ranking, however. Blacks were legally free, and penetration of the upper but not the uppermost stratum was now possible. This feature of the system, while benefiting some, also served to hinder full awareness of exploitation. The fact that Blacks were at times paid more than Hispanics for the same task also tended to disguise exploitation while raising a barrier to multiethnic labor unity. This was evidenced in the 1934 strike, which received almost no support from Blacks, widening the breach between them and Hispanics, who were in the forefront of the labor struggle.

Historical differences might also have contributed to the divergent perception of the relations of production. West Indians had a longer history as plantation laborers, as rural proletarians. This showed in, among other things, their consumption patterns in dress, furniture, food, leisure, and so on. There was also evidence of it in the relatively large number of non-kin-based organizations, such as UNIA, the Burial Scheme (a mutual aid association), and such lesser groups as the Onward and Upward Society and the Forward Growth Society. The need among West Indians to approximate value standards set by whites left them with a dilemma; they felt enlightened but ill at ease.

In contrast, most Hispanics who came to the Atlantic coast came from a long tradition as *campesinos* (peasants). Even though some had labored on coffee plantations in the highlands, the relationship they had developed with their employers was more personal than were the ties between West Indians and their colonial and postcolonial employers (cf. Wolf and Mintz 1957). Furthermore, unlike West Indians, they had an active attachment to the *patria*—their country—and its political machinery. These factors, among others, seem to have contributed to an attitude of national and personal confidence, despite the fact that their lifestyle seemed pedestrian, if not primitive, compared to that of West Indians.

Blacks' view of Hispanics was in stark contrast to the way they perceived Anglo-Americans. They saw their cultural relationship to Anglos as continuous in contrast to the discontinuous relationship with Hispanics. A feeling of kinship with Americans was the closest one could come to being British, at least in the corrosive setting of the plantation—although Americans were certainly not regarded as equal to the British. In any case, the upward path from common laborer to supervisor was one that some Blacks felt they could traverse socially if not economically, in the next generation if not in the present one.

Hence, Blacks were accused of "passive cooperation" and "identifying with the company" (Melendez and Duncan [1974]1977, 66; see Bryce-Laporte 1962, Kepner 1936, Olien 1967). This was partly instrumental loyalty, for like Jamaicans in other parts of Central America, Blacks were so "cocky being British" that comparatively they really did not care that much for the Americans (Kepner 1936, 169–71).

From the perspective of capital, instrumentality was perhaps the guiding principle of the plantation experience, legitimized by the "religion" of economic development on the heels of the Industrial Revolution. The deprived condition of ex-slaves, their descendants, and disenfranchised campesinos combined to form the ideal conditions for the manipulation of color and culture in the interest of capital accumulation. Black laborers, desperate to survive and even to advance according to standards set by their exploiters, stepped on their own and on white Hispanics who worked beside them, even as they deferred to white Anglos who paid their wages. Blacks and Hispanics were in turn manipulated by the Anglos who used color, culture, citizenship, and whatever else suited the growth of profit. By the 1940s and 1950s, when United Fruit abandoned the Atlantic region, the economic energy underlying race, color, and culture manipulation would become even clearer, for as the following chapters show, Blacks began to esteem Hispanics as soon as they were recognized as holding the key to socioeconomic survival and advancement.

THREE

TRANSFORMATION OF THE PRODUCTIVE SYSTEM AND RACIAL HIERARCHY

The settled and superficially hopeful existence of laborers on the Atlantic coast did not endure. Banana disease, labor conflicts, and the promise of easy land concessions conspired to transform the entire social and economic structure of the region. Banana production reached its peak at the beginning of the 1920s, after which production in South and Central America shifted; while exports from other banana areas increased, exports from Limón declined steadily (see Table 3).

Leaf spot diseases (*Fusarium cubense* and *Cercaspora musae*) were the main cause of the decline, but important political and economic factors were also involved. A key factor was the mounting protest coming from government, labor, and private citizens regarding the discriminatory policies of the Company, which favored West Indians over Hispanics. And then there was the problem of soil exhaustion, making cultivation at increasing distances from the main transportation arteries an unprofitable necessity. To stem the decline, United Fruit took two measures.

First, the Company planted cacao, a crop purportedly used as a medium of exchange from pre-Spanish days up to the nineteenth century (Blom 1935). To increase profits, the Company allegedly used force to discourage cacao cultivation among Jamaicans, who had been planting the crop in Costa Rica long before it became economically appealing to the Company. Cacao flourished for a while, and in a bow toward agricultural advancement, bananas were planted to shade the cacao trees, resulting in a temporary increase in banana exports at the same time.

The second measure was to encourage subcontracted independent cultivators and to sublease Company farms. The rationale was typical of monopolistic capital: shift the rising cost of production to the primary producer, while the Company monopolized marketing, a practice common in colonial plantations in parts of Africa and Asia (see Greaves 1968, 112–13).

TABLE 3
COMPARISON OF BANANA EXPORTS BY COUNTRY AND YEAR
(IN BUNCHES)

COUNTRY	1900	1913	1929	1932
Columbia	273,883	6,277,540	10,300,021	7,363,000
Costa Rica	3,332,125	9,366,485	5,784,724	4,313,000
Cuba	845,942	2,327,536	3,682,900	4,651,000
Honduras	4,772,417	8,238,726	28,221,463	27,896,000
Jamaica	7,173,890	11,419,281	22,020,877	20,360,000
Nicaragua	1,324,727	1,639,120	4,160,700	3,378,000
Panama[a]	2,125,709	5,185,530	4,722,426	3,600,000

[a]The figures for Costa Rica and Panama are somewhat misleading since fruit grown in the Sixaola district of Costa Rica is exported through Panama and therefore credited to that country. In any case, production in both countries was affected by the Panama disease (Kepner 1936: 67).

HISPANICS WIN JOB PREFERENCE

Added to this unstable and declining economic situation was a rising challenge to Black primacy in the labor force: an increase in the immigration of Hispanics. Some came from Nicaragua, but most were from the Costa Rican highlands (Fernandez, Schmidt, and Basauri 1976, 90). They began to arrive in the 1920s in delayed response to the banana boom; wages on the Atlantic coast were at times five to six times higher than in the highlands (Biesanz, Biesanz, and Biesanz 1982). Latifundismo in the highlands, coupled with the decrease in coffee production in the early decades of the twentieth century, were major factors pushing Hispanic workers into Limón. Also, with World War II came the suppression of credit to *cafetaleros* (coffee growers) and the close of the European market. Cafetaleros had the land but could not absorb the labor, and land was plentiful in Limón—a factor that was to become a growing source of contention between Blacks and Hispanics in later years. By 1927 there were more than 13,000 Hispanics on the Atlantic coast, and by 1928 approximately 45 percent of railroad employees were of Hispanic extraction (having Hispanic names) (Koch 1977, 10).[1]

As the ethnic pot thickened in the early 1930s, a significant new political element entered: the state. The national government insisted that Costa Rican nationals be given more employment and higher positions (Kepner 1936, 176–78). The mood encouraged a number of petitions. One that was remarkable for its anti-Black rhetoric was submitted to Congress in 1933 by 543 white residents of the Atlantic region. It decried the "economic crisis besetting the country" because of the "invasion of the cities of the Meseta Central" by Blacks and the preference given to this "inferior race" by the United Fruit Company. The petition insisted on a law prohibiting the immigration of Blacks (Archivo Nacional, *Congreso* No.16753, 1933).

This was a period of crisis, and although much of it could be attributed to the reverberations of the worldwide Depression, white Costa Ricans, from top to bottom, pointed the finger at Blacks. On April 10, 1934, *La Tribuna* reported that the government would no longer issue entrance visas to Blacks. On December 10, 1936, Congress passed an initiative requiring the use of executive power to guarantee "the preferential treatment due Costa Rican workers in the banana industry in this country" (Archivo Nacional, *Congreso* No.17726, Document No.1, 1936).

Leon Cortes, elected president of Costa Rica that year, prohibited Blacks from going beyond Turrialba, the town that stands between the white highlands and Black lowlands. At Turrialba the trains changed Black crew for white before entering the supposedly racially homogeneous Meseta Central.[2] Blacks caught in the highlands were occasionally rounded up and sent back to the Atlantic coast. More and more of them resorted to part-time peasant cultivation, and some upgraded their skills as they could. Meanwhile, Costa Ricans enjoyed preference in employment and wages, and competition was further reduced by a 1942 executive order prohibiting Blacks, once again, from entering the country (Beirut 1977, 153–154, cited by Bourgois 1985, 180).

Banana operations came to a screeching halt on the Atlantic coast in the early 1940s; a German torpedo allegedly sank the last banana boat in 1942. By this time, the Company had decided to relocate, and again the government helped by providing land on the Pacific coast. The relocation was not, however, complete: Some administrative activities, including the port and railroad operation, remained on the Atlantic coast. Abaca (Manila hemp) plantations continued to operate, and a wide expanse of land was planted—unsuccessfully—in rubber.

The relocation of the Company and the prohibition against the western movement of West Indian labor meant stiffer competition among ethnic groups in Limón. By 1942, when the last shipment of bananas left the Atlantic terminus, Hispanics were already prominent in independent farming as well as in the better positions in law enforcement, transportation, and, of course, local government. But Anglo-Americans still controlled the economy; they owned some farms, and ran the railroad, hemp fields, and processing plants that together constituted the main source of employment.

A few years later, the state nationalized the railway. With a government-owned railway as the hub of economic activity, increased benefits to Hispanics radiated throughout the Atlantic region. Perhaps the most important new economic niche for Hispanics in the long term was commerce. When United Fruit left, it closed its commissaries, which until then had virtually monopolized the grocery and dry goods trade, leaving the market open to newcomers with access to capital. The Chinese, who had been gradually moving into commerce since the early decades of the twentieth century, shared the market with Hispanics. Blacks, having neither access to capital nor, some would argue, the inclination for business, became even more dependent consumers as they gravitated to the urban areas.

Many Blacks left the country, barred from employment in the new plantations on the Pacific coast. Few, if any, returned to their native islands. Migration reports published by the Registrar General's office in Kingston, Jamaica, for example, show no arrivals from Costa Rica between 1935 and 1945, but note fifty-one departures for Costa Rica. Most Jamaicans, it seems, left Costa Rica for Panama or the United States. Protests from nationals made Costa Rica increasingly inhospitable to them. Without the United Fruit Company to lean on, the vulnerability of their position became all too evident; they now depended on the very people they had disdained.

BLACKS AND THE 1948 CIVIL WAR

The period from 1942 to 1953 was a watershed in the transformation of the Atlantic region, and the impact of events was multiplied within the context of national economic and political transformation. As early as the late 1920s, the power held by the descendants of the cafetaleros had begun to atrophy, and whatever development took place outside the United Fruit Company came through the infusion of foreign capital. As the influence of foreign money grew, so did the burgeoning proletariat, openly antagonistic to the ruling oligarchy (Bell 1971, 9). For Blacks caught in this period of structural change, the decline and ultimate demise of the plantation regime meant severe hardships, right up to their first opportunity for political participation in 1953 and beyond.

Political control of the Atlantic region by Costa Ricans crystallized after 1948, the year Jose "Pepe" Figueres seized power. Tomás Guardia, elected in 1940, was pressured by the Communists in his government to institute sweeping changes aimed at repairing a growing social disequilibrium. But Figueres's radical coalition of social democrats, students, and sons of the establishment demanded changes that would ironically return the country to petit capitalism and a completely self-interested ruling class.

The pressures exploded in a civil war in 1948; with some help from Blacks on the Atlantic coast, Figueres emerged victorious. Partly as political payback, but also for humanitarian reasons, Figueres encouraged Blacks to accept citizenship, courting them in subsequent elections. Yet as Kathleen Sawyers Royal (1977), Guillermo Joseph (1982), and others have observed, Blacks still remained outside the positions of power. Now fully under Hispanic control, they experienced increasing economic disenfranchisement and displacement. Unfamiliarity with laws, coupled with an increasing need for cash, caused many to sell to incoming Hispanics untitled land to which they had usufruct rights. Many ended up in urban Puerto Limón, slowly sinking into poverty as the economic world around them changed.

Services once controlled by Americans or West Indians came under the control of nationals. For example, the state education system replaced the one Blacks had fashioned after the Jamaican model; Spanish replaced English as the language of business, government, and interethnic discourse.

HISPANIC DOMINANCE AND CULTURAL LOSS

The radical transformation of the Atlantic may be summarized in two points: (1) the transference of the means of production from a foreign enterprise to the state, accompanied by increased small-scale independent production; and (2) the transference of de facto control of the province from the foreign enterprise to the state. In effect, Limón, a closed, dependent enclave under the plantation system, became a national appendage.

For West Indians, reaping the badly needed benefits of citizenship meant at least partial cultural incorporation.[3] They were now compelled to attend state schools, something they had boldly resisted. The government had long complained that the reluctance of Blacks to send their children to Spanish schools prevented the state from imparting to them Costa Rican sentiments. We are reminded of Bourdieu's (1977) observation that "the symbolic power to impose the principles of the construction of reality—in particular social reality—is a major dimension of political power."

Hispanics guarded the economic gate, and their values, transmitted through the education system, were now the passport to participation. But the lens of Hispanic values was never completely accepted in actuality or in principle; first- and some second-generation Blacks resisted viewing the world in that way. From the point of view of the young and mobile, however, resistance was and is nothing but a haunting vestige of the "days of British superiority," an obstacle to socioeconomic advancement.

For the purposes of discussion, patterns of incorporation, as manifested culturally and as they define the present position of one racial group vis-à-vis another, may be observed in four areas: language, nationality, marriage patterns, and ideology.

ENGLISH LOSES POWER

English, previously the language of prestige, now has some negative value. This is understandable, because Spanish is not only the language of power and prestige but also of access to a livelihood. While the advantages of bilingualism are recognized in some quarters, it was not until about 1976 that it was encouraged in school. As recently as 1976, some Black teachers charged Black students fines or pinched them for speaking English in school.

As the linguistic field has become dominated by Spanish, the structure of English (or English Creole) has changed accordingly. For example, the question is no longer phrased, "How old are you?" but "How much years you have?"—a Creole translation of the Spanish *Cuantos años tiene usted?* Or take the 10-year-old pupil asking the English teacher if she has to "copy the date." The child asks, *"Tiicha, wi af tu kopiar di fecha?"*—in this case, not just structural influence but partial relexification. Both forms of change indicate deep acculturation.

The question of the national identity of Blacks, for a long time unchallenged, was the main theme of a 1978 conference on the situation of Blacks in Costa Rica. The related question, allegiance to state, however, is now moot. In a conversation with a 35-year-old Black male on my first visit to Limón, I expressed my understanding that most Afro-Costa Ricans were descendants of Jamaicans. He promptly retorted: "I am a Costa Rican." I was to become even more familiar with that attitude. Responses to questions about Jamaican heritage varied from mild hostility to polite acknowledgment or nostalgia. After fifty or sixty years of living in Costa Rica, some still dream of visiting their idealized Jamaica. Others, mostly the young, see allegiance to Jamaica as an obstacle to becoming Costa Rican.

Loyalty to the state is not in doubt—a feature in which Costa Rica resembles other multiethnic Latin countries (Hoetink 1973, 153). In a small village on the south coast, I had occasion to witness a heated debate between a Jamaican visitor and three Afro-Costa Rican males regarding the relative merits of being Costa Rican or Jamaican. After a few beers, the Jamaican let slip a few derisive remarks about Costa Rica. The result was a fists-first encounter. Obviously not all Afro-Costa Ricans would physically defend their country against an opinionated Jamaican, but many would agree with them that "this is our country" and "it is the freest country in the world."

In contrast to European immigrants in Costa Rica, the allegiance of West Indians to the state is less the result of open-arms acceptance by whites than it is part and parcel of the ongoing struggle to establish a place in the shifting sands of the Diaspora. In essence, uprooted as they are, Blacks are willing to bend in order to sink their roots where the soil is fertile. This is expressed in, among other things, changes in marriage patterns.

AN INCREASE IN INTERMARRIAGE

Before the 1950s, West Indians married almost exclusively within their own group. In 1978, however, of 218 households sampled, 6.5 percent of all unions were racially mixed and 45.2 percent of all respondents were positively disposed toward interracial unions. A few Black women thought Spanish men were more helpful economically and more loving—even if not always passionate. And some women desired unions with Hispanics so that their children would have *piel claro* (clear skin).

Black males who were favorably disposed to mixed unions portrayed Spanish females as more tolerant, more encouraging, and more supportive. One Mr. Taylor, for example, divorced his Black wife and married a Hispanic woman. He recounted that when, occasionally, his landlord comes to demand late rent his present wife will "stand up to him [the landlord] and make him cool his butt until we have the money." His former wife, he said, would "beg the landlord and blame him [Mr. Taylor]."

Young children, too, have inevitably learned to value color and race. The following comment by a young Black woman about her nine-year-old daughter is not unique: "She don't like Blacks and I don't know where she get that idea from. She always asking me in the streets why is it that Negroes so *feo* [ugly]. The other day she told me that she wanted a new father [parents were separated] but not a Negro this time."

When the prestige culture referent was the geographically distant British, West Indians affected the ideal but lived the actuality of their own cultural patterns. Now they cannot ignore national pressure. But acceptance of Hispanic values by no means characterizes the entire Black community. Recently there has been a move to stem the tide of cultural assimilation, while emphasizing socioeconomic integration. Even so, the move is spearheaded by the "Negro elite," who find it difficult to muster grass-roots support for issues defined in racial and cultural terms.

An Ideology of Equity

Besides the control of economic opportunities by Hispanics, one powerful reason Black nationalism is doomed to debility is the very character of state ideology. Costa Rica is a social democratic polity. As such it is an exponent of the ideology of total social incorporation—irrespective of race—through equal opportunity for all. This ideological stance is predicated on the *policlasista* concept—the idea that there should be no separation of the polity other than by class—introduced by Figueres after the 1948 civil war and it incorporates elements of the colonial Spanish notion of corporate society. Bombarded with this ideology through various media, Costa Ricans find it difficult to admit that there is racial discrimination, in spite of overwhelming evidence of its pernicious presence. Furthermore, many Afro-Costa Ricans subscribe to the ideology of equal opportunity and view any discrimination against Blacks as social rather than racial. A successful Black farmer aptly sums it up this way: "If you carry yourself like a decent person and respect the Spanish, you can reach anywhere in this country. We don't have racial discrimination here, what we have is social discrimination. I can't mix with a man who carry himself indecent and don't show any ambition. The Spanishman feel the same way."

This point of view is borne out by the fact that 69 percent of 218 survey respondents agreed that while there is social and racial/color discrimination against Blacks, there is nevertheless equal opportunity, at least in education and employment. Like all ideologies, the notion of equal opportunity is validated by observation of individual cases, not by knowledge of underlying structure. Afro-Costa Ricans can always point with pride and hope to a few who have "made it." The ideology, in a phrase, co-opts the dissident and rewards the supporter. To the supporter, Black nationalism is provincial ingratitude. Hence Blacks may say, "I have only Spanish friends," or refer to West Indian cuisine as "poor people food."

Limited possibilities of upward mobility have, in recent years, propelled a few Blacks into skilled and white-collar positions in transportation, petroleum processing, banking, retailing, civil service, and the independent professions. Class alliances have, therefore, begun to emerge and seem, so far, to take precedence over ethnic solidarity. The fact that 82 percent of Blacks surveyed by the author believe that there is strong discrimination among Blacks themselves is an indication (weak though it is by itself) of the weakness of ethnic cohesion compared to intragroup class differentiation.

THE LEGACY OF THE PLANTATION SYSTEM

The similarity between white-Black relations in Limón today and white-Black, superordinate-subordinate structures found throughout the Americas would, without the historical dimension, lead one to conclude that Blacks have always been at the bottom vis-à-vis whites, or at least perceive themselves that way. For, with the exception of brief periods in Caribbean history, when Asian indentured workers replaced emancipated slaves in places like Jamaica, Trinidad, and Guyana, Blacks have traditionally assumed the lowest position in society. In Jamaica, for example, as newly freed Blacks retreated from the sugar plantations, the East Indians brought in to replace them took over the bottom rung of the social hierarchy, stigmatized by their immigrant status, by the reputation of the plantation, and by their acceptance of lower wages.

Where indentured labor did not constitute a significant segment of the labor force, as in Barbados and other islands of the Lesser Antilles, Blacks have occupied all lower levels of the subjective as well as the objective hierarchy. Hard work, thrift, and the strength of a relatively unfractured cultural tradition have propelled most East Indians further up the class scale. But even after the dismantling of the colonial political structure and the rise of Black leadership, more Blacks still live at poverty levels. In the Anglophone Caribbean, then, Blacks as a national group have outpaced other groups politically but have been outclassed economically.

In Costa Rica, Blacks began as favored workers with self-perceived cultural and social superiority vis-à-vis Hispanics within the plantation community, then moved into a position of both economic and cultural inferiority in the postplantation era. After the transition of the 1940s and the political incorporation of the 1950s, individual Blacks achieved intermediate positions in regional politics and in economic standing, but collectively they remain on the margins of Costa Rican life.

The other side of the coin is that the successful transition from migrant laborers to Costa Rican citizens is a living example of the resilience of Africans in the Americas. Alongside the economic and political dimensions mentioned above, the creative, if divisive, manipulation of cultural symbols played as crucial a role in the transition as it did in the plantation.

No doubt, had the plantation remained the economic mainstay of the Atlantic coast, the demographic composition of the work force and the province in general would have continued to move toward increasing conflict—only an expanding opportunity structure could have contained, or perhaps stabilized, the ethnic friction arising out of the use of a culturally and racially mixed labor force. However, natural conditions conspired with the technical limitations of banana cultivation to make this a moot point.

The ethnic factor was nevertheless a very potent fuel in the process of change. Protest against West Indians forced the state to pressure the Company into granting more and better positions to Hispanics. A local newspaper, *La Tribuna*, carried the following statement on September 3, 1930: "In its Costa Rica concession of 1930 the United Fruit Company promises, in filling any position of office worker, operator, or laborer, to give the preference to a Costa Rican 'when in its judgment he possesses equal ability and capacity with one of another nationality,' "(Kepner 1936, 178). As mentioned earlier, a growing nationalism, beginning around the latter part of the Depression, formed the backdrop to protests directed against Company control of such vast quantities of national resources, and against their discriminatory hiring practices. As Costa Ricans became victims of an increasingly polarized, foreign-controlled economy, they began to demand a return to the egalitarianism of family agriculture and small business. Both foreign capital and Black labor were seen as obstacles. It is understandable, therefore, that acceptance of Blacks came only after they had given their blood in the 1948 civil war.

That it was plantation activity that conditioned racial group relations and social hierarchy rather than the other way around seems clear. Yet the role of prior historical attitudes cannot be ignored. The stage for the plantation social drama was set, not in the immediate postemancipation plantation system, but in the slave plantation. The colonial experience of Blacks as well as Hispanics had established codes of evaluation and classification of color, rank, and prestige that were later reenacted within the modern capitalist plantation setting. The perception of race, color, and culture in terms of a hierarchy of values on the United Fruit plantation was primarily a function of position within the plantation structure, but the codes of evaluation were four centuries in the making.

When Blacks were favored over Hispanics by the owners of the means of production, the white skin color of Hispanics did not prevent Blacks from regarding their Hispanic labor-mates as inferior. The obvious conclusion is that it was not a matter of race per se, but of the integral part race plays in power relations and economic competition. In addition to protecting their economic position, through their flaunting of British culture Blacks were expressing allegiance with Great Britain, a superior power that had molded their subservient worldview for over four centuries. As soon as Blacks lost their position of superiority, a reevaluation of Hispanics followed, with many of the symbols of prestige now drawn from Hispanic culture.

The process by which individuals pursue their material and ideal interests involves evaluation, formation of strategies, and constant modification, allowing for emphasis and deemphasis of different aspects of culture or ideology, contingent on the individual's position in relation to the locus of power. But the manipulation of symbols, whether they be of race, class, or culture, does not by itself explain this complex multiethnic social process. The conditions that bring groups together and that keep them together are of equal if not greater importance in understanding why groups are the way they are and what course they are likely to take. Referring to the tendency to grant explanatory powers to ethnic heterogeneity, Wolf (1982, 379) cautions that

...this heterogeneity must itself be located in the *organization of the labour process*. The diverse groups brought together did, of course, make use of distinctive cultural forms to build ties of kinship, friendship, religious affiliation, common interest, and political association in order to maximize access to resources in competition with one another. Such activity, however, cannot be understood without seeing it in relation to the ways different cohorts of the working class were brought into the process of capitalist accumulation [emphasis added].

Four

SPACE AND SOCIAL INEQUALITY IN LIMÓN

As with most places undergoing regional development, Limón has its own unique relationship between population distribution and social inequality. Urban areas, in addition to being the center of resources (jobs, education, entertainment), are perceived as the center of civility. Therefore, a move to an urban area represents, in and of itself, social upgrading. Because cities are so perceived, their distribution and the movement of individuals between them have much to tell about the ranking of individuals.

Becoming and remaining part of a social stratum involves far more than such objective criteria as income, occupation, education, and family background; ideas concerning personal decency, dignity, honesty, and ambition come into play as well. The entire process is complex and fluid; the precise parameters are not always easy to define unambiguously, even for the insider. By asking informants how they made such evaluations, I tried to define the process. However, each evaluation and classification is qualified by the context in which it took place, and no study as limited as this can cover all important contexts. What I describe, then, is a mere outline of the system, developed by an outsider with the generous conscious and unconscious help of insiders. As a consequence, the social hierarchy is presented as if it were more fixed than it is in actuality.

The system of stratification I portray defines social class in terms of the dynamic relationship of groups of people to the means of production in the total society. However, the focus is on the status and prestige relationships among the peasants, proletarians, small-scale farmers, and professionals who constitute the Black community. The emphasis is, therefore, on intraclass rather than interclass relationships, with special attention paid to classification according to local knowledge—much of which occurs within what I broadly call the dominated class—and its implications for social mobility. But the social activities of this group are heavily constrained or facilitated by its position within the broader system of class relations, a fact that confronts the analyst at every point, particularly with regard to the almost coerced transmission of culture and social values downward and the manipulation of these values in efforts to move upward. The argument can be generalized to the Caribbean and indeed to all the postcolonial societies (see Worsley 1984), but important sociocultural features set Costa Rica apart from similar Caribbean territories.

THE INEQUALITY OF SPACE

The relationship between the distribution and articulation of population centers and social mobility is illustrated by a brief examination of urban-rural migration. Limón province is one of the few regions in Costa Rica where, in recent times, migration has increased both to and from rural areas. The movement is bifurcated along ethnic lines: Afro-Costa Ricans are drawn to the towns primarily in search of jobs and education, while Hispanics are attracted to the rural sector in search of land and agricultural jobs. The process shows the economic interrelatedness of the two groups; indications are that the movement of Blacks to the towns facilitates the movement of Hispanics to the rural areas. First, a brief historical background.

In the nineteenth century, population centers (and services) on the Atlantic coast sprang up in response to the demands of the banana industry. From the outset, the plantation was laid out to provide farm areas and administrative and shipping centers, a rural-urban pattern that ultimately influenced the social and physical structure of the community, as well as the division of skills, services, and amenities. The banana plantation was not exactly a "factory in the field" (Mintz 1959), like the sugarcane plantations; bananas did not have to be processed, they only required transport from field to port and from port to market. The main nonagricultural operation took place at the port, which, with its administrative functions, formed a kind of urban headquarters.

This institutionalized separation left a lasting impression on the sensibilities of the work force. The plantation was a sort of social womb; it molded the cultural and economic life of workers as it forged their consciousness. Everyone knew that culturally and economically the town represented the symbolic center of the world.

Since the early days of the plantation, many rural dwellers (along with the few upper-level plantation employees and later farmers and peasants as well) have also maintained urban residences. But it was difficult to get from some rural areas to Puerto Limón. A writer in *El Correo del Atlantico* of March 4, 1951, observed, "It is easier to travel to the United States and back than to travel to such places as Talamanca, Sixaola, Puerto Viejo, and Cahuita" (plantation sections south of Puerto Limón). All important services were located in the town, but transportation operated to serve the needs of the plantation rather than the needs of labor, hence the need for dual residences. Over the years this trend increased. Women often remained in the urban area for the greater part of the school year so that they could "school the children." Until recently the province's only secondary school was in Puerto Limón.

In the initial stages of railroad construction and plantation development, workers who pioneered virgin areas stayed in the bush for weeks, sometimes months, at a time, going to town only as a form of rest and relaxation from the backbreaking work and steamy environment. They also had to see their women occasionally, for the arrangement that kept the men in the bush and their women in town was a constant source of domestic strife, aggravated by the threatening fact of scarce women.

The structure of plantation society, then, set the foundation for and encouraged the emergence of a set of activities and accompanying values based on the division of space. These values would later form part of the cognitive map used in evaluating social prestige. The separation is reminiscent of Sydel Silverman's (1966) portrayal of central Italy, where the village-countryside contrast gave way to a civility-uncivility contrast in the evaluation of social prestige.

Unintended though it may be, the hierarchization of space is a central cog in the machine of labor exploitation. The concentration of services in any specific area is not necessarily proportional to its gross economic contribution to the national economy. The Talamanca coast, for example, produced 28 percent of the national income from agricultural export between 1974 and 1977 (Inter-American Development Bank 1978), yet it is one of the least serviced areas in the country. In Table 4, four levels of settlement in the province are designated by letters A through D in descending order. The Talamanca coast has only C and D level centers.

This is a somewhat unjustified simplification of the urban-rural contrast, for from the early days of the plantation, intermediate settlements sprang up along the rail lines and around the railway stops. In general, however, all settlements vary with respect to population, availability of services and amenities, and more importantly, with respect to racial composition and economic base. The layout may be conceived in terms of a hierarchical ranking of settlements according to the aggregate socioeconomic activity and relative size of the population (Berry and Garrison 1958; Brush 1953), with Puerto Limón as the hub of social and economic activity in the province. Map 3 shows how the levels of settlement for the province, described in Table 4, are distributed geographically.

TABLE 4
Functional Classes of Settlements in the Atlantic Zone, Costa Rica

ASSOCIATED FUNCTIONAL UNITS	LEVEL D	LEVEL C	LEVEL B	LEVEL A
Retail trade	Grocery or general store	Restaurant Tavern	Implement dealer Filling station Hardware store Food market Restaurant	Appliance store Lumber yard Drug store Apparel store Restaurant
Wholesale	———	———	———	Liquor
Finance	———	———	Bank Credit Union	Credit union Insurance agency Four banks
Trades and personal service	———	Tailor and seamstress	Auto repair Barber and beautician Shoe repair	Electric repair Photographer Dry cleaner Hotel Undertaker
Entertainment	———	Dance hall	Pool ball	Gymnasium Movie Stadium Public park
Transportation	———	———	50% paved roads	Night club Port Railroad terminal Taxi service
Communication	———	Mail delivery Public tele- phone only	Post office Telephone	Daily newspaper Telephone Radio
Utilities	Public water supply	Water supply Electricity	Water supply Electricity	All utilities
Manufacturing	———	———	———	Food processing Packaging
Professional service	Elementary school	Elementary school ——— High school ——— Health clinic	High school	Physician Dentist, Lawyer Veterinarian
Social service	———	———	Sanitation	Social security *Patronato* (domestic social services)
Government	———	*Deligacion* (police) Community organization Ministry of Agriculture Extension Office	*Municipalided* (autonomous county government)	Provincial government

MAP 3
ATLANTIC SETTLEMENTS AND RAILWAYS

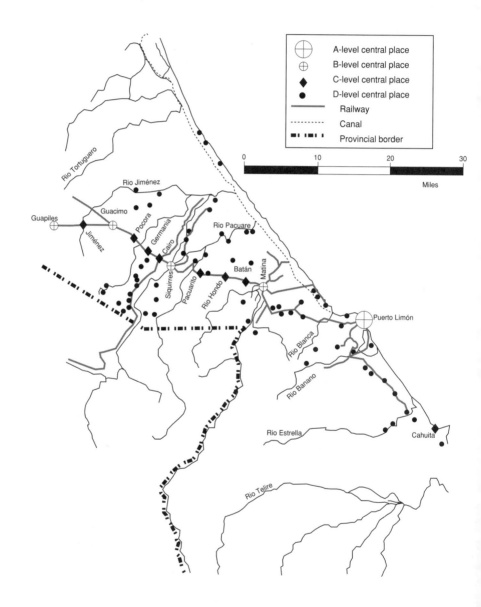

MOVING TO THE CITY

The movement of Blacks has been toward the service centers—Puerto Limón and San José, and most desirably, the United States. In 1973, San José absorbed 50 percent of the 8,644 emigrants from the Atlantic coast, according to a government census, which makes no ethnic distinctions. Since the 1950s, Blacks have moved steadily away from agriculture. As they move away, Hispanics move in, many appropriating land occupied or previously occupied by Blacks. Also, with the resurgence of the banana industry in the Atlantic region between 1964 and 1973, a large number of Hispanic immigrants (22,921 in 1973 alone, 38 percent more than the emigrants) came into the region, many from the Pacific coast. Many of these workers are disenfranchised peasants. The movement of population within the province is described in Table 5. The bulk of the rural-to-urban movement is from Talamanca and Matina—both predominantly Black areas—to Puerto Limón. The large number of emigrants from Guacimo to Pococi (5,764) is probably mostly Hispanic; few, if any, Blacks reside in Guacimo.

Why are Blacks abandoning rural economic niches for urban areas? For one, their United Fruit experience left them feeling only slightly more positive about agricultural work than slaves felt about the plantation after emancipation. To people with this background, the good life consists of a "clean" job, preferably in an office. Moving to the cities is a natural thing, particularly for young people.

The case of New Sligoville—a rural community of about one hundred—is illustrative. The village was established at the beginning of the twentieth century by United Fruit employees seeking independence from the plantation (Bryce-Laporte 1962; Purcell 1987). Initially, villagers relied on both wage labor and peasant cultivation of cacao and a few subsistence crops. When United Fruit relocated to the Pacific coast and the economy of the surrounding area declined, villagers came to rely solely on their small cacao farms for cash.

By 1976, 84 percent of all individuals born in the village between 1936 and 1962 had migrated for one reason or another. Significant migration began during the watershed period of the 1950s, sharply increased between 1966 and 1969, and has remained high. The reasons given for leaving are school, employment, or both. This emigration, although small in absolute numbers, has contributed to the abandonment of the all-important cacao farms and the virtual decline of the village. Every peasant parent wants something better for his or her children, and "better" means leaving the peasant plot. Individuals holding the few desirable rural positions (teaching, nursing, social work) do not usually reside permanently in the areas where they work, but ironically, they are rural role models.

The hierarchy of values corresponding to the hierarchy of population centers is expressed in, among other things, the manner in which the urbanite perceives the rural folk and vice versa. The country folk are, in general, regarded as lower class, unsophisticated, and backward. Told that I was living in a small peasant village, one urban acquaintance asked, "How a university man like you can live wid dem dark country people deh?"

The country folk, on the other hand, regard the urbanite as more refined and more knowledgeable—if at times morally injudicious. A middle-aged country woman commented: "You have de good and de bad everywhere but if you in town you know what goin' on an' you don't have to worry about getting the last o' everything." Yet the rural folk are well aware of urban confusion compared to the tranquility of their cohesive communities, enriched with a diversity that includes the landless peasant living next to the self-made country squire or the canoe fisherman sharing boundaries with the Black version of the *gamonal*—a rich farmer who stoically guards his "poor peasant" lifestyle.

The separation between town and country (or "lines"—remote settlements along the rail lines) is further complicated by a generational factor. Most first- and some second-generation urban dwellers maintain ties with the rural sector, still relying on some sustenance from their land holdings. In contrast, most third- and fourth-generation individuals are more independent of the rural sector, and even if they derive benefits from it, these may come through the older members of their household. For them, rural ties no longer bind.

BECOMING A "TOWN MAN"

As mentioned earlier, migration to the urban areas is regarded as social advancement whether or not the material conditions of the migrant have improved as a consequence. Donald, a resident of New Sligoville, migrated to Limón and took up residence with his aunt, planning to attend night school while working days. He attended school for a while and supported himself as a store clerk. Soon he lost his job and dropped out of school. He later worked as a maintenance helper on the docks but that also lasted for only a couple of months due, he said, to low pay and long hours. For months afterward, he could not find a suitable job. Asked why he did not return to the country to help his grandmother with her cacao farm, he explained that he could not live in the country: "There is nothing to do there." In fact, his grandmother agreed: "As long as he in town there you never can tell what may come his way. Verna [his aunt] know a lot of people an somt'ing might even come up at the hospital. If him come down here him can't go to night school."

TABLE 5
Internal Migration, Province of Limón

EMIGRATION	IMMIGRATION						
	Limón (Central)	Pococi	Siquirres	Talamanca	Matina	Guacimo	Total
Limon (Central)	—	282	329	26	99	17	744
Pococi	570	—	288	7	33	65	963
Siquirres	517	406	—	28	172	11	1,034
Talamanca	2,319	19	11	—	4	2	2,355
Matina	5,162	169	260	1	—	22	5,164
Guacimo	212	5,764	138	5	10	—	6,129
TOTAL	8,780	6,640	1,017	67	218	117	16,839

Source: Dirección General de Estadística y Censo. Censo de Poblacion, 1973.

Donald was part of a large network of men, several of whom played provincial football together and were members of a group appropriately dubbed "The Morning Noon and Night Domino Club." Their afternoons consisted of dominoes first and football next. Donald's day was fairly routine: He awoke late, ate, played dominoes until about 3:00 or 4:00 P.M., then went to the soccer field. He returned from the soccer field, ate if his aunt had already prepared the evening meal, or if not, he prepared the meal for himself and his two cousins. Occasionally he might have a drink at a nearby bar—if he or one of his friends had come into some *plata* (money). More frequently, however, hours were spent in burlesque conversation about women and sports, the group's favorite topics. Occasionally the evening ended with him wandering off to visit a girlfriend. Weekends were more hectic. Saturday night was likely to be spent at one of about five dance halls where salsa, reggae, and soul music put relaxed bodies into a rhythmic trance in which showmanship, style, and implicit competition conspire. Sunday might be spent at the beach or a *paseo* (picnic). Donald had become a "town man," leading a very easy, undriven, and improvident life in a tight job market not known for its generosity to young unskilled Black men.

The largest employer of nonagricultural labor in Puerto Limón, Junta Administrativa Portuaria y de Desarrollo de la Vertiente Atlantica (JAPDEVA), employs more than 3,000 workers, most of them unskilled. The promise of employment in this enterprise is so strong that a 1973 Cornell University study held that the availability of high-paying unskilled jobs in the transportation industry (port and railway) inhibits the motivation of young Limonese to acquire skills offered by the National Apprenticeship Institute. Consequently most of Limón's skilled manual workers are Hispanics drawn from the Meseta Central (El Equipo Cornell-Costa Rica, 1973, 10–17).

Limón is by no means an industrial province. In fact, in 1986 manufacturing enterprises numbered only seventeeen, employing some eight or nine hundred workers. Like most towns of its type, Puerto Limón has not been able to absorb the inflow of wildly optimistic opportunity seekers in productive work. Unemployment in 1986 was estimated at 9.5 percent, but some local leaders thought the rate for Blacks was at least 11 percent (no ethnic distinction is made in the national statistics). Yet, the rural young continue to migrate to Puerto Limón, and many of the better-educated Limonese migrate to San José, while people from all areas try to migrate to the United States.

As is usually the case, then, the organization and structure of the plantation society encouraged the development of hierarchical relations between population centers based on their economic and social function. The imperatives of life in such a system have engendered a set of values and expectations that outlived the plantation, to be reinforced later through the uneven development fostered by the state. All societies evolve some form of hierarchization of individuals based on one form or another of perceived or real differentiation. In the long run, whether a unit is classified high or low has less to do with its concrete human value than with how it is perceived by those in positions of power.

What is of interest is not whether a community is organized unequally but how compliance is exacted, particularly in multiethnic situations. In the case of Afro-Costa Ricans, compliance is largely exacted through a constricted occupational structure on the one hand and an evaluation system based on cultural factors of color, education, and material possessions on the other. But compliance is not absolute; Blacks have tempered the tyranny of color, culture, and material structures with moral concerns of their own, thereby resisting hegemonic control.

JOBS, MORALS, AND PRESTIGE

It has been observed that the occupational prestige hierarchies of similarly developed countries are alike and change little over time (Bendix 1970). In plantation societies or enclaves, occupational ranking and social stratification show certain parallels (Jayawardena 1963; Jain 1970). But when cultural and moral factors that permit or constrain mobility are taken into account, such parallels cannot be unambiguously drawn. The study of occupational ranking in Limón strongly suggests the need to go beyond considerations of the stability or instability of objective rank order to treat subjective and contextual factors of evaluation, which affect mobility in ways that can modify the part played by occupation itself.

Ironically, in the discussion that follows I have given occupational ranking heuristic primacy. This is done for several, primarily methodological, reasons: (1) occupation is linked to education; (2) it is a visible and public indicator of prestige; (3) it is a means to the acquisition of other symbols of prestige; and (4) the occupational hierarchy approximates the economic hierarchy (although an occupation such as farming may span the entire hierarchy relative to the magnitude of the investment involved and the lifestyle of the farmer). I arrived at a sense of the way Afro-Costa Ricans organize their prestige hierarchy by asking individuals to rate a set of occupations and observing the criteria they applied. It soon became clear that although occupation itself was used as an objective indicator of prestige, it was in no way a one-dimensional or independent determinant; other factors weighed heavily, and occupation was most important when it directly indicated level of education. When there is direct positive correlation between education and occupation, education itself seems to be

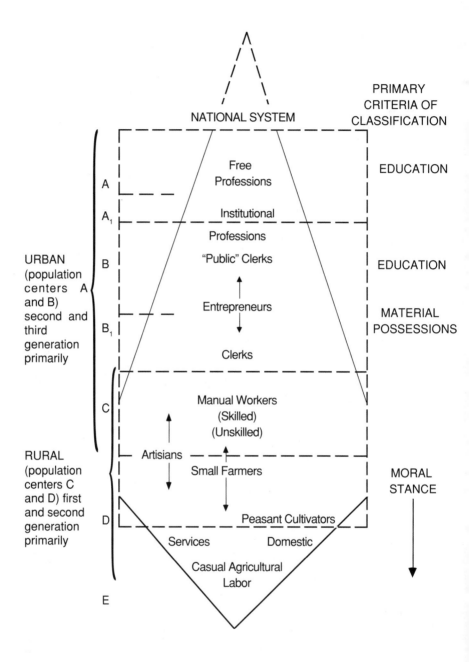

FIGURE 2

SOCIAL STRATIFICATION IN LIMÓN

SHOWING THE RELATIONSHIP AMONG OCCUPATIONAL RANK, POPULATION CENTERS,
AND CRITERIA OF CLASSIFICATION.

accorded greater importance. The question arises, then, as to which is more important in determining prestige. Most informants felt this that was an irrelevant question; an individual with high education will have a good job and much prestige while one with little or no education will not likely find a good job nor acquire high prestige.

Take the case of Harold, who graduated from a prestigious agricultural secondary school and then went on to the university. For financial reasons, his university education was terminated after almost two years. He taught high school for a while but gave it up because of disagreements with the school's director. After brief stints with various government ministries, including the Ministry of Agriculture, he finally returned to his village and decided to rely on the eight-hectare cacao farm he inherited from his father for his livelihood. When he was mentioned as an example for evaluation, informants consistently rated him higher in prestige than others who commanded significantly greater agricultural resources—referring to the fact that he was educated, one woman even commented that "dey must be *obeah* dat boy why 'im can keep a good job."

The complexity of social classification becomes even more apparent when the more symbolic criteria such as respectability, family ties, and religion are considered. By noting the factors considered by discussants as they located known individuals in the social hierarchy, and based on my own observation, a final occupational ideal prestige scale was designed (see Figure 2). The exceptions to this ideal model are many, and in the final analysis it is "how a person live that matters," I was told.

Embodied in the statement "how a person lives" is the notion of "living good" and its converse, "living bad." These are internal ideological categories that subsume ideas about honesty, personal disposition, ambition, good manners, decency, responsibility, and so on. These subjective factors constitute an important part of the total set of criteria considered when evaluating individuals. When, for example, a relatively poor high school director is said to be of a higher status than a wealthy businessman, it is not only because of his occupation, but also because he has not violated moral expectations of living good. At the upper end of the scale, however, these subjective expectations carry much less weight, for not only do the top occupations tend to place individuals in positions of power rather than mere prestige, but the folk have less of a chance to monitor their activities. Further, the idea of living good plays a greater part in the ideological expectations of rural than urban dwellers.

Class stratification touches all aspects of life, yet Limonese do not usually think in terms of economic class in considering a person's position in the society. Some individuals belonging to the second- and third-generation use the term *class* in a loose economic sense, and others use *middle-class* to refer to most workers in categories B and C in Figure 2 (and even in A at times). The use of the term in the general population, however, has much more to do with lifestyle than with economic position. This is partly due to the influence of the ideology of equal opportunity; people play down the distinctions but they cannot deny glaring status displays and distinctions in self-presentation.

For example, in response to a survey question, several elderly working-class women (both urban and rural) located themselves in the upper class. When asked why, they said they did not want for necessities, they lived a "decent" life, and they associated with decent people. To such people there are really only two classes: upper class (or "upper sects") and lower class. Lower-class individuals are unkempt, irresponsible, and lacking in ambition. They may at times be referred to as "dotti people" (*dotti* is the Creole word for dirty, meaning in this context immoral, unprincipled, unrighteous, and unconforming).

RATING THE OCCUPATIONS

To return to the hierarchy of occupations, the upper category, A on Figure 2, which includes all the "free professions," is the least debated. Doctors and lawyers in particular are "respectable, educated people." As one informant puts it:

These people you can go to for advice. They know what goin' on and them rub shoulder only with them own kind. . . . A teacher, now him not part a that circle but him is important too, for him have to set example for the children them. Him must be decent and respectful . . . With all these people now, them education is a life and death thing. . . . The doctor can save you life or kill you and the lawyer can send you a jail or make you go free. . . . But it not all of them good you know—like that Spanish one there that rob so much poor people land him nose rotten off before him dead.

This response implies not just prestige, it implies mystique and power, almost divine power—but note that abuse of power is self-destructive.

The distinguishing criteria for the levels of occupations charted in Figure 2 are not significantly different from what they would be in any Western country. In the mind of the Limonese, however, no job is fixed by reason of training or skill; the personal qualities of the individual are far more significant in evaluation than they would be in, for example, the United States. Consequently, the prestige of a person may be greater or lesser than the prestige normally conferred by the position itself.

Typically, among Afro-Costa Ricans, almost any clerical occupation is rated higher than a manual occupation—even if the remuneration is less—

a feature that the Anglophone Caribbean is rapidly outgrowing. One elderly informant proudly declared, "All my children dem work in office, man." A more staunch defiance of the plantation could hardly come from that voice. A distinction is made, however, between the run-of-the-mill clerical job and the more highly rated government or "public" clerical positions. The power or control over public services that civil service jobs entail makes them highly desirable.[1]

With manual occupations, income gains more importance as a criterion of evaluation, and the distinction between skilled and unskilled is not always taken into account. In fact, one could generalize that income as an indicator gains importance inversely to level of education. Yet, it is not income per se that is considered, but, as I was frequently reminded, how it is spent: what people own; whether they have a stable family; whether a man takes good care of both his "inside" and his "outside" children (in and out of his present marriage); the extent to which he drinks; whether he is known to be honest; whether he is a regular churchgoer or is active in the church; and other such moral considerations.

A central consideration is whether a man owns a house and, of less importance, the type of house. A man has not really demonstrated his manhood until he owns a house. He should also dress decently; a shabbily dressed person—particularly a woman—is not ambitious, and therefore is "low class." Further, a car accords its owner more prestige than a utility vehicle—even if the utility vehicle costs more and is income-producing.

At levels D and E on the chart, material possession and personal attributes show the greatest saliency as criteria of evaluation. Again, careful use of income and conformity to social and moral expectations are significant, bu it is primarily the persona that makes the difference at this level and not the education or the job. Some small-scale farmers in Point Cove, for example, contrast themselves with the wealthy Ashley family, whose source of income is farming and trading.[2] Villagers jump at every opportunity to note that the wealth of the Ashley family was not acquired through honest means. In contrast, one villager said of Mr. Walters, a subsistence farmer, "Everybody respect him . . . but if him go to the bank and want a loan nobody there don't know him."

For individuals like Mr. Walters, as for most other small farmers, prestige derives primarily from their position in the village. But this prestige, conferred by locals, is limited: They are subjected to a language, Spanish, which most of them do not master, and their sphere of social influence stops at the village boundaries. In contrast, although the Ashley family commands deference but little respect and prestige in the village, their sphere of influence and their overall prestige derive from wealth wrapped in relations exterior to the village. They are part of the provincial elite, a distinction declared by the size of their house and the dogs and barbed-wire fences that protect it.

The way farmers are evaluated holds true for fishermen: Boat ownership, is less important than personal comportment. Some fishermen work only during the lobster season, from October to December, but a good season can bring quite a fortune; and many Limonese still speak of a season in recent years when fishermen made so much money that some used 10-colon bills to light their cigarettes.

When women are employed, they are evaluated in the same terms as men. When they are not employed or otherwise engaged publicly but constitute part of a conjugal unit, their status is judged mainly in terms of personal characteristics and the social position of their male partner; that is, there is the tendency to treat the family as a hierarchical unit with prestige emanating from the household head. The occupation of the very small number of Black female domestics is rated very low, but the personal characteristics of the individual carry much weight. Women, however, view domestic employment the same way men view agricultural labor—it is to be avoided, except of course when it involves employment in the United States or with very rich Josefinos. Consequently, Black housewives prefer to employ Hispanic domestic helpers; the Black helpers are "too proud," they say.

RATING THE PERSON

Like small farmers and fishermen, *peones*,[3] unskilled laborers, vendors, barbers, artisans, waiters, "cookshop" operators, and home-grocery operators are classified more in terms of personal and moral qualities and the ability to acquire such obvious symbols of prestige as a house than by occupation. Factors such as age and popularity through civic deeds or organizations such as the Universal Negro Improvement Association (UNIA) or the Burial Scheme (a mutual aid organization) are also of far greater importance than actual occupation.

To illustrate: Mr. B is a tailor, but has also been the sage and distinguished president of the Jamaica Burial Scheme for several decades. He is reputed to have the answer to almost any question. A tall, dark-skinned matron entered his shop one evening in a state of rage. She had come to him to report that her house had just been broken into and to obtain advice. This was a matter in which the police could in no way fill Mr. B's role. The lady complained: "Ah know who do it... they tryin' to upset my life." For her, this was not just an attack on her material belongings but an attack on her person; not an isolated, impersonal crime against property, but an expression of "feelings" someone had been harboring against her. How then could the impersonal police deal effectively with such matters? Mr. B does; he advises and actively assists in nearly every aspect of local life, from health to housing, from religion to law, from child care to the care of the elderly. His prestige derives from personal lifestyle—decency, ambition, and living good—rather than from any consideration of occupation or income.

By this point it should be evident that there is really no sharp line between evaluating a person and evaluating a job. It follows, therefore, that similar considerations come into play when making decisions about social interaction up or down the social scale. The prominent place of subjective and moral criteria in evaluating individuals is an indication of how fluid the system of stratification—and therefore social interaction—has been.

Interclass social interaction is markedly more fluid among Blacks in Limón than in the Anglophone Caribbean. Limón's unique history helps to explain this. Built up over the course of a hundred years by the plantation system, the structure of Limón society has not provided the concrete conditions for fixed and unambiguous social strata within the Black population. Most people are manual laborers, and many with skilled or white-collar positions have close kin and friends who are unskilled and who, for various reasons such as church or lodge affiliations, function within roles that bring them in close social contact. Additionally, there is no real separation in housing among Blacks.

Also, the upwardly mobile are not likely, by reason of the ideology of solidarity, to move completely out of the ranks of kin and friends. Conditions for fixed social separation by strata are more available today due to the broadened opportunity structure and independence from solidarity ties. Yet there is still a functional need for solidarity, and the upwardly mobile are tied to those they left below through kinship and marriage.

In general, having a broad-based diffuse social network while at the same time remaining selective is one of the most valued characteristics of social interaction among Afro-Limonese. Its noteworthiness lies in the fact that it helps to slow the development of rigid class separation and provide a broader field for the use of kin and friendship ties. People associate with different groups at different levels and for different reasons (Jayawardena 1963, 10). As mentioned earlier, however, the tendency is still toward class crystallization and away from ethnic cohesion.

BALANCING THE MATERIAL AND THE MORAL

It would be misleading to treat occupational ranking as an independent aspect of social ranking in Limón, for people are evaluated and ranked even when they are not part of the set of recognized occupations. When their occupations indicate little about their social worth, culturally derived subjective factors such as dress or notions of honesty, etiquette, morality, and speech are freely brought into play. The principles of their application are much more difficult to grasp, however, than those of measurable markers such as income, although for the most part they function in tandem.

The principles governing the application of criteria in new circumstances, for example, are not fully accessible to an outsider only partially exposed to the body of cultural knowledge. Even insiders would be able to produce only intellectualized rules, for they do not contemplate the rules as an articulated body of conscious knowledge until questioned by the ethnographer. The particular instance—not the general rule—is conscious.

My data suggest, however, that the principle used to allocate prestige involves three factors: education; the associated idea of being *culto;* and the idea of living good. *Culto* is the Spanish term designating conformity to the dominant social code. The term—similar to the English *cultured* but with more of a behavioral connotation—is used mostly among young, urban Blacks. Rural Blacks use the concept of living good, which is related to but not identical with culto.

The prestige-conferring role of education is an immensely significant hegemonic tool, and it is certainly a common feature of all postcolonial societies. Carstens (1970, 8, quoted in Wallerstein 1979, 176–77) observes that for peasants in Africa "the surest way to achieve recognition and prestige in the eyes of the ruling class as well as from the local peasants is to participate in the externally imposed educational and religious institutions." The prestige embodied in education and in being culto is at the heart of making a living: It is tied to participating in stable wage-paying, primarily white-collar occupations, as opposed to small-scale independent ventures, especially in agriculture. Its roots are in the destruction of the old modes of subsistence and their cultural moorings, on the one hand, and the progressive imposition of a cash economy and its legitimizing ideology on the other. The underlying thinking is legitimized as "development" in the education process, so the student is intimidated into uncritical acceptance. It is, therefore, perhaps the most effective means of social control. When I asked why some people were reluctant to support a young left-wing Black candidate for deputy in the 1978 elections, most of my informants responded in one form or another that he was neither as *preparado* nor as culto as his opponent, a Black university graduate.

For people already brutalized by the plantation system and still stigmatized by race, the enticement to cleanse themselves through education or its trappings is dangerously attractive. A person who neglects his farm for a white-collar position that brings less material benefit than farming has no trouble justifying his position intellectually: the security of the job, the opportunity to associate with the "right" people, the ease of a clean job that will facilitate good health and longer life, and on and on. Soon, the intellectualized responses become the standard explanation, and the actual reasons become more securely concealed.

There is another concrete historical side to this struggle for emergence, wherever Blacks find themselves in postcolonial America. Cultivable land has always been in short supply, and many individuals give up farming for wage employment, a move that is understandable in light of the lesser security and lower prestige that subsistence farming brings in a society dependent on cash transactions. Naturally, therefore, even those who have opted for farming do not encourage their children to follow in their footsteps. In addition to the pressure of imposed economic necessity, West Indians have had to contend with a colonial ideology in which education and "moral life" held the promise of making the Black person—particularly the Colored middle-class—"equal" to the white person (see Austin 1983, 234–36).

Education has always been recognized by Blacks as not only the passport to mobility but—and perhaps more importantly—a means to become a better person: moral, decent, ambitious. Where education is a remote ideal, however, the concept of living good dominates. It is an aspect of what I call *solidarity*, consisting of a set of behavioral practices and expectations, that are a meld of African ontology and Christian principles, and which are in a dialectical struggle with the fissiparous tendencies of modern social change. Right living is above all a moral code. Having education and being culto also have moral components, for they are the molds and the signposts of "better people," and it is better people who keep the social fabric strong.

In applying these codes to the ranking of individuals, people mitigate the growing salience of material considerations. There is an implicit, humanitarian recognition in the system of classification: Not every ambitious individual can acquire material symbols of self-worth or even education. Consequently, moral/cultural judgment is integrated with greater force at the lower end of the hierarchy. The closer individuals are located socially to the dominant sector of the society, the more likely it is that the criteria used to evaluate them will be those derived from that sector. In their own subtle, perhaps subconscious, but no less important way, Blacks resist the tendency toward evaluating themselves by imposed standards—even while they participate in keeping those standards alive.

FROM SOLIDARITY TO EQUALITY:
WEST INDIANS JOIN THE MAINSTREAM

For West Indians, the inevitable consequence of being in the midst of radical historical changes on Costa Rica's Atlantic coast is a transformation of their own cultural principles. In three generations, many West Indians went from rural proletariat to peasantry and then to urban proletariat. Others went directly from rural to urban proletariat, and yet others went from rural proletariat to peasantry and have stubbornly remained the same. Whatever the changes in the economic sphere, however, political, and to some extent, social changes have combined with them to force cultural changes that affect the very foundation of their humanity. As Blacks become more absorbed into the mainstream of national life, the dominant cultural principle—what I call the principle of solidarity—is gradually giving way to the ideology of equal opportunity and its individualistic implications.

Solidarity is expressed among those who share a common agreement regarding values, goals, purposes, and interests. In this sense, its expression may be regarded as a cultural principle (Geertz 1973), the endurance and function of which depend on its being supported and facilitated by social practice. This differs from the kind of solidarity that is contextual, made necessary by a particular event but passing with the event, such as labor strikes and student protests. The underlying ideals of the latter are usually economic or political, not cultural. Rather than define solidarity as culture, I define it as ideology, an aspect of culture. The view of ideology used here distinguishes it from culture by (1) its function as a manipulative system of meanings, and (2) its ability to be transmitted from one society or group to another and, like social values, to be absorbed initially at a superficial level. For the purpose of this discussion, solidarity is being treated as spontaneously generated, while the ideology of equal opportunity, or *equality* for short, is imposed through the structure of inequality.

To the extent that there are common goals, values, and ideals contained in the idea of solidarity, it could easily be confused with an ideology of equality. In fact, what I call *solidarity* is what Jayawardena (1963, 1968) calls *human equality* in his discussion of ideology among plantation workers in Guyana. I prefer the term *solidarity* because it allows me to describe social cohesion without implying equality, and it permits a clear distinction between the ideology of peasant and working-class Blacks and the national ideology of equal opportunity or social equality.

These ideas do not apply to isolated social segments; equality is the ideology of the dominant majority. However, most middle-class and, in general, upwardly mobile Blacks have accepted it as the guiding principle of social life. The force of solidarity, on the other hand, is felt by and large in the rural areas, but the urban Black—particularly the rural emigrant— remains tied, though in an attenuated form, to its precepts. We are dealing, then, with two overlapping ideological foci within a general field of ideas.

Ideologies thrive on the logic of creative contradiction; they are, therefore, inherently ambiguous. The unity and equality stressed by solidarity are constantly threatened by *ambition*, itself one of the values that help to define solidarity. Ambition drives upward mobility, and mobility channels the individual, both geographically and socially, into the sphere of the dominant ideology of equality and away from the principles of solidarity— that is, away from intrinsic values toward extrinsic ones.[1]

SOLIDARITY AS A UNIFYING PRINCIPLE

An observer is not likely to hear an Afro-Costa Rican use the term *solidarity*, but will frequently hear the phrase: "We all one people." This is the signal phrase of solidarity. Its meaning changes along an inclusive-exclusive continuum in accordance with the context of use. Although it pertains to the Black community, it is not based solely on skin color. Other criteria include conformity to a cultural code of conduct, a degree of social and economic dependency on the community, kinship relations, and a host of other less determinate factors.

On a daily, nonconflictual basis, solidarity manifests itself in a number of ways. Although the care of children is the primary responsibility of the parents' household, all adults in the village exercise some responsibility and may reprimand or correct a child. Kin and ritual kin relations in the village are extensive due to intermarriage and generational depth. There is a high degree of interdependence, which until the 1960s was epitomized by cooperative, "day-for-day" labor. Almost everyone except the very old participates in recreational activities such as the weekly bingo games. Finally, an illness or any other misfortune is the active concern of all. Ultimately, kinship is at the heart of solidarity, for that is where the primary loyalties and obligations lie.

Solidarity is expressed most strongly in the context of its antithesis, *conflict*. The following incident illustrates one of its narrowest but most common usages. While doing research in New Sligoville, I was disturbed at my breakfast one morning by loud voices arguing in another section of the village. My hostess, Miss May, was as surprised as I was to hear such a wrangle at that time of the morning, so we both cocked our ears—as is the custom—before going out to investigate. As it turned out, Mr. Arnold's horse, tethered close to Miss Daphnie's house, had destroyed Miss Daphnie's plants. The *fuss-fuss* (quarrel) became increasingly heated and went beyond verbal insults to the point where Mr. Arnold entered Miss Daphnie's premises and threatened her with his machete. He told her: "Come outya make a lick [hit] you raas. [*Raas* is a Jamaican expletive.] Ah goin' show you who hav' talk pan dis raas 'ill." ("Why not come outside so that I can hit your [expletive]? I'm going to show you who has talk on this [expletive] hill.")

At this point, Mrs. Stephens, a "village mother," came out onto her veranda and attempted to dissuade the disputants. She began, "Arnold, now listen to me man, you know is not di firs' time you aas go in dat woman ya'd an destroy her t'ings. An' now you turn roun' want to beat her wid cutlass. A how unu so disgraceful. Unu make Satan rule unu man . . . . We *all one people* and we musn't behave like puss an' dog." The phrase is used here as an invocation of solidarity and injunction against conflict.

The roots of the conflict reveal the character of solidarity. Upon returning to the house, I discussed the matter with my hostess. I asked why she had not bothered to go out, as she usually would. She responded: "Me no business wid dem you hear sir; dat Arnol him t'ink him high and mighty. Him jus' set pan dat woman like a ticks pan aas behin'. Jus mek him stay deh, im en' no gwein to be good." Further inquiry revealed that Mr. Arnold did this because Miss Daphnie was not originally a member of the village but nonetheless got along better with the residents than Arnold, who, it is said, thinks he is better than the rest. Being an outsider, she was an easy person for him to "pick on."

My hostess felt that had the horse damaged the property of an older member of the village, Mr. Arnold might have been more amicable. Further, Miss Daphnie's only other kin in the village was her mother, who had taken up separate residence at about the same time as her daughter—both outsiders. Miss Daphnie had one thing in her favor: She was regarded as a "decent" young woman.

THE OUTSIDER: PRO AND CON

Two aspects of solidarity are noteworthy here. First, not being originally from a community potentially opens one to criticisms, abuses, and at times, virtual social disregard. There was a time, for example, when any stranger—particularly a Hispanic—visiting Point Cove had to, as they say, "swing low" (be humble) or be expelled from the community. There was a set of criteria for acceptance for membership in the community. The uppermost criterion was parish of origin; those who were from St. Elizabeth in Jamaica represented this category. The second criterion was country of origin: Jamaica (as opposed to other West Indian islands). The third was race/color: Blacks. The fourth and final was "nice" Hispanics—"hard-working and friendly ones." The newcomer was outside of the inner social sanctum, and even individuals not normally on the best of terms with community members would sometimes join in criticisms of the outsider.[2]

The social barrier thus created can be overcome, however, for while solidarity hinges on long standing in the community—long enough to permit participation in its gossip—other cultural practices also form the basis of this principle, including some to which the newcomer has access. The individual may conform to the code of "living good": being polite and humble, not boisterous and stormy; being ambitious enough to look presentable—though not to the extent of appearing to be better than the rest; "keeping the right company," and showing some recognition of and respect for "Christian morals." In addition, a married person with a family is usually more readily accepted, for the state of being single invites gossip about putative sexual activities. Conformity to any of these and the many other less determinate dictates of solidarity is likely to secure acceptance in a surprisingly short span of time.

Another noteworthy aspect of solidarity revealed in this incident is that being born into a community does not necessarily mean that the native's behavior will conform to the principles of solidarity. Although Mr. Arnold was a native and still has many kin in the village, his behavior was a clear breach of the normative code, not only because he frequently "fussed" with Miss Daphnie and others, but because he was regarded as a snob, what Miss May calls "high and mighty." He frequently referred to other villagers as "the poorer people dem . . . but for me." Although he had spent all his life in the village, he had no friends there and did not visit any household except his mother's, and then only occasionally. When I interviewed him, he said with a certain pride that all his friends were from "town" (Puerto Limón). His wife, who participated in the village's social life and was warmly regarded, was Hispanic and not from that area. It was rumored that Mr. Arnold thought of himself as the wealthiest person in the village, although neither his landholdings nor any other tangible measure seemed to support his claim.

The consensus was that Mr. Arnold did not "live good," unlike Miss Daphnie, who was a newcomer but who had managed to win the respect of others. She was a member of the *junta comunal*, participated in all village activities, and was a frequent visitor to the various older and respected families. She even had a friendly relationship with Mr. Arnold's mother. Knowing all this, Mrs. Stephens could readily reprimand Mr. Arnold for his misdeeds toward Miss Daphnie.

THE PENALTIES OF "LIVING BAD"

The antithesis of living good, "living bad," is a threat to the social order, not only with respect to links with the community but also with respect to familial relations. Mr. Timothy, a fairly successful grocer in Point Cove, had five sons and three daughters with his wife before she migrated to the United States. When she left, their eldest child, a son, was already 18. It was not long before Mr. Timothy "take up with" another woman, who started spending much time at his home. His second youngest son, Roy, who had given up *colegio* (high school) and a part-time job in order to assist with the *pulperia* (grocery store), expressed deep dissatisfaction with the new arrangement. He tried to rectify the situation with his father, objecting that this "stranger" was "rulin' evryt'ing."

Soon afterwards, Roy left home to live and work on his own. About this time, the eldest son, Victor, who had been employed in a skilled position by the railway company, left his job and returned to the village to farm. He asked his father to be a *fijador* (sponsor) for him so that he could secure a loan to get his farm going. His father refused, scolding him for having left such a decent job to do farming, for wasting all the schooling he had been given, and for having no ambition.

Meanwhile, Mr. Timothy's woman moved into his home, bringing five of her own children. It soon became evident that he was spending a considerable amount of money on the new additions to his household for he had by now begun construction of a new house in Puerto Limón. Rumors soon spread that he was lavishing his money on the woman and her children and refusing to help his own offspring. And when the new house was completed, it was gossiped that his new "wife" occasionally allowed her former (legal) husband to share the house it was said that Mr. Timothy was "fattening chicken fah mongoose."

These alleged occurrences, true or false, served to alienate Mr. Timothy's own children, and the degree of alienation became evident when he was forced by illness to spend some time in the hospital. His eldest and youngest sons, even after prompting from neighbors, refused to visit him.

A stepmother has always been a potential wedge among family members, especially where she affects the control and distribution of resources between the newly constituted affinal group and members of the agnatic group. This was precisely what happened, and why members of the community regarded this as "bad living." The ensuing gossip centered on the fact that at no time should the relationship between parents and their offspring be such that when parents are ill, the children are not present at the bedside.

Mr. Timothy never lost his social balance; he was a prominent member of the prestigious Burial Scheme and an avid domino player. Ultimately the net result of his behavior was some loss of respect, especially among older women. What is clear, however, is that his problem did not stem primarily from the taking of another woman, but from the neglect of his own children. As one of his sons commented, "If you own blood disban' you what you expec' stranger to do?" When his sons did not visit during his illness, everyone expressed sympathy, but few blamed the sons; it was retribution.

A COSMOLOGY OF DESTINY AND RETRIBUTION

The idea of retribution is central to the concepts of solidarity and living good. One lives good not just for its own sake but because living bad will inevitably bring "sufferation," if not to the subject, then to his or her offspring—the son shall inherit the sins of the father. The concept has greater force in rural areas, where the individualism that comes with urbanization and exposure to the totalizing commodity market has not yet completely taken hold. One cannot live good and at the same time be socially isolated.[3] The isolated and overly secretive individual is suspect; those who do not share their lives with the community run the risk of being accused of witchcraft or being "better than the rest." Such persons are not likely to receive the favors of the community in times of illness nor the highly valued big funeral,[4] the ultimate symbol of living good.

Retribution, ultimate and unavoidable punishment, intervenes in the decisions of every self-respecting conformist regarding day-to-day actions that may affect the lives of others in the community. Stripped of its Protestant moorings among Blacks, retribution suggests that history is self-correcting; man is innately good, but selfishness drives him to upset the natural order of things. Where this occurs, the equilibrating force of collective history steps in to effect rectification. This retribution should not be confused with the Christian idea of original sin, which posits a naturally sinful man and places the individual at the absolute mercy of an uncompromising God. The idea as expressed among Blacks—and this may very well be true for Blacks in general who have not yet suffered advanced assimilation to Western cosmology—is that man participates more actively in his own fate; the child is born free of spiritual and social handicaps, providing the parents did not impart their own transgressions to it prenatally. After birth, what you sow is what you reap. The concept is similar to what Price (1975, 36) discovered among Saramakan maroons: the notion that every event has a discoverable determinate cause, and that "man is the ultimate cause of evil in the world. . . . and just as misfortune stems from human wrongs, every offence will someday bear its bitter fruit."

Retribution fits well with the local understanding of predestination. If retribution means "what you sow is what you reap," then predestination explains the absence of what you would like to sow and reap but cannot. If desired goals remain out of reach, this was preordained—providing there is no spell of witchcraft operating, which would neverthless be partly the target's own doing anyway. In this ontological position, freedom and necessity are not at odds they are complementary, mediated by the actions of the individual as well as by those of the parents.

But there is yet another, more practical expression of this idea. Rather than try to change the world, everyone is obliged to try to live the best they can within it; there is a natural, harmonious order that man has the ill will to disrupt temporarily. To change a situation radically requires confrontation, but open confrontation is not a "respectable" thing. Open confrontation should be left to the "ignorant" folk —thus there is always a place for *obeah*. To be accepting is not to be weak; to "bloom wherever you are planted" is a mark of inner fortitude.

The idea of a self-correcting history in a world in which man should conform rather than transform is congruent with the Afro-Costa Rican notion of time. In daily activities, time is measured more by human and natural phenomena than by the mechanical clock. Alleyne (1985, 3) finds the same lifestyle among Jamaicans at home and notes that it correlates with structural features of the language: "In addition to tense in which some types of utterances may not be grammatically expressed, the language, perhaps with greater emphasis and significance, expresses whether an action is completed or not, whether it is habitual, repetitive, or whether it is prospective." This concept of time places little emphasis on the future. As one informant frequently commented, "You don't worry about what you going to reap, you just worry about what you sow."

As would be expected, retribution has wider cosmic applicability. In one of our frequent discussions about the condition of Blacks in Costa Rica, my hostess in New Sligoville explained that although most people felt that Jose "Pepe" Figueres, the leader of the 1948 civil war, had made life more tolerable for Blacks, her view was that he had also, unwittingly, unleashed a number of social problems for which the society would pay:

All my days I work hard an' never know a holiday. Even my late husband, God bless him soul, him work hard you see an' him never tek a rest. Is di same Calderon [head of the pre-1948 regime] who make us know feriado (holiday). Now is only after Figueres come dat we start to see all dis 'ardship . . . problem wid land, racism an' all dat. But is all over the world you know. *Dere is a circle, tings always come right roun'* . . . but it is goin' to be generations . . . I no bizniz wid dem you know mi dear, is only the Ruler las' forever.

Although statements such as this are imbued with a strong religious overtone, it is difficult to separate the religious from the secular. God, not man, rewards good deeds, but man, by the principle of self-correcting history, is coerced into taking action—secular and religious—to secure the smooth flow of life that follows from living good.

Is a lack of insight regarding the structural causes of poverty fostered by this cultural poverty? Arguably, yes, but it also forces the individual into a posture of responsibility. The lack of insight may be more related to the nature of historically determined purposive choice, choice outside the realm of their own ontology.

Under present conditions, the idea of self-correcting history seems to serve the uncontemplated function of bridging the gap between the present harsh reality of being at or near the bottom of the social hierarchy and the ultimate reality of the hereafter. During a water shortage at Point Cove, a meeting was held to discuss the matter, but Mr. Armstrong, usually a socially and politically active member of the community, did not attend. When I asked him why he was absent, he said: "I don't fight for not'n on dis eart' massah." This was largely an ideological statement because when the government had attempted to convert part of the village farmland into a national preserve, his interest in the hereafter did not prevent him from protesting. In a real sense, then, the ideology can be used to support inaction just as it can be used to justify and pursue active interest.

GOSSIP AS THE ENFORCER

Individuals are always careful that their actions are not overtly contrary to community codes of behavior, for that may expose them to unmerciful gossip, an important mechanism for the maintenance of solidarity. The actions of every individual, bar none, are closely scrutinized and talked about, and any breach of code constitutes material for "hot" gossip. The uninitiated outsider cannot but be amazed at the thoroughness with which individuals and events are scrutinized. "People here sleep with their eyes open," commented a young man in Point Cove jokingly. Gossip is the conscience of the community, the arbiter of moral dilemmas, the enforcer of values, and the prime social leveling mechanism. It has the additional function, however, of advancing prestige and protecting individual interest (Haviland 1977, 8).

In the same way that it is necessary to understand a speaker's knowledge of the world and cultural rules in order to understand his language (Keesing 1979, 14–37), it is necessary to be privy to the gossip of a community in order to understand the public statement about individuals and the nature of their social relations.

Mr. Morgan, a respected, soft-spoken 34-year-old carpenter, established a restaurant. Not long after, he began to find white powder and silver coins in front of the main door each morning. He realized that someone wanted his restaurant "out of the way." After several weeks a friend "pinched" him as to who it was. He then had to verify this before he could take action. He did not confront the person but instead went to his *obeahman*, or seer.

Word of his action spread by gossip. Weeks later, another small businessman fell ill; gossip had it that his ill fate was enough proof of his guilt. The offense continued for a while, but soon word spread that Mr. Morgan had taken steps to protect himself. Within a few weeks the powder and coins were no more. Here, the information to be transmitted by gossip seems to have been intentionally divulged.

Paradoxically, gossip is common knowledge to most insiders except, in some cases, the referent of the gossip. It is, therefore, a polite and effective manner of dealing with perceived contraventions of the moral order—it allows for the resolution of conflict without social disruption. The system seems to achieve conformity, therefore, not by the predictability of confrontation but by the fear of it.

A close cousin of gossip is the linguistic mechanism of *indirection*. In a group where social poise depends on the avoidance of open confrontation, indirection becomes the sine qua non of social interaction. As in other areas of the Caribbean, almost no conversation takes place among rural Blacks without some measure of it. If I were visited by individuals unknown to the villagers, someone would occasionally comment the next time they saw me alone: "So I see Government visit you, man" (if the visitor was a male),[5] or "So I see you *espousa* [spouse] come look fah you, man" (if the visitor was a female). Such remarks are expected to bring a protest and/or an explanation, enlightening the individual without the need for a direct question.

Concealment or discretion are commonly used forms of indirection. On the one hand, people take great care not to be obvious about acquisitions or purchases that could generate envy or accusations of "playing big shot." On the other hand, concealment or discretion avoids ridicule. A poor family will conceal a meal that is considered too poor: a meal of only ground provisions, for example. No respectable family will make a show of having dinner at 9:00 PM when every self-respecting person knows that dinner time is 6:00 PM Children are counseled to avoid "rattling the utensils" when eating late.

But no social group can deal covertly with all its many and varied problems; sometimes confrontation or open conflict is unavoidable, if not necessary (Jayawardena 1968). Here, too, gossip has its special part to play, for the chief weapon in a verbal battle is information heretofore confined to privileged ears. Making public such information humiliates the subject and evens the score. In this regard, gossip functions as a leveling mechanism.

According to rumor, Rachel, a tall, brown-skinned woman of about 30, the wife of a prominent grocer, was having a long-standing affair with a young man several years her junior. Her husband was supposedly well-aware of this, but his only reaction was to drown his troubles in alcohol. His inability to act was said to stem from the fact that a significant portion of his investment came from his wife's patrimony. Soon there was talk that Rachel had bought her lover a small business in another part of the province. Much of this was dismissed by the villagers with comments such as: "She no have no shame" or "a young blood she want." It was bad living, but discretion could save face. Furthermore, she was known to be a "nice woman," an "upper sect" person.

To the surprise of everyone, one sunny afternoon Rachel confronted a young woman named Maria in the center of town and accused her of "playing with" her husband—a phrase commonly used to describe casual sexual affairs. Maria pleaded innocence, but Rachel was incensed and took the opportunity to scold her unmercifully: "You couldn' keep you pickney father but you wan' play wid mi husban'; is what' wrong wid you mek yu can' fin' yu own man."

Enraged, Maria accused Rachel of being two-faced and proceeded to make public alleged details of Rachel's clandestine affair previously only in the gossip pipeline. This was the crucial step; now that it had become public, Rachel, who up to this point had been regarded by villagers as being of a higher social stratum, could no longer maintain social balance; her prestige was threatened. The next move was up to her, if she wanted to regain equilibrium. Restoring her image was particularly important, because not only had she been accused of activities that were proscribed for married females but these were the activities most closely associated with a woman's respectability (cf. Wilson 1973).

In a matter of days, the word was out that Rachel had filed charges in the courts against Maria. Forced to appeal to any source of vindication possible, she appealed to the courts, an extracommunity institution and one in which her higher social rank and her extracommunity network would perhaps gain her some sympathy. This outside norm, imposed historically through the articulation of the local community into the broader social system, not only facilitates freedom of choice but also has the contrary function of threatening the vitality of solidarity.

Ambition Works to Divide

As migration, mass communication, and education pull the rural areas into the mainstream of Costa Rican life, keeping individuals within the circle of the old canons becomes more difficult. The historical dynamic of the society, indeed the world economy, pecks away at the cultural underpinnings of these communities. How this is effected in the long run—in the face of contradictory ideals and expectations between one sector and the other—leads to another aspect of ambition a principle of solidarity.

Indeterminacy and contradiction within the ideology make it possible to have an abiding emphasis on solidarity in a social field marked by individualism and self-interest. The individual who lives good is an ambitious individual; according to the local definition of ambition, one who swears, is unpresentable, does not work hard, and shuns "Christian" principles is a no-good, unambitious person and not fit to "mix with decent people." There are frequent reminders to young people not to "keep company" with such types.

But at the same time, ambition permits discrepancy in the expression of solidarity, for ambition also means not letting opportunities slip by. Ambition, therefore, determines upward mobility on the social scale. One informant identified a lower-class person in the following manner: "Well sometime you jus' don't know, but I would say that is dose people who don't 'ave no ambition. Yu see dem on di street wid dem 'air not comb an' dem look untidy, yu know. *Dem not upward looking.*"

Ambition is a product of Blacks' desire to escape their structural position; the set of values embodied in the phrase "to have manners" must now be realized in the wider society—in the context of the ideology of equal opportunity. Those who do not avail themselves of opportunities are blamed for their own plight. Ambition, then, places the individual in a position that encourages assimilation of the two-tiered power model of society as the natural order of things. The unevenness of life chances is taken to be a product of individual effort and merit, rather than an outcome of the social structure.

In addition to the structural barriers to social mobility, however, there are cultural barriers that can be equally compelling in their function to maintain solidarity. The case of Mr. Morgan, the young carpenter mentioned earlier, illustrates a cultural barrier. With a loan from the bank, he had built the best restaurant in the village. It was patronized primarily by outsiders, Hispanics and Anglos. It was rumored that Mr. Morgan was becoming a "big shot" because he did not want local people in his restaurant. So when he began to see coins and white powder at the entrance each morning before opening, he realized that his attempt at upward mobility was not to the liking of some members of the community; the use of obeah to impede his progress was testimony enough. Mr. Morgan's business improved after he obtained protection, but there are tales of some who were not that fortunate.

Mr. White, for example, had been selling homemade bread for many years. When he was not delivering by bicycle to his nearby customers, he plied his trade on the commuter train between Limón and the Estrella Valley. He soon expanded his business, opening a small combination bakery and shop. Business thrived until a Chinese man opened another bakery a few doors away. Mr. White's bakery began to decline and continued to do so at about the same rate that the Chinese bakery was improving. He soon found that all his customers were now "supporting the Chinaman." Mr. White finally had to close his business, explaining that "Black people don't like see dem own people prosper." The phenomenon is part of what Peter Wilson (1973) calls "crab antics," but it also brings to mind Naipaul's (1969) story of the Black baker in Trinidad whose bakery could not thrive until he employed a Chinese person as a front (see Chapter 6 for further discussion of Black business).

Crab antics are also present, though to a much-reduced extent, when an individual attempts mobility through educational opportunities. It is believed that without proper protection a child who is doing well in school is likely to be "tampered with" by envious individuals. Miss Laura's 16-year-old daughter Jasmine was said to be doing rather well in *colegio*, but she complained frequently of having headaches. For a while, each time she complained, she was treated with the usual herbal medicine—cerasse *(Mormordica charantia)*—to "clean out" her blood. After a few months, Miss Laura decided that it was not just a simple headache but that someone "was putting their hand in her life." She visited a seer who told her that a not-too-distant neighbor was responsible. Miss Laura had suspected this all along, for that particular neighbor had accused her of "thinking she no walk 'pon God eart' since her pickney in college."

EDUCATION PROVIDES AN EXCEPTION

Still, individuals who attempt to better their position through education are more readily accepted and deferred to than those who choose the path of commercial ventures within the community. One need not search too far for an explanation: A business is successful because it draws its resources from the community. People recognize this; the comment is often made that "ah don' want nobody get rich off me." Furthermore, a person who becomes rich threatens the perception of relative equality. If the owner of a successful business is a "nice" person, however, she or he may be tolerated and even liked.

Education, on the other hand, is not perceived as drawing on the scarce resources of the community. Moreover, the path of mobility through education leads away from the community and therefore does not remind villagers of their own social and economic insecurity. Crab antics are intended less to pull the individual down than to prevent him or her from advancing at the material and psychological expense of others, for those who rise can usually avoid being pulled down by fulfilling the expectations of the solidarity community. Thus, solidarity allows for inequality.

On the surface, solidarity seems to be a barrier to initiative and mobility within the community. In reality, however, it seeks to define mobility rather than prevent it. Its obstructive quality results not from its nature but from its functioning in an economic structure where only a few are able to overcome the inherent obstacles. What Blacks object to is not upward mobility per se, but its threat to kin and personal loyalties and its imposed hierarchy of values and modes of behavior which plant the seeds of discrimination. Perhaps the strongest evidence for the breakdown of solidarity is the disappearance of cooperative labor, caused by the commercialization of labor in even the most rural sectors and the increasing emigration of the young.

As Afro-Limonese migrate into the urban areas, they leave the orbit of solidarity and move into that of the ideology of equality. Elements of solidarity survive in the urban areas, but mainly among first-generation Black residents. The shift from solidarity to equality is therefore symptomatic of and part of a broader socioeconomic and cultural transformation of the Black population.

EQUALITY OF OPPORTUNITY: IDEOLOGICAL INCORPORATION OF BLACKS

A unique feature of the history of West Indian migrants in Costa Rica is that their position in the country changed radically with the turn of events brought about by the 1948 civil war. All of a sudden these unwanted but necessary guests found themselves being courted in efforts to establish the Second Republic after the civil war. One of the ironies of this historical juncture is that the original intent of the Figueres effort was to stem the economic control of foreigners and protect the system of private enterprise and *minifundismo* that had characterized the nineteenth and early twentieth century (Bell 1971, 159).

It was ironic that, at least superficially, Blacks constituted an alien and unpropertied group that must now share the already scarce land and other economic resources. Moreover, their presence belied the popular boast that Costa Rica was a racially homogeneous society. But as events unfolded, Figueres's junta changed from revival of petit capitalism to extensive social reforms, still holding against corruption and foreign control (Stone 1975, 318–19). This was a rather sudden turnabout, joining forces with those few—some in the Communist party—who were expressing dissatisfaction with the rampant individualism and elite family control of that period.

This was where the seed of Costa Rica's social democratic system was sown. Figueres was well-aware that given this turn of events, plus the general political climate of antagonism to his policies at the time, the votes to be gained from a population of more than 19,000 Blacks could make the difference between consolidating the new regime or returning the old one.

It is difficult to say in a concise way what *social democracy* meant to those in control then, or what it means even now. Theoretically, it is described as an egalitarian system of distribution of opportunities and essential services within a framework of free enterprise. Figueres himself described it thus: "Socialism is the aspiration towards an economic order in which each gives the maximum of his capacity in the organized production of needs, in exchange for standards of life as high as the accumulated resources and the daily product of general work will permit "(quoted in Jimenez 1979, 156).

This system of equitable distribution was realized in an economic structure of state-controlled private enterprise. It was marked by respect for political and individual liberty under the watchful eye of the state—what Facio (1942, 163) calls *state liberalism*, akin to Engels's ([1894] 1976, 360) *aggregate capitalism*, in which the worker remains proletarian. And indeed state capitalism increased in the 1970s, serving the interest of the powerful and contributing to much of the political conflicts of the 1980s (Sojo 1984). My concern here, however, is not to criticize or explain Costa Rica's social democracy, but to explore, briefly, its meaning for Afro-Costa Ricans.

BLIND FAITH IN EQUALITY

The ideology is understood by Costa Ricans, Black and white alike, as one that guarantees egalitarianism and individual freedom. The visitor needs only take a taxi once in San José to become familiar with this theme. Those who remain doubtful after the cabby's lecture on the merits of Costa Rican equality are told that Costa Rica is the freest country in the region. Comparative reference is immediately made to the various right-wing regimes in Central America, stressing that Costa Rica never had a Somoza. Costa Rica does not have an army but instead spends its money on education and social services. And where individual liberty and standard of living are concerned, it is the "Switzerland of Latin America"—so the story goes. Costa Rica, they argue, has the highest literacy rate in Central America. Faced with this barrage, few are likely to argue the fluid relationship between the literacy rate and the average level of education of the populace, let alone the relationship between the rate of literacy, the preferential distribution of resources (including education), and the persistence of poverty among Hispanics, Blacks, and Native Americans.

By and large, Costa Ricans have accepted the idea of a free, egalitarian nation. Yet they are fully aware that this does not mean socioeconomic equality. For the most part, they see their society as one organized into a fluid status hierarchy that can be penetrated by any and all, irrespective of race or creed. This perception has led to the persistence of what Ossowski (1963, 109) calls *democratic optimism* in reference to the United States.

The vehemence of this ideal of equality can be partially attributed to two aspects of Costa Rican history. First, there is the brevity of the period between the Costa Rica of minifundismo and small, free commercial enterprises, and the emergence of large-scale, mostly foreign capitalism (Stone 1975: part I and II). Most Costa Ricans believe that the country, as poor as it was, never developed class divisions. But the collective memory of that historical period, characterized by minimal differential in wealth, has long outlived the reality. Second, the leaders of the 1948 civil war, in their attempt to justify the establishment of a democratic socialist state, played heavily on the traditional belief that marked wealth differential did not exist in Costa Rican society , except in the immediate pre civil war period.

The claim to egalitarianism arose at a time when even the Spanish *hidalgos* (nobles) eked out their own livelihood from the soil alongside the peasants, a period when Costa Rica was by far the poorest Central American territory. So entrenched was the faith in equality that it survived the rise of the cafetaleros in the mid-nineteenth century, only to be reinforced after the 1948 civil war in the social democratic ideology. The ideology serves to give credence to the mythical idea that the distribution of reward proceeds on the basis of achieved rather than ascribed criteria.

THE INDIVIDUAL, NOT SOCIETY, TAKES THE BLAME

For Afro-Costa Ricans, egalitarianism, besides attempting to deny racial discrimination, posits a society in which achievement is now claimed to depend solely on individual merit. In an attempt to provide the concrete conditions for the realization of these ideals, Figueres's Partido Liberacion Nacional (PLN) saw to it that racial distinctions were not made in the national census—such distinctions would be discriminatory, it was reasoned. In effect, the very history of Blacks in Costa Rica was denied by such reasoning. The evidence from places like Cuba and Brazil clearly shows that a mere ideology does not eliminate racial discrimination (Dzidzienyo and Casal 1979; Fontaine 1985; Moore 1988).

Some concrete steps were taken to pull Blacks into the mainstream.

Infrastructural improvements were allocated to Limón, where the population was, even then, still about 50 percent Black. Between 1954 and 1958, forty-seven schools were constructed, an increase of 950 percent over the number constructed from 1922 to 1951 (Rout 1976, 271). Large sums were also expended on roads and on agrarian reform, but the emphasis was on education, the primary mechanism for inculcating national values. As early as 1930, Secretary of Education Ricardo Fournier complained that the reluctance of West Indians to use the national school system in place of their autonomous privately run "English" school system made it difficult to "teach ideals and the sentiments of Costa Rica." (Kepner 1936, 166–67). Today, the autonomous Black-run schools have gone the way of cooperative rural labor.

The institutional political field also became accessible to Blacks. In 1953, Alex Curlin, the first Black *diputado suplente* (regional representative to the national congress) was elected. Since then, there have been six other Black diputados and one Black provincial governor. A Black man was nominated to the position of manager of JAPDEVA, the largest single economic enterprise on the Atlantic coast, organized for the administration of the government-owned port and railway complex and the general economic development of the region.

Whites and Blacks alike mention these facts as adequate evidence of equal opportunity for Blacks. Mr. Ramos, a resident of New Sligoville, was generous in his opinion on the matter:

We doin' all right. For we down here it not always good, for coco [cacao] prices go up and down, but we live though, for we can still get a penny now an' then. An' you see, this country free, man. You work when you want an' you can drink you liquor when you want. If I don't have the money I can go down Pueblo an' Missa Lewis [a grocer in the adjacent village] will give me anything I want....An' to tell you the truth we can't complain, for now we own people them gettin' big position in this country: look pan [at] Joseph at Northern [JAPDEVA is referred to by Blacks as "Northern," the name of the railway company when it was controlled by the United Fruit Company], him is the manager; something we think would never happen a Costa Rican. Now you see Black man neck and neck with the white man.

Yet, Mr. Ramos, who shares a dilapidated two-room shack with his common-law wife and two children, did not seem to be benefiting from the new order in any objective way. Mr. Lewis, the Black grocer referred to by Mr. Ramos, also offered his analysis:

You can learn to be a tailor, you can learn to be a simple mechanic; right now I like the way I see the government is going because we did not have all these opportunity and you will still see them [young men] running about and you ask them what are you doing for you'self? They tell you, nothing, nothing! And why? Just because he is lazy; because you have opportunity all over....My mother and father died when I was in second grade, but I never give up trying until I make it today.

The optimism that Blacks lavish on the political and economic system is demonstrated by the steady pattern of support for the PLN. A 1965 survey showed some 75 percent of Black voters steadily supporting that party. The figure represents the highest percentage of support by a single ethnic group for any political party (Mergener 1965, 49; see also Denton 1971, 72–79). In 1974, only 43 percent voted for the PLN, with 57 percent divided among five other political parties. And in 1986, the main opposition to the PLN successfully fielded a Black candidate, for the first time seriously challenging the PLN for Black support.

With urbanization, greater participation in the educational system, and a nationalist surge in the 1970s, Blacks have assumed a more critical posture and have become less reliant on the good will of a single political party. The shift in party support is, in some measure, an affirmation that equality is a national rather than merely a party commitment. In fact, expanded educational opportunity for Blacks, even under the conservative government of the early 1980s, is further affirmation. But ironically, it is through education that the ambitions of Black Costa Ricans are realized, pulling them away from the domain of solidarity.

SOLIDARITY VERSUS EQUALITY

Upward mobility within the country ipso facto requires migration to the urban areas, where the ideology of equal opportunity is most fervently accepted. It is not that there is no expression of solidarity among urbanites; it lingers there but in a changed form, as evidenced by, among other things, the emphasis on convivial drinking, a social practice based on sharing and close social intercourse, and in which notions of manhood also find expression (cf. Jayawardena 1963, 48–52). As one Afro-Costa Rican put it: "We drink with *orgullo* (pride)."[6] Many of the more philosophical aspects of solidarity are still alive among older urbanites, but positivist education and the demands of urban individualism have taken their toll among the young.

The impetus for change in ideology and values springs from the nature of power relations within which Blacks must function if they are to achieve upward mobility. Thus, in the urban setting, rejection of the often overblown claims of the social democratic ideology is likely to be encountered, not in the working class proper, but primarily among the young lumpenproletariat and working class who, while not inclined to ride the rising cultural nationalist tide, are nevertheless acutely aware of the constraints of color and race. Similarly, we find believers and nonbelievers in the rural areas, and the division seems to correlate with class and generational differences.

Solidarity and equality have several contrasting characteristics, among them:

1. Each ideology dominates a different social strata. And whereas solidarity explicitly attempts to control upward mobility, equality explicitly promotes upward mobility but implicitly imposes arbitrary limits on it.

2. The knowledge that community members use to maintain solidarity is transmitted primarily through close personal and kinship networks. Social practice within the domain of equality, on the other hand, promotes, even requires, competition and individualist striving.

3. Solidarity is not contemplative while the ideology of equality is contemplative and intellectualized. It is therefore likely to show a greater degree of idealism.

4. Solidarity is intolerant of divisive economic but especially social disparity. Equality, on the contrary, implicitly encourages socioeconomic disparity by not explicitly recognizing the inherent structural support for inequality.

The importance of these ideological positions to the process of social mobility and increasing inequality among Blacks lies in the point of congruence between the two: Solidarity requires ambition, which under present conditions has to be realized through education, and education is also a requirement to take advantage of equal opportunity. In other words, contrasting features notwithstanding, solidarity impels and pushes some of the mobile into the realm of equality, thereby unwittingly facilitating social change.

In the realization of ambition, mainly through education, the psychological tie is made to upward mobility and its attendant ideological transformation. For the Afro-Costa Rican, the meaning of education is not exhausted in its implication of social mobility. The concept of the proper and complete person is tied up with the role of education. To illustrate, we can look briefly at the meaning of the words *illiterate* and *ignorant*, as used by Jamaicans in Costa Rica. The meaning of *illiterate* is not confined to what it denotes: ignorant, uneducated, unable to read or write. It is used in a broader connotative sense: being "uncultured," uncouth, and even lacking such moral qualities as honesty and human decency. A person who publicly violates social decorum may be brushed off with "you no see 'im illiterate," meaning he knows no better, whether or not he is in fact able to read. An unfriendly person may be regarded as illiterate and uncivilized or ignorant. The word *ignorant* carries all of the above connotations, but it specifically refers to someone who is boisterous, loose-tempered, and publicly disrespectful—showing a lack of superego control. Education is for Blacks what baptism is to the sinner. Commented one elderly male informant: "I have to agree with Shakespeare. Ignorance is the curse of God. Knowledge is the wings on which we fly to heaven." And, as if to confirm its redeeming efficacy from the other side of the ethnic fence, a local Hispanic attorney remarked with pride that Costa Rican Blacks were some of the nicest people he had known, "especially the educated ones."

The national ideology of equality ultimately espouses the credo of equal opportunity. However, it simultaneously legitimizes inequality by accepting not just the class structure but a set of values that says Blacks must cleanse themselves culturally before they are accepted. The ideology of equal opportunity does not endorse racism per se, but it insists on conformity to a white culture. A similar situation obtains in Cuba and Brazil. In Cuba, despite the ideals of the revolution, and in Brazil, despite the well-rooted ideology of racial democracy, there is still an inverse correlation between darkness of skin and power (Dzidzienyo and Casal 1979; Fontaine 1985).

The ideology of solidarity, as a blueprint for action in today's world, would no more allow an effective escape from the clutches of postcolonial degradation than equality. Solidarity bears striking similarities to Peter Wilson's (1969) "reputation," a cultural response to colonialism characterized by the ethos of equality and associated with the lower stratum. Wilson suggests reputation as a national ideology for the Caribbean, and he mentions Grenada's Eric Gairy as an example of a leader who gained power based on its values. But the history of Gairy's politics has shown precisely why such a nationalist ideology by itself does not serve the interest of the collective.

Gairy gained power not by promising long-term structural change but by exploiting grievances between entrenched white planters and privileged colonial government officials on the one hand and the downtrodden Black labor and peasantry on the other. Without a plan, once labor became organized and the immediate grievances no longer dominated the political consciousness, Gairy had to resort to charisma, authoritarianism, and clientelism, replacing a white plantocracy with an equally exploitative Black commercial elite.

Costa Rica's class and ethnic structure would not allow for a similar dynamic. Blacks hold strong allegiance to the white-controlled nation, but even if that were not true, they still would not have the political base to ride to power on a nationalist ideology. They have little alternative but to find their place within the existing structure, although they need not sacrifice their culture. Under present conditions, however, the ideological transformation from solidarity to equality is part of a profound ongoing cultural change, a value transaction inherent to this type of adjustment.

PATTERNS OF SOCIAL MOBILITY IN LIMÓN

The radical change in the relationship of West Indians to the state after 1948 meant that, at least in theory, it was now possible to transform their status from unwanted plantation residue to rightful citizens. Afro-Costa Ricans could now be integrated socially, politically, and economically—but only through channels made accessible to them by the dominant society.

Ascendance to white-collar positions by way of the educational system has been the preferred route to integration. The second most desired route is migration—both internal and international. Migration may be a means to achieve education, but more frequently its goal is higher wages and a higher standard of living. International migration is particularly desirable, not only for the economic reward but for the knowledge of the world and the prestige that come with it. A less desirable and less traveled path of upward mobility is the establishment of independent business ventures.

Choosing a means of social mobility is strongly influenced by the type of historical cognitive conditioning that Blacks have experienced and by the constraints inherent in the politico-economic structure. In most cases, the choice is based on decisions that are quite rational within the breadth of the individual's understanding of the social and personal circumstances. To a great extent, however, the choice is uncritical and conformist and therefore perpetuates dependency.

THE CHRISTIAN CHURCH: AN IDEOLOGICAL SEEDBED OF SOCIAL MOBILITY

Afro-Costa Ricans who write about their culture frequently refer to religion, folklore, education, and the family as the cultural cornerstones of the Black community. Kathleen Sawyers Royal (1977,19) observed: "The church played an extremely interesting role in Limón. On the one hand, it was the medium which gave life a sense of meaning. On the other hand, it was a means of cultural alienation, causing sectarianism which in turn impeded a unified political organization....the church was the center of culture, where the dramatic arts, elocution, and above all music, flourished." In 1978, Father Robert Evans, in a speech on "The Church in the Cultural Development of the Negro," pointed out that "the church has as its special mission that of the Teacher without distinctions of sect or denomination. It has accomplished a valuable task and an undeniable mission with respect to the culture of the Black Limonese" (1978, 8, 9).

So deeply embedded is the Protestant church in the lives of West Indians that it is difficult and certainly unnecessary to say where its religious role ends and its social and political role begins. The impact of Christianity on Black society, on relations of power and domination, on momentary liberation and respite, and the overall direction of change deserves far more attention than this work affords.

The Christian church is of particular importance in the emergence of Afro-Limonese society primarily because of the social wilderness into which West Indians were initially transplanted. They could not draw on the social and religious institutions of the Hispanic sector, for geography and ethnic bias prevented intercourse. Furthermore, Blacks were Protestants in a Catholic country. Even so, it seems the social and spiritual need for religious institutions in the relative isolation of the Atlantic coast would have guaranteed the establishment of Protestant worship in any case.

The first Baptist church was established in about 1888, the Methodist in 1894, and the Anglican in 1896. The Salvation Army appeared in the first decade of the twentieth century, about the time the Seventh Day Adventists and Jehovah's Witnesses arrived. (Even the French patois-speaking plantation workers from St. Lucia and Martinique established their own Catholic church in Costa Rica, long before Hispanics found the Atlantic coast hospitable.)

Both the African-derived *puk-kumina*[1] and Protestantism had their special place then as they do today. Many individuals participated in both simultaneously without manifest contradiction—though to the assimilated and to white Christians, the mere Africanness of the deeply expressive puk-kumina embodied a violation of Christianity. With its divination and healing practices, puk-kumina appealed mainly to the working class and peasantry—although some members of the upper class secretly took advantage of its services. But Protestantism was attractive to all social levels; it was decent. Consequently, most social activities centered on the Protestant churches, which were the arbiters of religious as well as social excellence.

Informants speak with obvious nostalgia about the elaborate concerts, harvest celebrations, talent competitions, debates, elocution contests, and so on, that were staged exclusively by the church. For most people, the church provided the first exposure to collective learning, systematic memorization and recitation, acting, reading, and even poetry. Some Afro-Costa Ricans believe that their rate of literacy is so high because they have been "reading the Bible all along." Sunday school was a must for the offspring of all self-respecting parents. It provided not only religious but social education as well.

Mr. Walters's experience is characteristic of many first- and second-generation West Indians. He is now a fairly successful farmer and a respected community leader of sorts. He said that he came to Limón and "got a little education, English and Spanish, but most of it was English, and it was all in the church [Seventh Day Adventist] and on my own. Most of the time we had to help with the farm, so that cut into schooling, but our church insists on education of the young people, and we grew up in the church. I love reading and I used to go down by the sea shore and sit on a rock and just read to the wind day in and day out."

He recalls with satisfaction how, when he was called upon to speak—without prior notice—about the social problems besetting Limón at a meeting held at the Universidad de Costa Rica, he did not falter, for his church had prepared him.

The role of the Protestant church as an educational institution can best be understood in the context of a semiautonomous plantation society whose real interest in education ended with minimal on-the-job training. Initially, Limón had no schools except those provided by West Indians themselves, the famous "veranda" schools, as they were called.[2] When state schools were eventually provided, Blacks had to be educated in a language not their own, one they defensively called the "bird language." Few competent Hispanic teachers could be found for the Atlantic coast. The combination of factors led Blacks to resist sending their children to "Spanish" schools. It is said (but not substantiated) that the United Fruit Company also resisted the establishment of state schools on the grounds that the West Indian workers, once having learned Spanish, would become too politicized. In any case, the West Indians' sense of cultural superiority manifested itself in resistance to the state school system.

The Protestant churches had long-established schools, which in effect supplemented the existing veranda schools. All emphasized the three Rs: readin', ritin', and 'rithmetic. Veranda schools were also associated with the church, for in some cases the school principals were also church principals. In fact, these schools were not strictly secular institutions; uncritical Bible study was routine, and there was no skimping on the institutionalization of religious doctrine.

By 1927, Limón had some thirty-three private schools and the astonishing distinction of the highest literacy rate in the country. The economic hardship of the Depression years brought significant changes. The ability of parents to keep their children in veranda schools diminished, and some closed. The church schools, though threatened by the increasing rate of social integration, continued to be instrumental in the social and moral life of the province. In fact, though transformed linguistically and otherwise, the Episcopal church still runs the most outstanding private school in Limón today, with English as part of its curriculum.

Naturally, as the state school system gained ground, the role of the Protestant church in secular education diminished. The church's impact on the social and moral fiber of the society has not, however, suffered quite the same fate, for the heavy exposure to and insistence upon church education among the first and second generations had a profound effect on the enculturation of the present generation. The church helps to mold good, decent, conforming citizens.

The conforming conservatism of the Baptist church, for example, is illustrated by its members' attitude toward a recent minister. Trained in the United States, he was given to liberation theology. He was criticized for this, but, more tellingly, he was criticized for the manner in which he dressed: He often wore jeans, T-shirts, and athletic shoes (rather appropriate dress for the tropics). A dress code has always been important to the church. The idea that "Sunday best" clothes are worn only to church and other important occasions such as funerals and weddings is still quite current. It is not unusual for worshippers to stay away from church for the lack of appropriate attire, while for the more fortunate the church is the main stage for sartorial display.

The early kinship between Protestant ideology and the capitalist ethos has left its mark on the church in Limón. A successful Christian is a better Christian, for economic rewards are regarded as a blessing from the Almighty. Although members are enjoined not to be greedy—"It is easier for a camel to go through the eye of a needle than for a rich man to enter the kingdom of heaven"—prosperity is a blessing. The economic success of its members ensures the viability of the church, and ambitious people are more likely to be attracted to a prosperous church. Upward mobility is therefore subliminally emphasized and reinforced.

As in the society, the considerations of hierarchy are not merely material; a tradition of association with the symbolism of secular power is a key factor. The Episcopal church, for example, derives much of its prestige from its association with Great Britain, and this prestige feeds back into the community. As one informant described it:

The name of the church has a lot to do with it; you have a lot of outstanding families who were Seventh Day Adventists, and just because they were Seventh Day the people them never used to give them the recognition they deserve. You notice is who used to go to St. Mark's [Episcopal], Baptist and Methodist, those were the outstanding church—and not even Baptist so much. In the other churches the families have to be real outstanding to get recognition.

Inside the church, the seating arrangements followed a time-hardened hierarchy. The more prominent members in the society—and hence of the church—sat in the front pews. In some cases the same families occupied the same set of seats for several decades, other members tacitly acknowledging their rank by not using their seats. The offspring of these prominent families were usually participants in the choir in their younger years, assuming various church offices later. Rear seats were usually occupied by marginal members—marginal for the day, such as latecomers or those who perceived themselves to be improperly dressed, or marginal in terms of their religious status at the moment, for example, temporary "backsliders" or transgressors. In terms of status and prestige, then, the church reflects the community. Because the church was the primary source of early education, the arrangement of unequal relations and its accompanying values became part of a cognitive model for social mobility in the secular world.

Motivation for upward mobility is balanced by the requirement of "living good," so that it is possible for a church member who is conforming and active but poor to have a fairly high status. Such status may not be fully recognized until the individual's funeral, the event that perhaps most potently recognizes status within the church. The duration of time the body is kept in the church for viewing and the length and size of the funeral service are directly related to the socioreligious status and popularity of the deceased and the grieving family.

Visiting patterns reveal status divisions also. In spite of the ideology of brotherhood under God, close friendship across status lines outside of kin relationships is the exception rather than the rule. Following a fading tradition, a lower status person who visits across status lines is received on the veranda, while the inside of the house is reserved for special guests and close friends. A young woman confided that her own father (a preacher) was rather surprised when he discovered that she received her guests inside her living room. As a child growing up in her father's house, she said, this practice was forbidden. In times of illness, however, some visiting across status lines does take place. Lower-level members visit upward, bringing with them, where possible, gifts of agricultural produce; upper-level individuals, particularly church officials, visit downward, bringing good wishes and a prayer.

In ideology as well as practice, the church reflects the model of hierarchy it absorbed from the society. As an educational institution, it reinforces the hierarchy, making members "fit" for society even as it cleanses them for heaven. The role is paradoxical, for while the church supports the notion of brotherhood, it instills in the believer a sense of superiority vis-à-vis the sinful masses and a desire to climb the social ladder. By doing this, however, it prepares the individual for a psychologically, socially, and economically competitive world.

EDUCATION: SALVATION WITHOUT SOLVENCY

Plantation heritage qualified Blacks for little beyond agricultural labor. The more fortunate, such as railway and port workers, had some skills; there were mechanics, linemen, drivers, dispatchers, and so on. In addition there were a few white-collar workers: clerks, timekeepers, telephone and telegraph operators, and a few bookkeepers. There were also those who had developed what I call independent skills: carpenters, masons, tailors, cobblers, teachers, and, not to be forgotten, healers. The plantation phaseout left many of these individuals employed, but those who were employed in direct plantation activities—and particularly the young—had cause to worry.

The experience of their parents left them little or no cause for pride in agricultural employment. Nor were they likely to move into peasant or yeoman agriculture as their parents might have done. Besides, little land was readily available to the poor. Therefore, by the early 1950s, young Blacks had begun to think of betterment almost exclusively in terms of nonagricultural means. Peasant farming was a partial alternative to wage labor among only a small minority.

Although many individuals who had productive farms have simply abandoned or sold them to pursue wage employment, the lack of agricultural endeavors cannot be attributed solely to this; there have always been problems with agriculture among the poor. In the first place, many Blacks acquired land by simply squatting on and cultivating it. They never bothered to obtain title; even if they wanted to, many did not know how. Consequently there has been a long-standing pattern of Blacks losing their land to Hispanics familiar with the tenure laws of the country—a problem exacerbated by the influx of immigrants from the Meseta Central following the completion of the San José-Limón highway in the mid-1970s. (The Institute of Land and Settlement initiated a program to remedy the problem of entitlement in the 1970s, but its effects were limited.) In addition, individuals and families who occupied land still under the jurisdiction of the United Fruit Company until 1978 had difficulty making long-term plans due to uncertainty as to the ultimate disposition of the land.

The insecurity of untitled holdings and the perennial problem of insufficient land made obtaining loans and technical assistance difficult, if not impossible. It has become all too clear that without state assistance, small farmers cannot be competitive in a country where industrial-scale farming is becoming the norm.

Today, in spite of the fact that agriculture gets much ideological encouragement and some real support from the state, there is minimal interest in it among the young. Of 218 households surveyed, only two adults under the age of thirty indicated agriculture as a career choice, and only one had access to more than one hundred hectares of land. Similarly, in interviews among rural elementary school children (ages 8–14), only three boys (two Hispanic and one Black) out of seventeen indicated a desire for a career having to do with agriculture. Of eighty-four elementary school students (sixty-four Blacks and twenty Hispanics) interviewed in the urban area, none indicated farming as a career choice.

Mobility, in general, is in a direction away from the traditional occupations of Blacks in the region. The Afro-Costa Rican epitomizes Rex Nettleford's comment that *"the obvious answer for the African or black Jamaican is to sink his racial consciousness in the wider greater aspirations to acquire education and other means of making himself economically viable"* (1973, 53–54, emphasis in original). Seventy-eight percent of all adults surveyed saw a good education as the path to upward mobility for their offspring. But can aspirations be satisfied through the existing infrastructure provided by the state? And perhaps of even greater importance, how much of an obstacle is the class position of parents, in terms of both attitude and access?

Obviously, equal opportunity in education regardless of class position is a myth, especially beyond the elementary level. Middle-class parents take for granted that their offspring will choose a noble profession, more as a matter of maintaining the family name and increasing their prestige than as a matter of self-improvement. Working-class parents, however, may cherish aspirations that are sometimes unrealistic. They are influenced largely by incomplete or distorted knowledge of how the opportunity structure functions, on the one hand, and on the other, by role models whose backgrounds, and therefore life chances, are dramatically incompatible with their own. Furthermore, the content of the educational process itself, removed as it is from the reality of its own socioeconomic context, instills values and aspirations that are unachievable ideals. The result is extreme frustration (see M.G. Smith 1960, 332–54 for the situation in Jamaica). In Limón, role models are professionals, politicians, or others in white-collar positions. The imposing image presented by these individuals, inclined as some are to flaunt the symbols of their position, is profoundly influential in the course that upward mobility takes.

Class background can be decisive in determining who makes it to the university. In spite of improved access to higher education with the opening of a second university in the early 1970s, it is still evident that few Black students come from very poor families. And those who are from poor families have, for the most part, found themselves in special circumstances.

Maria, for example, who grew up with her maternal grandparents, peasant cultivators, in New Sligoville, managed to go to the university after high school in Limón. In high school she lived with an aunt in Limón, returning to the village on weekends (she was one of the fortunate Black female students who didn't have to drop out). When she was accepted to the university on a small scholarship, she was fortunate to be able to live with her mother, who works in San José. But for these fortuitous circumstances, a university education would have remained only a dream.

The widening access to higher education has brought home to Blacks the problem of the cultural chauvinism and racism upon which their educational integration is based. Critical comments come not only from Black intellectuals but also from Hispanic thinkers. Quince Duncan (1975, 25-26) summarizes Abel Pacheco's appropriately critical statement:

The Black goes to the classroom, and struggles to master the culture of the majority. Shirley Bell was educated as if she were not a Black woman. They did not prepare her to accept her reality and by so doing liberate them of the prejudices. They inculcated in her the fallacy, the grand fallacy, of the magical force of education; the great myth of the automatic liberation from all oppression....Shirley represents the young of Limón whose prospects are limited by the color of their skin, or simply by being from Limón Her diploma ended up at the bottom of a chest, useless.

Failure of the economic infrastructure to absorb the newly educated, coupled with the realization that "Spanish" education/culture does not automatically free one from the miasma of racial prejudice, has produced a new set of demands on the society. These demands are being voiced, paradoxically, by those who have themselves benefited most from the process of incorporation: professionals and university students.

ADEQUATE BUT NOT EQUAL: ASPECTS OF THE EDUCATIONAL INFRASTRUCTURE

The basic infrastructure necessary to facilitate mobility through education is present, even if somewhat limited.[3] Education from elementary through high school is theoretically free, but ancillary fees can still be prohibitive. Many students, particularly males, drop out of school to work and help support the family. Others drop out when they lose hope of gaining appropriate employment; all around them they see examples of high school graduates who have had to settle for the same jobs as nongraduates. Puerto Limón has a fairly high illiteracy rate (17 percent) compared to that of other provincial capitals (Casassas Simo and Osorio Ponce, 1977, 37–40). Available figures from the province suggest that illiteracy is much higher in rural areas (such as Talamanca and Matina); 75 percent of the work force has only primary education (El Equipo Cornell-Costa Rica 1973, 21–22).

The picture at the higher education level shows a lack of congruence between ideology and realization. According to figures made public in

1973, only 0.2 percent of Limón's population made it to the university—representing 1.0 percent of the university population, while Limón's population is around 6 percent of the nation. Limón had the lowest percentage of university students of all the provinces. As would be expected, rural provinces have the lowest proportion of university students.

It is difficult to derive full meaning from these figures in the absence of data regarding qualifications of students, number of applications made, criteria of rejection or acceptance, and so on. It can be easily assumed, however, that a significant part of the explanation for the low participation is related to class and, more than likely, race. In Costa Rica, Blacks and Hispanics alike see language skill as one barrier to admission and adequate performance of Blacks. Finally, the geographical location of Limón in relation to San José—where the universities are located—cannot be discounted.

The long and rocky road to higher education leaves festering frustration and discontent in the Afro-Costa Rican population. Much of Costa Rica's national and international prestige rides on its genuine commitment to education, but the national ideology of equal opportunity portrays the system as more open and accessible than it actually is. The high literacy rate that is often mentioned effectively obscures the inequities. As the main vehicle of upward mobility, education is limited. As an ideological tool for acceptance of the status quo and as a means of instilling national values in the young, it is more than adequate, for these functions are achieved more effectively at the lower levels of the educational system. At the higher levels, however, education does tend to render the social system more transparent, and here lies a central paradox: At the lower levels, education presents the social system as ideal, while at the higher level it serves the unintended function of helping to expose the contradictions and provide the basis for critique. Hence educated Blacks are more acutely aware of the inadequacies of this path of upward mobility.

"KEEPING SHOP": INDEPENDENT COMMERCIAL VENTURES

Commerce has been perhaps the least pursued avenue of upward mobility among Blacks. In the urban centers as well as in most rural areas, most of the larger and more successful businesses are owned by Chinese, though there is a growing number of Hispanic entrepreneurs. Blacks do own businesses, but they are for the most part small pulperias, restaurants, and "cook shops," one or two bakeries, and a few bars. Some exceptions are a medium-size hardware store, two dry goods stores, and a rather large restaurant and dance hall. Chinese own the movie theaters, restaurants, hardware stores, hotels (the Episcopal church, which is predominantly

Black, owns a large modern hotel), dry goods stores, most of the better bars and grocery stores, and supermarkets. They also control the very large clandestine lottery known locally as "chance."

A few wage-employed Blacks have been diversifying their options by buying houses in newly developed areas and converting part of the house into a small pulperia. In some cases the wife or grown children run the pulperia while the husband continues wage labor or farming. Because this is a rather new development, it is difficult to hazard a guess as to its impact on the economy of the Black sector. Occasional small "home enterprises" are found in the downtown area also, but these tend to be even smaller in scale, ranging from the marketing of bread (baked in a small bakery at the back of the house and sold through a living room window) to the selling of a few farm products displayed on the veranda.

There is a saying among Blacks that "Chineman [Chinese] run business but Black man keep shop." But the question of why the Chinese managed to become successful entrepreneurs while Blacks did not is still unanswered. Both groups entered the plantation arena as laborers, yet by the 1920s the Chinese were well-established in small businesses. One difference may have to do with historical exposure to the type of sociocultural activities that engender and reinforce self-reliance rather than destroy it. Another consideration might be that Blacks went to Costa Rica—as they went to Cuba or Panama—not to put down roots but with the intention of returning to their homeland after accumulating some cash. Also, the generally favorable disposition of Hispanics toward the Chinese as contrasted to Blacks may have affected the climate for entrepreneurial support.

Then there is the problem of the relative absence of entrepreneurial skills among Blacks, and the difficulty of obtaining capital. Blacks who have tried to obtain capital through the banks have complained of their inability to meet the requirements, which involve the patronage of prominent individuals as much and perhaps more than the ability to repay. The case I describe below, although exceptional in its success, hints at some of the limitations—both cultural and economic—to breaking into the world of commerce.

Ronald, a teacher, and his wife, Marcia, a university student, came to the exceptional conclusion that the path to independence in Limón was not through working for someone else, but working for themselves. In the mid-1970s, Marcia left the university and with their small savings established a modest fried chicken business, housed in a small roadside stall. In addition to the fried chicken, she sold sodas, cigarettes, and minor items such as chewing gum. The business did rather well, as it was ideally located on the main commercial street close to the municipal market.

Ronald continued to teach as the business flourished under the magic hands and attractive personality of Marcia. Soon she opened another shop in a front room of their apartment, employing a young female relative as assistant. After two years at the first location, they found an even more appropriate and larger shop, upgraded the store into a roadside cafe, and diversified their products. As business grew, a third shop was opened, and Ronald gave up teaching, bought a small pickup truck, and occupied himself with the necessary hauling and delivery.

During the 1977 lobster season, Ronald bought two boats and contracted them out for fishing, but he was much less successful at this. Nevertheless, he was severely criticized by some of his peers for being greedy. In commenting on this, he observed that although Garron (a wealthy Hispanic businessman and landowner) had about sixteen boats compared to his two, Garron was never criticized for being greedy. This was crab antics at work.

In 1978, Ronald had the opportunity to purchase a large cacao farm with a house and other amenities, but he needed significantly more liquid assets. He asked a friend who knew the seller to inform her of his intention to purchase and to request time to obtain a bank loan. She agreed. In the meantime, a Hispanic from the Meseta Central made her an offer, and in addition, took the land documents, offering to process them at no cost to her. Meanwhile, the bank processing Ronald's loan needed the documents in order to finalize the loan agreement. Ronald's competitor learned of this and held on to the documents, at the same time increasing his offer. What was considered a prime investment opportunity was lost to a shrewd, aggressive competitor with ready capital. In one instance, Ronald had crab antics working against him; in another he had the lack of capital and business know-how.

Two basic trends are discernible in the efforts of Afro-Limonese to establish independent ventures. One is the move from wage employment, through the accumulation of savings, to private investment. The other—which concerns mostly successful rural small-scale farmers—is the move toward diversification of economic activity to open pulperias, and, in a few cases, to become middlemen in the cacao trade. The latter activity, however, is restricted to a very small number of individuals and is for the most part confined to the Talamanca corridor.

It soon becomes evident that, but for the exceptional few, upward mobility through entrepreneurship is not pursued with any vigor. It is less evident that although many Blacks say that "Black man can' do bizniz," the factors contributing to the lethargic state of this aspect of Afro-Costa Rican life are many, deeply entrenched, and bewilderingly complex.

In discussing social stratification in Trinidad, Braithwaite (1953) identified six factors he felt inhibited the development of lower-class businesses: (1) conspicuous consumption; (2) a personality type not amenable to sustained continuous activity; (3) the opposition to restrictive occupations; (4) the influence of "pratique" relationships, wherein intimacy tends to disregard market relations, and in which market relations do not cross class lines; (5) the female-dominant household in which socialization fails to develop the type of male personality necessary to assume the responsibilities of business; and finally (6) the low regard for "dirty" work.

All of these factors in varying degrees apply to Costa Rica, but they still do not by themselves account for the lack of Black businesses. In the first place, conspicuous consumption, the product of that perverse marriage between marketing techniques and the ideals of bourgeois self-definition, plagues the poor of all shades of skin. Notable exceptions are the Chinese and East Indian migrants throughout the Caribbean and the new Asian immigrants in the United States. And if we think that Blacks are not capable of sustained, disciplined activity, we should take a closer look at the Black peasant anywhere in the Americas. It is to Blacks' credit, however, that they are often reluctant to be regimented if it means their labor is exploited and their spirit weakened. It is in this light also that the low regard for dirty work must be viewed, even though business is not always dirty. As to the absence of a "responsible" personality due to female-led socialization, we might observe that some of the Caribbean's most astute business people are women (Carnegie 1983). The roots of irresponsibility among Blacks go beyond the matrifocal family; it is part of the slavery heritage.

To understand the special orientation of Blacks, it might be useful to make a distinction between business skills and ethics in the capitalist system and entrepreneurial skills and ethics in a more universal sense. Under capitalism, business skills and ethics presuppose the core motive of maximizing material gain. A universal understanding of entrepreneurship, however, does not require such an ideology. In its broadest sense, entrepreneurship is the ability to organize and direct an undertaking, assuming the risks involved for the sake of the desired gain. The ultimate goal need not be maximum material gain—or the gain may be diverse rather than singular. The organizer of a successful nonprofit organization is a good entrepreneur, and so is a higgler whose aim is to make money but who is keen to balance social obligations and cultural mores against the desire for profit. In keeping with this distinction, Black heritage might produce good entrepreneurs but not good capitalists.

Braithwaite (1953) hints at this cultural explanation in his discussion of pratique relationships wherein intimacy disregards market relations. West Africa is well-known for its astute traders, but this does not mean they are good capitalists. The African trader, like the Caribbean higgler or small-business person, is in the business of making a living, but this is defined differently from the capitalist idea of making a living. In the capitalist tradition, man is *homo economicus:* personal, social, and environmental relations are clearly subordinated to the ethos of individual accumulation. In the African/Caribbean tradition, making a living is organically tied to maintaining the society and the environment—and the spirit—as a whole.

This understanding is part of a monist ideology in which all categories of life—god, spirits, man, animals, and plants—form an organic whole (Keita 1979; Mbiti 1970). Sharing is therefore more important than accumulation, and pratique relations more important than market relations. These cultural traits form, in a historically attenuated manner, the bedrock of the ideology of solidarity in Costa Rica. Although the persistence of the African ontology may be good for social cohesion and perhaps even for business, it is bad for capitalism.

The other aspect of Black heritage that inhibits business is far more obvious; indeed it is what this book is really about. It is the myth of intellectual inferiority bequeathed by colonialism, a myth that legitimizes exploitation and makes self-esteem a slave to bourgeois expectations. Until three decades ago, for example, Black skin was rare behind a bank counter in the West Indies, and it was not likely to get unbiased attention in front of the counter. There was simply little or no experience and even less encouragement for the poor Black who wanted to start a business. And for some who started, the noncapitalist ethic made them uncompetitive in the capitalist market.

Then there is the problem of collective self-esteem. In postemancipation Jamaica, for example, mobile Blacks left the wide-open niche of retail trading to the Chinese, because they were preoccupied with social status and therefore went for more highly regarded white-collar jobs. Finally, one cannot discount the part played by the particular historical conditioning Blacks experienced, which motivates self-improvement through means other than independent ventures.

MIGRATION AS UPWARD MOBILITY

For Caribbean and circum-Caribbean peoples, migration has traditionally helped to shape patterns of coping with harsh life conditions and circumventing local constraints on upward mobility. Although migration is sometimes viewed as a means of coping, it is also appropriately viewed as a self-improvement strategy. The majority, no doubt, migrate initially to cope—depending on how coping is defined—but many emigrate from conditions in which they are doing better than coping.

The presence of West Indian migrants in Costa Rica represents just one step in the quest for self-improvement; they continue to display a well-founded sense of restlessness. This should be no surprise—for West Indian poor, "to move is as ordinary and expected a thing to do as to be sedentary" (Carnegie 1983, 12).

INTERNAL MIGRATION

Migration within the province of Limón was discussed in Chapter 4. I limit the discussion here to migration from Limón to the capital, San José. Internal migration in Costa Rica is tied primarily to two related factors: employment and education. The distribution of employment opportunity and education is determined by historical patterns in the national and international distribution of tangible and intangible resources. Because the emphasis on development has been on the Meseta Central, it is quite predictable that Blacks seeking opportunities should direct their attention to San José. In addition to the concentration of investment in that area, it is the seat of the central state apparatus, itself a residual employer of labor, with approximately 15 percent of the total labor force (Costa Rica Ministerio de Culture 1977, 39–60).

At the same time, Limón, despite its distinct economic importance to the nation, has the lowest salary scale of any province except for the northern zone, which is inhabited mostly by Hispanic peasant cultivators. Despite its relative poverty, Limón today is less a source of cheap labor than it was in the 1950s, when United Fruit abandoned the area. Those were particularly lean years, and Blacks sought opportunities wherever they could; many women, for example, emigrated to San José, where they worked as domestic maids in return for a meager wage and room and board.

Just living in a city such as San José has its own inherent value. It places the individual within the range of diverse possibilities and options, such as employment, education, social opportunities, social refinement, and all the other benefits of city life. Both the immigrant and the Limón resident recognize that it takes special skills not only to live in the city but to take advantage of its services, and this recognition has given rise to a set of social brokers who position themselves at hotels frequented by Afro-Limonese when they visit the city. The rural-urban brokers lighten the burden of being a country bumpkin, and worse, a Black country bumpkin.

Although for the most part employed at lower white-collar jobs and manual labors, Blacks in San José do enjoy the competitive advantage of speaking both English and Spanish. As in Limón, however, few engage in entrepreneurial activities. The visibility of a few successful Blacks in the city employment structure creates the false impression that Blacks in general are doing well economically.

Upward mobility through internal migration in Costa Rica is similar to that in other Third World nations where development is interpreted as

Westernization; the search for educational and job opportunities is all-consuming. The distribution of postprimary educational institutions, therefore, follows the distribution of urban centers, and the educational quality of such institutions tends to be in direct proportion to the level of urbanity in the area in which they are located. Moreover, because of the nature of the distribution of job opportunities, those who migrate to urban areas in order to further their education are forced to remain there. The net result is a constant drain of human resources from the rural areas and a concomitant partial disintegration of economic and social ties.

INTERNATIONAL MIGRATION

As with other areas of the Caribbean and South America, international migration has remained a most desirable life strategy. The main destinations are the United States and Canada. During the 1950s and early 1960s, large numbers of Afro-Limonese women were contracted to work as household helpers in the United States. As expected, initial migration to the United States was to provide the groundwork for the later emigration of relatives and friends, pulling, as West Indians do, kinship ties into the heart of the migration process. Today there are few families in Limón that do not have close kin or friends in the United States.

Kinship networks have been instrumental at home, too. Children of migrant parents are left in the care of relatives—grandmothers, aunts, older siblings, and at times the remaining member of the parental couple. But although the migrant parents usually move swiftly to have their children join them, the arrangement has occasionally created irreparable disharmony between marriage partners and problems with the socialization of children left behind. This is not a unique phenomenon and certainly deserves closer study, along the lines of Gonzalez's (1969) analysis of Black Caribs and Price's (1970) discussion on Saramakan migration and marriage.

Still, with all its inherent problems, international migration is perceived as perhaps the most desired means of mobility for adults. Without exaggeration, it could be said that should restrictions be removed, Afro-Costa Ricans (and Hispanics too) would flock to the United States in waves, as did Cubans permitted to leave by the Castro regime in the 1970s. As Greaves (1968, 113) puts it, the desire to travel is among the determinants of individual motives for accepting capitalist conditions. As many Afro-Limonese put it: "You have to travel to know."

The theories applied to the phenomenon of migration span the spectrum of major theoretical formulations in current social science (see Bryce-Laporte 1980, Chapter 8). Yet there seems to be little effort directed toward understanding the individual conditions and attitudes of those who move in the context of the structural factors affecting movement as a whole. For example, it is misleading to suppose that Caribbean migration to the United States is motivated by economic necessity alone. Undoubtedly economics has been and remains the crucial factor; members of the middle class often move with or without their accumulated capital. The underlying impetus is not economic necessity but a historically acquired bourgeois notion of moral and social self-improvement, a notion that posits the satisfaction of basic needs alone as unambitious.

Political considerations, too, may come into play, as in the case of migration from Cuba and more recently from places like Haiti, Nicaragua, and El Salvador. But, to reduce all explanations to economic or political causes would be to miss the vast array of social and cultural factors that impinge on the process leading to the final act: The distribution and availability of social opportunities, kinship relations, questions of race, national allegiance versus individual and family interest, and desire to travel all come into play.

As encompassing as its motives are migration's effects; it affects those who move as it affects those who receive the movers and those who are left behind. Its long-term effect is felt on the nature of ethnic and class relations of both sending and receiving countries. Allen and Smith , writing of Asian and West Indian workers in Great Britain, observe that "they are integrated into the system in such a way that without them the structure of existing class relations would be critically affected" (1974, 40). Indeed the class structure of societies in the Americas is founded on migration; Black migration no less. When Afro-Costa Ricans resort to movement, whether for escape, betterment, or enrichment, they are simply resorting to a life strategy inherent in the African diaspora.

Fighting the Stereotype

It would be truly exceptional if most Blacks—in Costa Rica as elsewhere in the Americas—did not aciduously pursue one form or another of upward mobility; it is a psychological necessity. Blacks find themselves in societies where all that is deemed valuable is based on the hierarchization of natural differences bundled into an economic rationale. Dark skin signals poverty, indolence, and lack of intelligence and sophistication, all traits perceived as downright primitive. This is a legacy of colonialism. So even if Blacks did not need the material gains of upward mobility, they would still have to strive to save their cultural and personal dignity by putting the lie to stereotypes held by whites. Sociologists from Rousseau to Talcott Parsons have rightly agreed that inequality is a sociocultural necessity; but the issue is whether inequality must always be molded into moral oppression.

The overwhelming emphasis on education as the main vehicle of mobility is based partly on a realistic assessment of the requirements of a modern technological society and partly on a drive toward those areas of economic life that promise greater prestige. But people are somewhat imprisoned by their historical experience; the overriding desire for white-collar positions seems to be a reenactment of the status/prestige organizational characteristics of the plantation system. Manual labor is unattractive because the plantation experience with its strict dichotomy—manual labor is slave labor, while nonmanual labor is free labor—has no doubt left that particular impression of the world on Blacks' minds. Their perception of opportunity, status, and prestige, then, is influenced not only by their often inadequately informed assessment of the opportunity structure, but also by the cognitive fossil of the plantation hierarchy.

With respect to migration, the willingness of individuals to migrate to find opportunities—even at the expense of national allegiance—speaks to the often disregarded fact that the concern of the West Indian masses is neither cultural, national, nor ideological identity; the main concern is self-improvement. Add to this David Lowenthal's (1972, 5) comment that the main theater of West Indian activity is neither the area as a whole nor any territorial grouping, but rather the particular land that is home, and it becomes evident that there are really two theaters of activity: the land that is home and the land that provides social and economic improvement. There is no apparent contradiction between having a house, land, family, and friends in one country and working and living for decades in another (cf. Lowenthal 1961). Similarly, for the mobile there is usually no apparent contradiction in appealing to the values of the dominant majority in order to secure the standard of living desirable for self and family. The dilemma is that Black success in the mainstream of a predominantly white society inevitably entails some degree of dependency—cultural, political-economic, or both.

SEVEN

THE INEQUALITY OF LANGUAGE IN SOCIAL PRACTICE[1]

S poken language has become the primary means by which we express our interpretation of experience, but it is also a pivotal signifier by which we evaluate and categorize those we encounter, whether we do this consciously or not. In Costa Rica, a multiethnic, multilingual society, the use of linguistic symbols as indicators of position and aspiration is a predictably complicated affair. Race and color combine with multilingualism to sharpen the social markers. Understandably, therefore, they have become important vehicles in ongoing efforts toward self-improvement among West Indians.

In discussing the relationship between language and social structure, my intention is not to describe the languages spoken at various levels of the society but rather to examine some of the social contexts in which language functions as a marker of social status and prestige. A secondary concern is with language as an indicator of the relationship between geographical space, type of economic activity, and level of acculturation.

MULTILINGUALISM ON THE ATLANTIC COAST

There are three main languages used in Limón province: Spanish, the official state language; Standard Limón English; and Limón Creole, a changed form of Jamaican Creole.[2] Until the post–civil war (1948) period, Jamaican Creole was the main language spoken by Black employees of the United Fruit Company and Black peasants. There were certainly those Jamaicans who, for reasons of status and/or occupation, preferred to speak Standard English, but because the plantation context dictated that they communicate with the laboring class, their use of Standard English was restricted to communication with their social or occupational peers, North Americans and Britons. A Jamaican druggist who practiced medicine in Limón in the latter years of the plantation regime observed that upon his arrival in the early 1920s, he had to modify his language from Standard

106

English to Jamaican Creole "because many of the people with whom I came into contact could not understand my speech." Today the language field is far more diversified. About 73 percent of Blacks are bilingual, and 80 percent speak and read Spanish (Headley Mullings 1983, 195).

There has been an increasing and interesting change in the relationship of the three languages, according to Wright-Murray's (1974) description. As acculturation influences a three-dimensional language situation involving Spanish, Standard Limón English, and Limón Creole, Limón Creole is gradually collapsing, resulting in a two-dimensional situation involving Spanish and Standard Limón English. At the same time, North American English is replacing the Jamaican flavor of the English spoken by the young. From my own observation, the few third-generation Blacks who speak Standard English do indeed speak American rather than Jamaican Standard.[3] It is what they are taught in the schools, and it is what most English-speaking visitors use.

The totality of English spoken, however, may be viewed in terms of a continuum from Limón Creole at one extreme to Standard English at the other, with most speakers commanding only a restricted zone of competence. According to Woollard (1978, Essay 1) and again supported by my own observation, the majority of speakers fall in the range shown in Figure 3. (There is a generational differentiation in the use of codes: The Limón Creole end of the continuum is spoken largely by first- and some rural second-generation migrants, while the Standard Limón English end is spoken by third-generation and some younger people such as English teachers and a few others who have studied English beyond the usual level required in the schools.) Accepting Woollard's conceptualization, I use English to refer to the entire continuum, while Limón Creole and Standard Limón English are used to refer to their respective extremes.

As mentioned in Chapter 2, English was once the main vehicle of social prestige among Blacks. A person who mastered Standard English could not go unnoticed in the plantation system, especially as the majority of laborers spoke only Jamaican Creole, not having had access to the education necessary to acquire Standard English skills. Skin color and education mediated the prestige scale, increasing the status of individuals according to their perceived proximity to whites. This situation remained without significant change up to the end of the 1940s. Few Blacks even attempted to learn Spanish until Hispanic hegemony in the region made it a necessity. As would be expected, the impact of the change in hegemony was greater in the urban areas. In the rural areas—especially where proletarianization is slow, and where there is steady emigration of first- and second-generation Blacks—Standard English and Limón Creole have remained the dominant languages. In order to highlight the relationship between geography and

FIGURE 3
LANGUAGE CONTINUUM

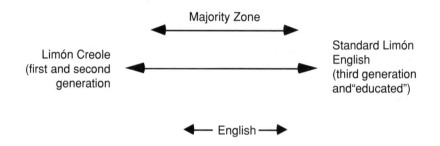

social change, let us examine the language situation in three different types of communities, ranging from small rural villages to the provincial capital.

NEW SLIGOVILLE: ENGLISH DOMINATES

The village of New Sligoville is representative of the language situation in most rural areas. Miss May, the head of the household in which I lived when I worked in this village in 1978, was a Jamaican-born widow about 62 years old. Neither she nor her mother, Mammy, spoke Spanish. Mr. Percy, the third permanent member of the household, was a Jamaican-born man about 74 years old. With several of his brothers and sisters, he joined his parents in Costa Rica when he was about 12 years old. He was bilingual. A temporary member of the household, Doña Rosa, was a female Hispanic who lived with them while she worked on land she rented from Miss May. She spoke only Spanish. In a household of four, then, there were two English monolinguals, one Spanish monolingual, and one bilingual (or trilingual, if we separate Limón Creole from Standard Limón English).

Despite Miss May's inability to speak Spanish, she routinely engaged the few Hispanics from the village and adjoining areas in brief conversations whenever they stopped by to purchase candy or soda—which she sold at home—or simply to say hello. Mr. Percy, her brother-in-law, sometimes had to interpret for her, but this was only when precision was crucial. Her competence in Spanish, as well as speech, extended only to the infinitive and third-person forms of the more commonly used verbs, and the names of a few familiar objects and foods. Yet her competence as a receiver (i.e., her comprehension) far outweighed her skills as a speaker. Miss May frequently engaged in extended conversations with Doña Rosa, whose knowledge of English was about equal to Miss May's knowledge of Spanish. Doña Rosa had attempted to learn English with the use of recordings, but with little success. Admittedly, I marveled at the first such conversation I was privy to. They were preparing dinner and, while peeling green bananas, launched into a discussion of Doña Rosa's plans to plant plantains (*Musa paradisiaca*) on a piece of land she had leased from Miss May. Following is an excerpt from the conversation.

Miss May: "You know Doña, the rain goin' start soon so you mus' get you *eejo* them [*hijo* = son] to clean an' fork up the finca before it start."

Doña Rosa looked at her questioningly and she repeated, using arm movements to clarify: "The *yuvia* [*lluvia*] man, pronto. Once it start you no sabe when it goin' *termina* an' you can' make plantain sucker stay on the ground too long, them will rotten."

Doña Rosa: *"Jorge me prometio desde no se cuando Mi' May pero cho, ese muchachito mio siempre esta preocupao, con que yo no se. Dios sabe*—not'ing. *Tiene tiempo porque no esta trabajando en este momento, y no tiene finca....Bueno, a ver semana entrante.* Nex' week."

Miss May: "I did think you say you was goin' gormandize the coco nex' *semana*."

Doña Rosa: *"No mang, como el viejo* [her husband] *todavia se queda en su espalda en el hospital mejor que dejar Jorge trabaja mientras que yo paso dos dias alla."*

They sometimes continued for almost an hour like this, casually shifting from subject to subject as the occasion afforded. Each questioning look from one to the other met with clarifying arm movements, voice modulations, repetitions, and substitution of words and phrases. In actuality, they had spontaneously developed their own pidgin, founded not on verbal symbols alone but on the long-established affinity and mutual knowledge that characterize as such a relationship. Neither of them mastered the other's native language, but they mastered communication.

Miss May's mother, a wiry, energetic, mild-mannered woman in her late eighties, spoke even less Spanish than her daughter, but her English spanned the continuum from Creole to Standard. She used Standard English mainly in church and Burial Scheme activities. The church in her neighborhood had long been inactive, but when she waxed sublime she still used a register befitting a Baptist deaconess. She occasionally listened attentively to conversations between her daughter and Doña Rosa, but maintained a dignified silence.

Mr. Percy, on the other hand, was one of the few first-generation Blacks in the village who was fluent in what he often turgidly referred to as "grammatical" Spanish. He learned it while employed as a cacao buyer during the late plantation period. He had also worked as a farmhand for brief periods alongside Hispanic peones. Imbued with a sharp sense of propriety, he was as proud of his Spanish as he was of his "Queen's English."

In turn, he was respected not only for his language ability but for his vast, though at times fanciful, knowledge of history and world affairs. He had been the judge—a local police agent who settles minor disputes and helps investigate local crimes—when New Sligoville was the demographic and commercial center of that part of the Estrella Valley. Later he was several times president of community juntas. He was regarded as something of a community leader, but his prestige was attenuated by his regular participation in raucous domino games with younger boys, sometimes involving money. His language skills had nevertheless placed him at the heart of community affairs.

This household is atypical of Black households in this small rural village in one respect: Spanish was frequently spoken. Although a good number of adults in the village spoke some Spanish, few had mastered a speech code as close to the standard as Mr. Percy's. Except for three other households having racially mixed couples (husband Black and wife Hispanic in two cases and in one, the reverse), English was the main and, in most cases, the only language spoken in the home. Interestingly enough, in the case of racially mixed couples, Spanish dominated, even when the Hispanic member of the union spoke some English. And if the offspring of such unions learned Limón Creole, they did so mainly in social interaction with their peers and other English-speaking members of the community. Almost every child, however, spoke some Limón Creole, and all spoke Spanish, the language of state education. On the whole, children in New Sligoville and vicinity rarely communicated with their peers in Spanish; "Spanglish" (the term applied to the lively Spanish-English syncretism common throughout the province) was the usual mode.

DIVISON BY AGE AND RACE

The various domains of language in the community were distinguished by, among other factors, generation, education, and race. In general, Hispanics spoke Spanish and Blacks spoke English. But third- and some second-generation individuals, having learned Spanish in school and Limón Creole at home, had the advantage of both, depending on context. First-generation exceptions like Mr. Percy, however, by virtue of their knowledge of the language and culture of both ethnic groups, had access to most speech codes within the total linguistic system and could therefore function comfortably in more domains than most villagers, young or old. The domains of each language overlapped, however, as Figure 4 illustrates.

It would seem reasonable to assume that in communities such as this, leaders would be drawn from individuals who fall into the overlap zone. This was not the case. Seventy-four-year-old Mr. Percy was in a leadership position of sorts, but although he qualified linguistically, he was out of the generational range. With increasing acculturation and decreasing social autonomy, the villagers gradually relied on the nonresident Hispanic school teacher as their representative to outside agencies. When I asked Mr. Percy why the teacher was increasingly placed in a leadership role, his response was that it is better to have a "Spaniard" represent you when dealing with government representatives and agencies. The strategy goes beyond language capability; it is a shrewd alliance with the dominant ethnic group.

But English was the functional language in this community. In contrast

FIGURE 4
RELATIONSHIP BETWEEN LINGUISTIC DOMAIN AND GENERATION

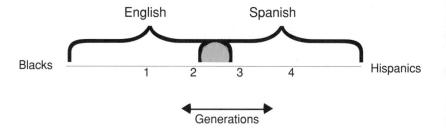

to the more urban communities, English was used in all public gatherings during my stay in the village. In the past, the village had boasted vibrant community organizations, but the only regular public gathering at the time of my visit was the weekly bingo game. Although comments or protests were made in Limón Creole, there was nevertheless some Spanish infusion. And because of the manner in which Spanish was used, its inclusion seemed intended, consciously or unconsciously, to pique the interest of participants while adding a touch of humor and contrast. The calling of bingo card numbers and types of winning positions, such as *cuatro esquinas* (four corners) almost always involved some Spanish. The calling of numbers was occasion for individual creativity. The following are a few of the calls, which combine Spanish and Limón Creole into a poetic form of Spanglish: "El numero back a di door—four/ El numero big boot—*doce*/ Cincuenti, que bola—*cincuenta*/ Veinti bela—*veinte*/ Marti con clavo—*setentiuno*."

Even the elderly, who do not normally speak Spanish, know enough to function at a bingo game, as in other language domains outside of the village. As the elderly usually say, "God be praise, mi can buy mi *pan* [bread] in Spanish."

POINT COVE: SPANISH MOVES IN

In contrast to New Sligoville, where English clearly dominated, Spanish was taking a firm grip on the community in Point Cove. In 1978, about 9 percent of the population of approximately 1,400 was Hispanic. In addition, there were such Spanish domains as a school, a bank, a health-care clinic, a police station, and an agricultural extension office. Hispanics had assumed a very active role in what used to be an all-Black community (Palmer 1977). There were Hispanic cacao buyers, fishermen, police, peones, and one pulperia owner. Spanish was used in most pulperias, since even Black-owned stores occasionally employ Hispanic or young Black assistants who are more conversant in Spanish than in English. Most such individuals, however, do speak some Limón Creole, so that the elderly who speak no Spanish have no real problems making purchases—or protests.

Three factors seem to account for the pervasiveness of Spanish: (1) the growing number of Hispanics and their level of integration into the day-to-day life of the village; (2) the larger number of young people between the ages of approximately ten and thirty remaining in the village; and (3) the fact that this is a prime cacao farming and trading area with a relatively high level of commercial activity and extensive outside contact.

Factors Supporting English

Nevertheless, when a group of young men congregated, whether to play dominoes, play music, or simply talk, the language was usually Limón Creole, except when a Hispanic was present. And even then, if a non-Spanish speaking foreigner was also present, as is often the case since young American and European tourists frequent the village, Limón Creole or English might still be spoken in deference to the stranger. In fact, the unceasing presence of white tourists helps to retard the encroachment of Spanish while simultaneously slowing the sagging prestige of English. White is a legitimizing color.

Perhaps of greater importance in shoring up English was the strong Black nationalism among young men in the village, a feature understandably absent from New Sligoville because there was less of a consciousness of cultural challenge from the outside. The nationalism that served to preserve Point Cove's culture arose out of the confrontation between the cultural challenge of Spanish and the deep tradition of stern independence that characterized its history.

There were a few young men, some with higher education—a restaurant owner, a teacher, two Ministry of Agriculture employees, and a few others—who were inclined to use Spanish more than English, especially when speaking in the presence of strangers. But Standard English still carried some prestige; those who were therefore comfortable with it were less inclined to speak Spanish than their Creole-speaking peers.

The insistence on Spanish was more pronounced among young Black women. I frequently spoke to a young female assistant at a pulperia who always used Spanish. I had begun to assume that she did not speak English until I saw her, in the company of other females at a local Saturday night dance, speaking very expressively in Limón Creole. A fair conclusion: Spanish is a component of respectability, especially in formal situations.

A Question of Prestige

The respectability factor is as relevant for Hispanics as it is for Blacks, for although many Hispanics manage fairly well in Limón Creole, some are reluctant to use it in communication with foreigners and middle-class Blacks, unless some rapport has been long established. One encounter with the local police was to fix this firmly in my mind.

Toward the end of my first week in the village, several of my belongings were stolen. Within the hour, little detective work by local acquaintances identified one of the two individuals responsible. The culprit confessed but would not reveal the name of his accomplice or where the stolen items were hidden, and the local police seemed quite uninterested. This placed me in a position of having to be persuasive in Spanish—a draconian task for me even when calm. With a calculated combination of threats and pleadings, I eventually prevailed on the police and the items were soon recovered.

Throughout the incident, which lasted about two hours, no English was spoken—except in my most frustrated moments when the aim was not communication but rather expression. The following week in the center of town, the same officer approached me asking for a ride, as all the buses had left. This time, he spoke unblemished Limón Creole. I was later to hear Hispanics speak Creole, mostly to elderly Blacks (but sometimes to their younger Black friends). A local social worker explained to me that it is frequently done out of respect for elderly Blacks. The police officer's insistence on Spanish was due partly to the fact that the occasion was official; he therefore needed the security and authority that the official language conferred.

In multilingual Costa Rica, Spanish is the language of power as, for example, the "formal code" in a monolingual society would be associated with positions of power (see Bloch 1977). No individual lacking a command of Spanish is likely to assume a position of leadership in relation to the dominant Hispanic sector, and this is becoming even more true with the increasing dependency of Black communities on the Hispanic state.

THE LANGUAGE OF POWER

During my stay of several months in the village in 1978, all of the few public gatherings I attended were conducted in Spanish, and discussions were usually dominated by Hispanics in spite of their minority status in the village. A meeting to discuss the unsatisfactory condition of the village water supply was presided over by a Hispanic, a senior clerk in the local bank. When it came time to suggest possible courses of action, only the Hispanics and a few younger Blacks spoke. A letter was drawn up by Hispanics to accompany a petition. It was later submitted to the appropriate government authorities by a Hispanic accompanied by a young Black male. This young Hispanic was urged to convey the petition to the authorities because he knew them personally, but he, in turn, suggested that the young Black male accompany him. At no time did Blacks assume a central role in the debate, even though they far outnumbered Hispanics at the meeting.

At a subsequent parent-teacher meeting, the head teacher of the school, a young Black male, stressed that the concerns of such a meeting pertained to all, and that all should express their opinions. An elderly Black woman immediately responded: "Usted sabe que yo no hablar Espanol."[4] ("You know that I do not to speak Spanish.") This brought some laughter, but everyone fully understood the powerlessness that the humor was meant to make bearable.

Like many older Blacks in the community, this woman's already limited competence was diminished by her insecurity. And many who have comments to make at public gatherings restrain themselves only to hold their own "meetings" on their way home and in the secure company of peers. It is a form of retreat, and the frustration and powerlessness is particularly marked in a community such as this, where Blacks boast a robust tradition of independence and self-sufficiency.

As in most Black peasant and working-class homes throughout the province, English was used in the home in Point Cove. Occasionally, however, Spanish, Limón English, or Standard English might be used, depending on which member of the household was addressed. After visiting Miss Elsada's household of seven (only one of whom was first-generation and all of whom were fluent in Spanish) regularly for a month, a pattern of communication emerged. The eldest daughter, a twenty-six-year-old presently attending high school at night and who had previously spent some years in the capital, San José, preferred to speak Spanish. This was also true, but to a lesser extent, of a younger daughter who was a regular high school student. To the mother, Miss Elsada, I had a clear choice of Spanish or English. With a twenty-three-year-old daughter who had lived and attended high school in the Central Valley, and who now had a son fathered by a Hispanic, I had a choice of Limón Creole or Spanish. With the younger children I spoke Limón Creole or Spanish.

Several factors influenced this choice. Miss Elsada was first-generation, raised in an English-speaking home, but she later developed extensive contact with Hispanics. All her children had been schooled in Spanish but had ample exposure to Limón Creole both in and out of the home. The daughter who spoke mainly Spanish had extensive contact with Americans, which I concluded made her self-conscious about her own brand of English when talking to English-speaking foreigners.

The eclectic language preference and practice in Miss Elsada's household typifies the changing sociolinguistic reality in Limón: Young people, of high school age and older, having been schooled in Spanish, are more confident in its use, especially when speaking with outsiders. They have been led to think that Limón Creole (or "mek-a-tel-yu," as they call it) is "bad" language—"banana language," "braad talk." Yet those who can speak Standard English display a proud willingness to use it in situations where others would opt for Spanish—as was demonstrated over and over in the choice of languages in interview situations.

The presence of a tape recorder usually elicited the interviewee's best speech—if it elicited any at all. An elderly woman in New Sligoville, known for her uninhibited fealty to Jamaican Creole, agreed to the use of the recorder but commented: "I no laik dem sop'n de yu know sah, dem mek yu taak too braad." (I do not like those things, they make you speak too broad.) She then proceeded to tell me about "a nice brown skin girl" who "speak so good" but when she was recorded, "sound braad and flat like banana talk" when she was recorded. Even those who, try as they may, find it difficult to speak Standard English or Spanish have assimilated the myth of "good" and "bad" talk and the hierarchy of Spanish-English-Creole. This causes an inhibiting tension in all but the most unselfconscious speakers, such as preteens.

PUERTO LIMÓN: DOMINANCE OF THE PUBLIC SPHERE

The language situation in Puerto Limón was generally similar to that in Point Cove. But, because of the markedly greater degree of occupational specialization, language usage was more clearly defined in relation to social stratum and social context. Few clerks, teachers, or young white-collar individuals, particularly women, in Puerto Limón, would opt to do an interview in a language other than Spanish. The imperative of Spanish in formal situations was true even for those who, under other circumstances, would not hesitate to speak Limón Creole or Standard Limón English. Males, for example, seemed more comfortable speaking Limón Creole and even Standard English when they could.

With the growing demographic dominance of Hispanics since the early 1970s, most business enterprises and all governmental institutions operate in Spanish. This fact and Spanish education are the two most powerful agents in the change from English to Spanish in the public sphere.

Unlike the two rural areas, Spanish is becoming the language of the domestic sphere in Puerto Limón also. The exceptions are where there are dominant first-generation members in the household, where language is part of a nationalist posture, or in some cases where the household head is working class. The main reason for this is strategic: In this critical socializing context, English or Limón Creole would place children at a disadvantage in school, where they must function in Spanish. (This gives urban children an advantage over rural students.) Parents might speak Limón Creole with friends but, as they say, "we try to fight it at home" because the children must be brought up "right." When, in the mid-1970s, there was a proposal by nationalist Blacks and a few Hispanic supporters to institutionalize Creole in the schools, many—particularly older Blacks—objected on the grounds "that the children were not being brought up just for Limón but for the world."

The social structural necessary for achieving competence in the official and prestige language is more evident among women. It is usually the young and mobile mothers who insist that their children speak Spanish at home and who themselves more readily elect to speak Spanish as a mark of respectability. Donald, a young civil servant, had revealed in discussions with me that while he and his wife, a clerk, tried to bring up their children in Spanish, they frequently spoke English at home. When I visited the home for the first time, however, his wife spoke only Spanish. Even though Donald occasionally switched to Limón Creole, the conversation invariably went back to Spanish, and his wife spoke no English at all during the visit.

There is evidence of a slight change in this attitude, however. With growing cultural nationalism since the mid-1970s, there has been some effort to preserve English. Consequently, many mothers who previously spoke only Spanish to their children now try to teach them not Limón Creole, but Standard Limón English.

Responses to a survey question regarding language preference are summarized in Table 6. The question specified preference rather than language most frequently used, but individuals who do not use a particular language would hardly identify it as their preference. Many people, particularly in the urban area, who gave English as their preference were people also competent in Spanish. It can be assumed, then, that the percentage of people who used Spanish in their daily activities was far greater than the figure for preference suggests.

As the table shows, the preference for Spanish was far greater in the urban area. This is indicative of the degree of acculturation and the extent to which urban life has come under the influence of the national institutions. More to the point, however, it suggests two related factors: (1) the extent to which language and mobility are mutually supporting (mobile Blacks are to be found mostly in urban areas)—indeed, the highest percentage of preference for Spanish (55 percent) came from the most affluent area of Puerto Limón surveyed; and (2) the preference for a language is an indication of national allegiance.

Comments made by respondents were enlightening in this regard. Most people who expressed a preference for English commented that they did so because it is "our language" or because it is their *lengua materna*. The overwhelming comment from those who identified Spanish as their preference was, "Es lo que domina." ("It is the dominant language.") A few said that it was easier to speak. One female respondent, however, gave a very revealing, if not surprising, response: "El Español es más decente." ("Spanish is more decent.") *Decent* could be replaced by *prestigious*. By viewing class in behavioral terms, she represented a significant proportion of urban Blacks. This woman might very well have said: It is part of what we aspire to, therefore it must be better and more decent than what we are leaving behind.

TABLE 6
LANGUAGE PREFERENCE AMONG BLACKS IN LIMÓN

	RURAL	URBAN
SPANISH	19.1%	50%
ENGLISH	74.5%	50%
NO PREFERENCE	6.4%	—
NUMBER	87	130

LANGUAGE, COLOR, AND STRUCTURE IN LIMÓN

Limón Creole provides a wide range of variation along a continuum from the old form, or Jamaican Creole, to Standard English (Wright-Murray 1974). These variations are not all accessible to all Blacks. For example, first-generation Blacks would not speak the same variant of Limón Creole that the fourth-generation group speaks, while the fourth-generation group would not have access to the Standard English used by older Blacks. As mentioned earlier, however, there is evidently rapid change occurring throughout the continuum. The influence of the Spanish language and Hispanic culture has given rise to a process of relexification and phonological modification, with accompanying structural changes to accommodate them.

Many children can make no distinction in pronunciation between initial position /j/ and /dz/ (e.g., "yo-yo" and "jo-jo" would be produced in the same way), having fricativized [j] for both consonants as in Costa Rican Spanish. A child is not likely to say, "Him ave trii yiez lef fe tun ten," as would be said in Jamaican Creole, but, "Falta trii yiez im get ten." ("In three years he will be ten.") The structure is changed to accommodate the Spanish verb *faltar* (to need, to be lacking) (Woollard 1979).

Changes in form are accompanied by changes in the meaning of experience, which translate into changes in the perception of the social structure. Young children have come to associate color with language in a more profound way than adults. Because Hispanics are regarded as white, children regard all whites as Spanish speakers and are therefore surprised whenever they encounter whites who speak English. A British woman teaching English to kindergarten students in Limón found that initially the children spoke to her only in Spanish. The reason for this was revealed later when a four-year-old said: "A Diana le quiero, porque aunque es blanca es negra porque hable Ingles." ("I like Diana because, although she is white, she is really Black for she speaks English.") Clearly, these Black children regarded English as their defining tongue and therefore felt an affinity for those, Black or white, who shared it.

LANGUAGE AND SOCIAL PERCEPTIONS

The language-color dichotomy extends in a somewhat ironic manner to perceptions of the social structure: Children recognize that whites belong to the dominant socioeconomic sector and Blacks to the dominated. Consequently, it is not unusual to have children, innocently trying to retain their dignity, cast aspersions on anything Black. A young woman confided that in her attempt to have her two children (ages eight and ten) identify with

Black culture, she bought her daughter a Black doll. To her amazement her daughter refused to use it, complaining that it was too Black. As the mother explained it, the child ill-treated the doll and finally threw it away.

The entire meaning system of color, race, and language as part of the child's cognitive world deserves further, in-depth study. Why, for example, do some children brought up by Black (or light-skinned) Spanish-speaking parents see themselves as non-Black or express dislike for things associated with their Black heritage? How early, and in what social context, do they begin to perceive conflict in and derive meaning from the race/class structure of inequality?

It seems that even if these children speak Limón Creole or Standard English, aspects of meaning are rooted in Spanish. Woollard (1979, 18) has observed that meaning rather than form seems to be primary to the children's linguistic system. She gives the following examples of two conversations that illustrate this:

Teacher (using a picture of a clown): "What about the clown?"
Child, aged six: "The *payaso?*"
Teacher: "Yes, we call him the clown. Can you say clown?"
Child: "*Payaso.*"
Teacher, pronouncing carefully: "C-l-o-w-n."
Child tries hard to imitate, but her lips form a /p/.

Teacher (teaching the English names for the days of the week): "What are the days of the week?"
Child, aged seven: "Sunday, Monday, Tuesday...Saturday.
Teacher: "Which days we don't come to school?"
Child: "*Sabado.*"
Teacher: "Say it in English."
Child: "*Sa*bado. We don't come to school *sabado.*"

In the first example, the reason for not associating the word "clown" with the idea of a clown as conveyed by the word "payaso" may be that the child has never heard the word clown before and needs time to assimilate the meaning. Be that as it may, to the child, the idea of a clown seemed not to be contained in the English form. The second example is even more revealing, for although the child could produce Saturday in a mechanical listing of the days of the week, when it came to associating form and idea, it was the Spanish form of the word that was used.

It may be possible with in-depth study of cognition to derive a relationship between meanings rooted in Spanish as illustrated here, and (1) the association of Spanish with white and English with Black, and (2) the tendency of Black children socialized in Spanish to seek to identify with Hispanics while regarding Blacks as ugly and inferior.

As the experience of these children lamentably demonstrates, with each new generation, Blacks lose, bit by bit, the ability to apprehend their world through the vehicle of English in its manifold forms. For it is not simply the linguistic form that changes when they substitute Spanish for English but the meaning of their experiences.

Like English, the Spanish used among Blacks also has its variations, but the range seems much narrower than for English. In general, Blacks tend to speak a more formal variant of Costa Rican Spanish, standard rather than dialectical. This is no doubt the influence of the medium through which the language is acquired. Among most Blacks, for example, syllable final /s/ remains [s] in contrast to the modification to [h] among the Hispanic Limonese. Further, the familiar *tu* form of the second person singular pronoun is frequently used by Black speakers but is rarely heard among Hispanic Costa Rican speakers, who use the familiar pronoun *vos* instead.

Nevertheless, there are Blacks— particularly those who learned Spanish outside of the schoolroom and the young whose confidence permits variation—who have picked up colloquial forms used by Hispanics. In contrast to the above formal markers, there is the stereotypical *es que* by which Josefinos identify Limonese Blacks. Limón Blacks frequently use the phrase at the beginning of sentences to mean "it is because," "the reason is," or merely as a "starter" such as *uhm* in English.

Manipulating Language in Multilingual Society

Between Spanish and English, then, Blacks do have access to a range of codes, and the code used in any context is determined not by the given context alone but also by the competence of the individual as a function of his or her social position. Although a context may demand a particular code or language, the individual may not be able to produce it. There is, therefore, frequently a conflict between the contextual demands and the competence of the individual, and this, in turn, may affect the status aspiration or pretense of such individuals. Unable to avail themselves of certain public services, for example, they might rely on lawyers or brokers who at times, having selfish interests, cause them to lose land and other assets.

The other side of the coin is that some people try to take advantage of their ignorance of Spanish. Mr. Johnson, a Jamaican-born man of about sixty-five, was being served with a court order by a Hispanic police official who explained—in tortured English—that the order directed Mr. Johnson to build additional sanitary facilities on his premises. The policeman began to read the court order, written in Spanish. Immediately, as if struck by a sudden revelation, Mr. Johnson stopped him and said, *"Yo no entiendo nada* of what you are saying," ("I do not understand...") The policeman continued to read, and upon completion asked Mr. Johnson to sign it. Mr. Johnson emphatically said, "No! I can't sign what I don't understand." To this the policeman countered: *"Si usted no lo firma, yo se lo firma. Si usted no lo hace lo que exige el orden, la ley se le hace cumplir. Yo soy la ley."* ("If you do not sign it, I will sign it for you. If you do not obey the law, the law will make you comply. I am the law.") Mr. Johnson then retorted, *"Usted no puede firmar para mi* [you cannot sign for me]; even in the court they have interpreters." The policeman responded, *"Dice la ley, señor, yo lo firmo para usted. Tome."* ("The law says I can sign for you. Here, take it.") Mr. Johnson, reluctantly conceding defeat, forced the policeman to explain, after which he signed and took the order. The policeman said good-bye, and Mr. Johnson climbed the steps to where I was sitting, commenting, "He gave me the word and I must obey; the Bible says that you must obey the law."

Because Spanish is the language of officialdom, Blacks trained in the administration and dispensation of such services learn their skills in that language. Consequently, in discussions touching on the technical aspects of such matters, Blacks are likely to make the immediate switch to Spanish. They are able to use Spanish words and phrases for which they do not know the English equivalents. I sat often in an insurance agency office run by a young Black man whom I had come to know very well. Occasionally several young men would sit and converse in Creole. As soon as a client entered, my friend would, apparently unconsciously, switch to Spanish for the transaction, then return to his Limón Creole conversation.

The manner in which Spanish and English reflect a separation of the domains of social activity, and the relative ease with which people are able to shift codes, is a clear indication that, like the various levels of social activity, the languages together form a single system of discourse, a system that, taken in its totality, gives an indication of hierarchization of social contexts as marked by language use.

Earlier I stated that women, particularly the young, are more inclined to use Spanish as a mark of respectability. Men become accomplices to such display when it suits their purpose as, for example, when a man approaches a female stranger with the intention of winning her friendship. The choice of language is usually Spanish. The situation demands a certain display of style and a showing of his best qualities.

A group of middle-class men between the ages of twenty-five and thirty-five were drinking and conversing in Creole in a bar in Puerto Limón. A young, neatly dressed brown-skinned woman passed by, and one of the men initiated a conversation with her, in Spanish. Throughout the conversation the woman stood captive, responding with yes and no, while the young man tried aggressively, in his most embellished Spanish, to woo her into a date. As soon as she continued on her way, the young man's friends began to chide him: "What a way you just 'mash up' the Paña man language on her, eh. You soun' like you was born taking Spanish." It was evident from the comments that she was competent in English; nevertheless the situation demanded that this man display his knowledge of Spanish. Apart from the fact that to speak Limón Creole would have made him seem only ordinary, people believe that Spanish is more lyrical, more romantic.

Creole is reserved for friends already won, and particularly for males. I was frequently in the company of a white British female researcher and found that on such occasions some of my young Black male acquaintances addressed us in Spanish, whereas outside of her company they addressed me in Creole.

The choice of language, codes, and registers in Limón's multilingual field is determined not only by contexts, but by the choices available to sectors of the society in accordance with their position in social structure and their intentions of upward mobility. It is not only those languages, codes, and registers to which people have access that are determinant, but certainly those from which they have been effectively barred by reason of class, color, and age. Conversely, inequities in the process of language acquisition reinforce the unequal social structure in ways so much more efficient than if language difference were absent. As a sociopolitical process, the intermingling of languages is far more than the sum of the parts.

Limón Creole, Standard English, and Spanish, as they function in Limón, are part of a total social semiotic system from which elements are drawn and spun into communications fitting the various fields of social life. The first-generation peasant who can barely purchase her bread in Spanish is also part of the Spanish linguistic field and at times may even attempt to use ignorance of Spanish to her advantage. A restricted code or a creole language may do for its users what the elaborated code or formal language does for the dominant class. On both sides there is exclusion, exclusion that is both parent and child of inequality.

But as Bourdieu and Passeron observe, "Official language sanctions and imposes what it states, tacitly laying down the line between the thinkable and the unthinkable, thereby contributing towards the maintenance of the symbolic order from which it draws its authority" (1977, 21–22). The informant who commented that Spanish is "more decent," and those children who found it difficult to associate meanings learned in Spanish with English forms, are joined in their assimilation of the authority tacitly imposed by official language. The assimilation of imposed meaning is perhaps the final word in passive cooperation with domination—intentional or not.

Some anthropologists argue that language assimilation is not the heart-breaking or soul-destroying thing others claim it to be (Gellner 1964, 165, cited in Worsley 1984, 250). True, to the people involved, the change of language may seem a small price to pay for advancement and acceptance. But the power relations and color prejudice that surround the change count for more than mere irritation; the situation brings with it, particularly for Blacks, other experiences that are truly soul-weakening, if not soul-destroying.

Linguists at times speak of the equality of languages and codes, but they are really thinking of culturally relative communication, which does not take into account the class rooting of languages and codes. Once a language becomes articulated at the lower levels within a system of social and cultural stratification, its function must be viewed as part of the totality, and therefore itself stratified.

EIGHT

COLOR AS SOCIOECONOMIC VALUE

olor is a more imposing symbol of evaluation than language, even though it does not permit the range of subtle symbolic manipulation that language does. Individuals may possess varying competence in several languages and codes, which they can summon according to the demand of the particular context or intention. They obviously cannot, however, change their color to fit the context, although in some Latin countries (Brazil is the prime example) the calculus of color meanings is bafflingly complicated. Color, nevertheless, includes a consortium of social symbols and social acts, such as type of hair and mixed marriages, which permit manipulation. A Black person who marries a Hispanic may be making a conscious color choice and a fair-skinned woman with kinky hair may only need the help of a competent hair stylist in order to "pass."

As in the United States, Blacks in Costa Rica constitute a minority in a white-dominated society—97 percent white, 2 percent Black. But unlike the United States, where the slightest evidence of Black blood designates one as Black, in Costa Rica, as in most of South and Central America, a combination of Caucasoid features and Hispanic cultural traits may allow a person with evidence of Black blood to be regarded as white.[1] Therefore, people with similar physical features may fall on both sides of a blurred ethnic divide, depending on other socioeconomic factors such as a network of friends.

Yet, the line of separation in Costa Rica is not as fuzzy as in, say Brazil, with its more than twenty designations of color tones, or in Cuba, which Fidel Castro in 1976 declared to be Latin-African (Dzidzienyo and Casal 1979, 4, 24). Naturally, because positions of power and privilege are controlled by those who are phenotypically and culturally white, upwardly mobile Blacks tend to value white features; they can be transacted toward advancement.

To be sure, as in places like Brazil, economic factors, too, play a part in gaining admittance into the dominant group. Although well-off, dark-skinned individuals are not accepted as Hispanic, their wealth helps them to acquire Hispanic social and cultural trappings and thereby improve their chances of acceptance. This pathway is probably easier for light-skinned Blacks. As mentioned in earlier chapters, people who grew up in poverty can achieve relative acceptance through educational accomplishments. It must be emphasized, however, that while education and wealth open gates, the passage is limited without the required color and culture. And for those who do not possess material trappings and/or a high level of education, physical and cultural traits may be the only value they bring to social transaction.

Personality, too, plays a part in Hispanic-Black relations, but by itself it accomplishes little. This is so partly because of the way that economics, race, and culture are linked structurally. The more upwardly mobile Blacks are in closer contact with Hispanics, but Black-Hispanic relationships are, for obvious reasons, not as intimate as relationships among Blacks. Therefore, it is the surface characteristics such as color, education, and social values rather than the deeper personality traits that come into play. At the lower socioeconomic levels, there is usually less interracial contact, but where it occurs it tends to be based more on personality and behavior than on education and social values. It is noteworthy, too, that color is not only a factor in interracial relationships; it also enters into status relations among Blacks, although its significance is fast diminishing.

THE PERSISTENCE OF CONFORMITY

If the Costa Rican case has anything to add to our understanding of color inequality in the Caribbean, it is that the lighter skin color need not always dominate. Just as Blacks who were transported to Costa Rica brought with them notions of the prestige of the "Queen's English," so too they transported notions about the meaning of color in the social hierarchy, notions developed in the colonial West Indies and later nourished by the plantation system in Costa Rica.[2] The United Fruit Company, by the way it organized its productive forces, perpetuated the exploitative colonial tie between color and social hierarchy. In Costa Rica there was one important difference, however: The color strata were to a limited extent interchangeable depending on productive relations. As detailed in Chapter 2, the United Fruit plantation hierarchy was constituted of white North Americans on top, Black West Indians in the middle, and white Hispanics below.

With the demise of the plantation, the position of white Hispanics shifted from below Blacks to above them. This shift did not represent a contradiction within the overall structure and meaning of color. When the white North Americans left the region, the ensuing reconstitution of political and economic control resulted in the accession of white Hispanics to the uppermost ranks vacated by North Americans. Brown-skinned Colored Jamaicans still occupied their interstitial position between dark-skinned Blacks and whites, to be augmented later by a small but growing number of mulattoes. Smaller ethnic units like the Chinese, for example, did not need to be included in this schema. They had the advantage of fair skin but were perceived as neither part of the reshuffling nor as referents in the evaluation of color as a symbol of prestige and social mobility.

Today, Black Costa Ricans respond variously to questions about the importance of color in efforts to improve their life conditions, but the majority admit that color is and has been a factor. The recognition, however, is strongest among the young (under fifty), whose chances depend more directly on the wider Hispanic society than do those of their elders. For one thing, many elders still cherish a flickering sense of superiority and a denial of racism. It is primarily the young who complain about job discrimination, who mention the clubs in San José (and, until recently, in Limón) where Blacks are not welcome. It is the young who complain about schools in San José where their children are not wanted. And it was young professionals who, after decades of relatively silent endurance, made the issue of discrimination the theme of a national conference in 1978.

Because many Blacks as well as Hispanics feel there is social but no racial discrimination in Costa Rica, they argue that Blacks can improve their position by adherence to the codes of social decency, hard work, and diligent study. One individual insisted:

The Black man is not ambitious. He does not take opportunities when they come his way. We should follow the white man . . . for the white man has always been successful. That is why whites have used Blacks; it was the natural course of things. They took Blacks from Africa because Blacks could not defend themselves. We Blacks must now try to gain some of the superiority of whites.

With the departure of United Fruit and the consequent ascendancy of local Hispanics, there has until recently been some "passing" by mulattoes and a few "Jamaica brown-men" still in the area. Today this rarely occurs, although I occasionally encountered a mulatto who preferred to be regarded as "Spanish." With racial divisions as fluid as they are, it takes little more than light skin, straight hair, and appropriate social credentials.

Within the Black community itself, color is used as a symbol of prestige, but only by a few who tend to use it in combination with Hispanic cultural traits. The more pervasive tendency is to downplay Black cultural features and to assert that "we are all Latins" or "we are all Costa Ricans," as opposed to being West Indians.

It follows, then, that present social conditions do not undermine the colonial notions of color hierarchy, but reinforce them. People today still speak of "nice clear skin" and "good hair"—though I am not aware of mothers squeezing the noses and lips of their children to "make them look good," as once was done in the United States and the Anglophone Caribbean. Such reinforcement in its most ominous form seems to have penetrated even the system of education. The process occurs directly through the use of educational material written exclusively in Spanish, and, of course, about Hispanic cultural themes. Even graphics are molded in the Spanish image.

Consequently, some young children come to think, for example, that *"el negro es feo"* (ugly).[3] An eight-year-old girl, on leaving with her sister to visit their grandmother, commented with a frown, *"Vamos a abuela a comer comida negra; que pereza."* ("Let's go to grandmother's to eat negro food; what a bore!") The child did not pick up this attitude at home, for her parents were confidently Black-conscious. But it is not only among children that Black culture and its symbols have lost value. A young Black man told me, *"Soy negro en el piel pero en conciencia, no."* ("I am black in skin but not in mind.") The comment was a defensive, contextual redefinition of allegiance, provoked by an incident in which other Blacks accused him of fraud involving land.

There is also the opposite position on the issue of color and Black culture. Occasionally, a Black claims to like nothing white. Tomás, a mulatto whose father is Hispanic, commented that his neighbor's children, all fair-skinned with curly hair, were *guapo* (literally, handsome) but said, "Dem should be darker, me no like not'n too light, me no even wan' see not'n white." In New Sligoville, I took photographs of a group of children between the ages of about nine and fourteen. One photograph, in which one of the subjects was Hispanic, was underexposed. As soon as the Black boys in the group discovered this, they burst into laughter and one remarked, "Is the Spanish boy spoil the picture"—yet it was quite natural to them that the Hispanic boy should be included in the photograph in the first place.

This attitude is not unusual among children in the rural areas, for although they interact less on a daily basis with Hispanics, they do so with more poise and confidence in their color and culture than do children in the urban areas. Urban children may have been exposed to more negative signals regarding race, color, and culture than those in rural areas. Rural children take the distinction for granted: They recognize the difference and even make stereotypical racial comments, but their interactions seem less burdened. The same can be said for the interethnic relations between rural and urban adults. The "peasant humility" of rural adults is balanced by an air of confidence that appears to have contributed to a smooth, if cautious, interaction. Relationships are defined more by individual characteristics and personality than by race or color. Still, fair skin, "good" hair, and other Caucasian features are valued, but are less a function of the acceptance of Hispanic values than of the survival of colonial values. Thus, perhaps because of differences in socioeconomic activity, the same symbols may no longer have precisely the same meaning among assimilated urban and nonassimilated rural Blacks. It is noteworthy, too, that those self-deprecatory comments blaming Blacks for their own plight do not usually come from the peasantry, but from members of the urban middle class, who forever wonder why others can't be as ambitious as they are.

COLOR AND CHOICE OF SPOUSE

Perhaps the most telling expression of the role of color in the structure of inequality occurs in the attitudes toward choice of spouse. Complaints that upwardly mobile Blacks are inclined to marry whites are commonplace. This is supposedly true in particular of professional Blacks, and because their numbers are small, such claims may be made on arguably good grounds. My survey (no control for class affiliation) of 218 households found that only 6.5 percent were mixed unions, but this is enough to trigger sharp comments from the more nationalistic. There is the story of a Black teacher in Limón, for example, who was engaged to a Black woman from humble background who was nevertheless considered a fitting bride for any man. Shortly before the wedding was to take place, he befriended a Hispanic woman whom he later married. Numerous people told me with open sadness that the Black woman ended up in a mental institution.

The former Black governor of Limón, who also married a Hispanic, was often mentioned as an example of the practice in high places. There is also the case of a successful businessman who married a Hispanic. The children regarded themselves as Hispanic until one day in school an occasion arose that required segregating students according to race. In spite of their protests they were placed among Blacks. The matter caused open conflict between teacher and parents, but it helped ultimately to uncover the question of identity for the children.

Discussions about mixed unions failed to reveal a clear sense of the personal and emotional considerations that go into the decisions regarding choice of spouse. The general feeling expressed by Blacks was that Black men marry Hispanic women because they perceive them as socially "better" and because it facilitates social acceptance in the wider society. Black women make similar choices for similar reasons, including the desire to "improve" the skin of their children—the old Latin solution of "whitening." The Hispanic, on the other hand, sees such marriages as Black acceptance of Hispanic culture and society. In fact, instead of resenting mixed unions, as is usually the case in the United States, Hispanics seem to view them as a good omen, as a sign of amalgamation, sociopolitical unity, and affirmation of their cultural superiority. This attitude is not unique to white Costa Ricans; the chairman of Cuba's Movement of National Orientation and Integration, established in the early stages of the revolution, expressed the feelings of many Cubans, indeed many Latin Americans, when he said that from interracial unions would emerge "new physical attributes and moral virtues" (Moore 1988, 47).

To the general public, it is the perception that counts, but even the perception itself is not as simple as it appears. Although there is fairly strong across-the-board criticism of upper-level Blacks who marry Hispanics, little or nothing is said about lower-level Blacks who do the same thing. Considerations of class enter into the picture. Poorer Blacks, perhaps because they feel left out, express mild resentment against those who are better off. And some argue that the choice of a Hispanic spouse is a rejection on the part of the upwardly mobile of the inferiority that Blackness symbolizes. No such feelings are directed toward poorer mixed couples.

In 1978, there were frequent complaints that the trend toward mixed unions was increasing among upwardly mobile Black females. This was not evident to me; there were one or two Black university students who had Hispanic boyfriends, but I knew of only two Black females of the middle class who had Hispanic spouses. There seems to have been a greater number of young working-class women who had Hispanic spouses.

However, upper stratum Black females often talked about the difficulty of finding *hombres preparados* (educated men), because when Black men graduate to the upper levels they marry Hispanics or migrate. To support their case, the women pointed to several professional women who were single, despite their preference, and to university-educated women who had married men with significantly lower levels of education. The women were quick to point out, also, that such marriages tend to be problem ridden.

The thorny social-structural and psychological problems involved in the acceptance of symbols of value such as color are evident in the efforts of Black men engaged in mixed unions to justify their choices; such explanations almost always involve the "struggle for advancement." One man said that his Black ex-wife was not supportive of his work, could no longer understand him, and was not politically aware—and he found that he was far more productive since marrying a Hispanic. Another, a teacher and small businessman about thirty-five years old, observed that his new Hispanic wife was far more helpful in developing economic independence and in general was much more frugal than his Black ex-wife. His Hispanic wife, he said, worked harder and demanded less. Still another, a man of about forty-five married to a mulatto, said the "Spanish woman give you more freedom and they not as nagging." He also said that Hispanic women tend to be more supportive of the male.

The explanations and justifications stretch into issues having to do with the alleged traditionality of the Black female and her alleged posture of dominance (rather than equality). Some also said that when the Black male reaches a certain social level, he is forced by circumstances—job or career, residence, social activities—to associate with (and marry) those of this new level, who are for the most part white. Interestingly, no one cited love as a reason, though, of course, the question was never directly asked.

Whether the motives behind the phenomenon of mixed unions have to do with changed values or simply changed social circumstances, they are for the most part rooted in the process of social mobility and inequality. Two mutually influential factors can be distilled from comments made regarding this topic. First is the notion, developed in the colonial experience and reinforced by an unequal opportunity structure afterward, that bettering one's position means seeking psychological and social alliance with the perceived bearers of authority and power. The alliance, in some cases, may be purely instrumental, but the instrumental may be motivated by material as well as psychosocial needs.

I am reminded of a story about the policy of a taxi operator, Mr. Mason, during the United Fruit Company domination of the region. Mr. Mason, who was Black, prided himself on serving whites only. To publicize his position on the matter, he painted a large white circle with his name in the middle on the back of his car. From then on he was referred to as "Mason in the white circle."

The second factor pertains to the change of value orientation that mobility engenders. Moving up the social scale means inevitably, even if reluctantly, assimilating part of the value system of the new social level. This value change, as well as the psychosocial alliance, is by no means confined to the attribution of higher social value to white skin and other Caucasoid features; it characterizes the more general process of value transaction and enactment within which status and prestige symbols are accepted or rejected depending on context and strategy.

Costa Rica: A Special Case

Even after the Black nationalist surge of the 1960s and 1970s, preference for the lighter shades of skin color continues to be common throughout South America, and to a lesser extent, the Caribbean. Not every Black person articulates such preferences—most perhaps do not—but all are affected by its importance in the historical process. When a young Black Costa Rican woman declares that she would prefer to marry a "Spaniard" so that her children may have *piel claro* (clear skin), she is expressing her understanding of a complex of values that have had a concrete historical role in colonial and postcolonial Western societies; degrees of wealth, privilege, status, and power have been, for well-known, if abhorrent, historical reasons, associated with shades of skin color.

It is not color per se that matters, but the perceived valence of rewards associated with it. The rewards are redeeming, for Blacks have come, through an inadequate reflexive awareness of their own history and the reluctant acceptance of the dominant interpretation, to be regarded and to regard themselves as the damned of the earth. As older Blacks frequently comment in moments of despair: "We niega people will never get nowhere." Others say, "We are as black as sin."

COSTA RICA'S COLOR CONTRAST WITH THE WEST INDIES

The importance to Costa Ricans of skin color and other white cultural attributes contrasts with their importance in the Anglophone Caribbean. In places like Jamaica, Trinidad, and other areas of the West Indies, the 1960s and 1970s brought a sharp decline in the value of light skin and European culture for Blacks. Black nationalism came late to Costa Rica (mid-to-late 1970s) and found less than fertile ground. Several related reasons come to mind.

First, the social place of color in Costa Rica, as in Brazil and Cuba, follows the well-known Latin model of race relations, in which the primary characteristics are denial and paternalistic assimilation (see Gledhill 1988). The West Indies, on the other hand, is closer to the Anglo model, in which the alleged inferiority of Blacks was viewed as fixed in nature, and therefore legitimate grounds for unequal separation—although places like Jamaica have had a fair share of denial even after the nationalist critique of the 1960s and 1970s.

Second, there is a difference in the racial composition of political, though not economic, power. In Costa Rica, Blacks are not only a minority, they do not in general hold positions of political power. Quite the contrary in the West Indies. With their numerical strength, West Indians who remained home were able to make inroads into political power beginning with the labor movement in the 1930s and 1940s and culminating with the independence tide of the 1960s. They were, therefore, strategically placed to put into policy and practice many of the nationalist ideas of the 1970s. In Jamaica, for example, a clear ideological break with colonial notions of high color and culture was integral to the Manley government of the 1970s. This, of course, should not be taken to mean that racism is not alive in the West Indies. A series of articles in *The Jamaica Record* as recent as 1989 (March 18 and April

2) showed that virtually all of the major sectors of the Jamaican economy—tourism, export agriculture, export manufacturing, distributive trades, and pharmaceuticals—are controlled by various shades of whites.

In Costa Rica, as in other Latin countries, denial and paternalistic assimilation continue to flourish. Blacks may not suffer the castelike racism characteristic of the United States, but they are coerced into denying much of their cultural dignity in order to find even a small corner in a white-dominated society. The difference means that Latin Blacks must first cleanse their consciousness of paternalistic assimilation, for if cultural whitening makes them at home politically, they are not likely, ultimately, to feel at home with themselves. Yet, for Blacks in the Americas, the reality of a syncretic identity is part of the normal process of being and becoming (Nettleford 1978, 9–12). But once the symbols of racial conflict outweigh the more organic symbols that previously defined their identity, they can no longer manipulate the dominant values with ease.

KINSHIP, VALUES, AND SOCIAL MOBILITY

Much has been written about the nature, structure, and organization of the family and household in the Anglophone Caribbean. The effort has concentrated on identifying and explaining structural patterns that typify the region, patterns grouped under the label *matrifocal family or household*. But questions remain, and for the most part they have to do with whether those patterns are attributable to mating patterns (M. G. Smith 1962; Simey 1946), to historically imposed economic factors (R. T. Smith 1956; Rodman 1971), to cultural survivals and reinterpretation (Herskovits and Herskovits 1937, 1947), or possibly to some combination of specific historical and socioeconomic factors (Mintz and Price 1976; R. T. Smith 1988).[1]

The major structural features identified for most of the West Indies are also discernible among West Indian migrants in Costa Rica, and the concerns regarding class and culture are also relevant there (see R. T. Smith 1988). However, rather than join in the discussion of those concerns, I would prefer to deal with aspects of family and household that are more directly related to class and social mobility.

In one form or another, almost all ethnographies link West Indian kinship organization to economic marginality, a link that is undeniable in most instances. However, except for R. T. Smith (1956, 1988) and Mintz and Price (1976), the authors do little to explain how that marginality influences the dynamism and resilience so characteristic of kinship and household relations in the region. Part of the reason may be that scholars tend to search for structure and organization—an imported theoretical legacy—and therefore miss the effects of individual efforts to cope with difficult but changing conditions. People do try to overcome constraints, and the strategies they use influence their domestic organization in ways that depend on their position in the social hierarchy. It seems fair to say, then, that an approach that pays attention to individual strategies can help illuminate the processes that lead to the broader patterns.

To that end, in the following chapter I discuss two aspects of Afro-Costa Rican adaptation that affect the organization of the family, as well as household size and composition. First, I review the results of a survey strongly suggesting that spatial movement, as an aspect of social mobility, coupled with the economic position of particular communities, affects the size and composition of households. Second, I present a brief biography of one family, highlighting its struggle against economic and social odds in an effort to achieve stability. The case suggests that in addition to the familiar constraints on family organization, the need to conform to particular sets of social values in the bid for respectability and prestige exerts its own share of structural as well as psychological stress. Before presenting these discussions, I offer a synopsis of the historical conditions surrounding the development of domestic organization among West Indians in Costa Rica.

HISTORICAL ROOTS OF FAMILY ORGANIZATION[2]

The first West Indians to arrive in Costa Rica were usually males. In addition to the harsh conditions, ignorance of what to expect was likely the main reason married men left wives behind and the reason women did not venture there on their own. Granted, other factors, such as caring for the very young and the very old, prevented many women from making the trip. Also, labor recruiters preferred males because, in their minds, labor conditions were more suitable for men.

In any case, once the laborers arrived in Costa Rica, they needed no one to tell them that the conditions created by United Fruit were for men and only the very hardiest of women. Workers had to endure long hours of clearing, digging, and lifting; torrential rain and scorching sun; mosquitos, scorpions, snakes, and sundry organic terrors of the tropics. And at day's end they were confronted with crowded dwellings and inadequate sanitation. Even as late as the first decade of twentieth century, a few men remember being startled at the conditions that greeted them upon arrival.

After the pioneering stage, when conditions improved somewhat, men were able to send for their women, and single women began to migrate on their own, although they usually traveled under the sponsorship of kin or a prospective spouse. Conditions improved slowly; even after the completion of railroad construction, most of the heavy work—indeed most of the work except for port activities—was distributed in the bush. Few women were allowed to brave those areas. Except for a few who performed domestic chores for the men, women stayed in the relative safety of Puerto Limón.

Understandably, this arrangement, combined with the scarcity of women, discouraged—though it did not prevent—the development of a stable family organization. The scarcity of women as late as the 1920s and the town-bush separation of the sexes led to some infidelity and rivalry. Many men who worked in Puerto Limón, some of them with prestigious jobs and relatively attractive life-styles, sought the sexual services of women whose menfolk were, by necessity, working in the bush. From time to time, a few women found this temptation irresistible, and some men, after sponsoring the immigration of potential spouses from Jamaica, eventually lost them to rivals who were better located geographically and economically. To make matters worse, some women had to go for several weeks without setting eyes on their men and the meager wages upon which they so thoroughly depended.

Not surprisingly, some of the women who knew where their menfolk worked and how to get there visited them on payday. Some such visits turned out to be rather eventful. There were spirited quarrels with men who gambled away their pay, secreted part of it for another woman, or as frequently happened, had taken more on credit from the Company store than they anticipated. On the other hand, there were couples who had to satisfy their starved sexual urges right there in the barracks, where privacy was a premium.

The imbalance in the sex ratio continued for some time,[3] and it may have helped to spur the development in Puerto Limón of prostitution, which became an integral part of the town's life. As accounts go, the demand for prostitutes was so high and some were so desirable that they could demand and receive more than half a week's wages from the less tight-fisted men. A few older men still have vivid memories of some very special *filles de joie* they knew back then.

With time, working conditions on the banana plantation and provisions for health care improved somewhat, and women immigrated in increasing numbers. Yet stable family life among West Indians was still difficult. The incidence of death and serious illness, due mainly to unsafe working conditions, continued to be high right up to the peak of plantation production in the 1920s; much of this occurred on railroad and road construction rather than on the plantation itself. Health care was poor and segregated. Some claim that it was occasionally safer to be treated at home for illnesses than to risk placing oneself at the mercy of racist doctors in the Company hospital. Poor health care, combined with unsanitary and crowded dwellings, inadequate or nonexistent schools, low income strained by an unethical credit system, and an arrogantly apartheid environment made the task of raising children Herculean.

Conditions were worse in the rural areas. The mostly white upper-level employees stationed in the towns benefited from better wages as well as proximity and access to health care and educational facilities. In the rural sector, the availability of unoccupied land that could be used use to supplement meager wages eased the burden; it not only helped to provide a higher standard of living but, in cases where the land could be shared or passed on to children, it helped to hold the family together.

As in all plantation systems, status separation did not evolve in Limón; it was established during colonization of the region by the differential demands of the plantation. Such separation, as discussed in Chapter 6, was built less on the hierarchical evaluation of skills than on the colonial-rooted status stratification of skin color and culture. These concerns affected all aspects of family life and organization.

To begin with, there were few women above the working-class or housewife category; the occupational structure did not permit it. The relative homogeneity in the status of women was so marked that an elderly professional Jamaican-born male who went to Costa Rica in the mid-1920s confided that: "Man, when I found that one girl that showed some refinement and intelligence—[looking at his wife of over 40 years] an' she still beautiful too you know—I had to hold on to her." His wife was a teacher, as were most of the "refined" women. Some were practical nurses, seamstresses, or hairstylists, and, of course, there were the "high-class" wives of the brown-skin Jamaicans. Unmarried women of this upper crust were objects of competition. If a teacher, or any woman of above-average qualifications, had brown skin, she was doubly desirable. If she married a dark-skinned man it would be because he was educated or because he "had something."

In the early years, status considerations in the choice of spouse and the upbringing of children were based not so much on the perception of chances within Costa Rica as on knowledge of the status system in Jamaica, where the majority intended to return. Granted, when the events of the 1940s and early 1950s changed the outlook regarding return to Jamaica, the system of status evaluation and classification, for the most part, did not change with it. And those changes that took place pertained mainly to the upgrading of Hispanics, structurally situating them in the position vacated by the North Americans. The old status considerations, therefore, continued to influence the choice of spouse, the upbringing of children, and in general, the opportunities of families and individuals.

Clerks, teachers, and church officials were rigidly careful about the mannerisms, attire, language, sexual liaisons, and social network of their daughters, and those values filtered down to the less fortunate but ambitious workers. Sons had more freedom because, for one, pregnancy did not affect them in the same way. Pregnancy could curtail "a good education," and no self-respecting young man should marry a woman already known to be with child. Attitudes toward premarital pregnancy were just an ideal, but they carried weight in that status-conscious environment. A pregnant girl was supposed to marry the "culprit"—if he was of acceptable standing—before knowledge of her pregnancy became public. But this path was still not the most desirable if the girl was very young and still in school. The alternative was temporary exile to Jamaica, another part of the Atlantic coast, or, in later years, to San José, until her baby was born. The baby was then left with relatives, or failing that, the mother would remain exiled until the child grew up. The wide acceptance (or in some cases, tolerance) of contraceptives and changing social and moral standards have made this practice unnecessary in recent years.

Indoors or outdoors, the daughter was carefully watched. Church activities were a must, but secular parties were by invitation only, and events such as the weekly dance held at the Universal Negro Improvement Association (UNIA) hall were out of bounds for "nice" girls. Besides school and church attendance, the only other moments of freedom for nice girls were Sunday afternoon walks, dressed in taffeta and Sunday shoes, their hair freshly combed and bedecked with ribbons. Daughters of the rural folk were even more constrained, confined primarily to church and school activities and maybe sewing lessons after graduation from elementary school. Some children were sent to Jamaica for further education, but this was a privilege accorded only to those whose families had the money, and primarily to males.

Much effort went into ensuring that female offspring did not end up marrying the wrong man. As soon as a daughter established a relationship that was potentially serious, the young man was expected to approach the girl's parents. He had to state his intentions to their satisfaction before the liaison could be openly sanctioned. It was of far less concern to parents, however, who their male offspring chose as partners; males were less subject to codes of respectability.

Among the wealthier peasants, the urban working class, and the emergent middle class, unceremonialized marriages have been and still are rare. This is important, because children of unceremonialized unions are discriminated against by some teachers and, to a lesser extent, prospective employers. Children born to parents in *union libre* (consensual union) usually carry the *apellido* (family name) of the mother only, and are therefore easily identified by anyone familiar with the Spanish naming system.[4]

Today, as in the past, economic factors are often not the main criteria for status distinctions and therefore are not of singular importance in the selection of mates. In urban areas these factors are, however, of some importance. Economic differences are less marked in the rural areas, where people rely more on aspects of behavior such as language, attire, and conviviality. The qualities of being hard-working, "steady" (not given to frequent conjugal shifts), and ambitious are especially important. Again, because economic differentiation is not very marked, the choice turns on behavioral indications of intention regarding mobility. For the most part, however, the young rural individual achieves mobility outside of the rural sector and therefore marries outside, where considerations of choice may be based mainly on such status factors as color, "looks," and occupation.

From the distribution of population centers to the distribution of the sexes, from the ability to afford the responsibility of a spouse to color and status considerations affecting choice of spouse, most of the factors affecting the establishment of a family or household are linked in one way or another with the history of the plantation. Although not born on the Costa Rican plantation, such factors were certainly nurtured and encouraged there.

VARIATIONS IN HOUSEHOLDS

The need to move from place to place for self-improvement always affects household composition and size. In the case of Costa Rica, this factor derives from the way plantation activities dictated a particular kind of distribution of communities (detailed in Chapter 4). People move wherever jobs are, but the movement is not necessarily permanent or one-way; it creates flexible ties that defy the conception of a bounded family unit even while they retard the development of rigid class separation among Blacks.

A survey of households in five separate communities in Limón shows significant differences in size and composition (see Table 7).[5] The differences are not large, but it is nevertheless clear that: (1) households in poorer communities tend to be smaller than those in the economically better-off ones; (2) there are differences in household composition and size between rural and urban communities; (3) there is no difference in size between rural communities of varying socioeconomic levels, although there is some difference in composition.

The socioeconomic ranking of the communities in question is based on the relative distribution of occupations in each (see Table 8), with due consideration given to their traditional place in the region's hierarchy of communities. Rather than name the communities, I rank them using the designation U for urban and R for rural preceding their numerical rank order. Table 9 shows the relative size and some selected aspects of household composition in the ranked communities.

Correlating the mean household size with the socioeconomic level of each community, it is clear that urban communities with a higher percentage of residents in the upper socioeconomic level have larger households. The difference is admittedly small, but it is nevertheless significant ($p < .05$). A similar difference in mean size is found between rural communities and the two upper socioeconomic-level urban communities. Therefore, it appears that the urban communities—at least those of the upper socioeconomic level—have larger households.

Between rural communities R-1 and R-2, however, the only difference encountered was in one aspect of composition: R-1 had a higher percentage (7.3 percent) of household members who were not part of the household head's lineal issue than R-2 (which had 5.5 percent). Further, R-1 had a larger percentage (4.1 percent) of grandparents living with their children, compared to R-2 with less than 1.0 percent.

The difference in composition between rural communities may be due primarily to two related distinctions in the characteristics of the two communities. First, there are more services in R-1. Second, R-1 is a very stable cacao and coconut farming community, whose members traditionally take great pride in their economic and social independence. Community R-2 is also a farming community, but on a much smaller scale; it is far less stable. This instability is partly due to the fact that, unlike R-1, most of its residents have only usufruct rights to their land. Furthermore, practically all of its young people have migrated. These factors suggest that people who would normally emigrate to live with relatives in the urban areas can and do remain in R-1 because of its stability and higher socioeconomic level.

With regard to the relation between rural and urban communities, it can be assumed that people migrating from rural to urban areas are more likely to seek out and reside with their better-off relatives, those who can accommodate them without much sacrifice. Households in U-1, the highest-ranked urban community, are larger than in other, lower-ranked, urban communities. The large size is accounted for by the presence of relatives who are not members of the household's nuclear family. They consist of collateral kin who have moved into town from the rural areas, and of grandparents and grandchildren—28.6 percent of the population of the community. In many cases, both husband and wife are employed, and so the grandparents assist with grandchildren and household chores. But the composition of these households (and indeed many of the other households surveyed) is not enduring; some collateral kin may stay only as long as it takes them to establish their own household, and indications are that some children spend long periods at other relatives' houses. Community U-2 also has a large mean household size, but its composition differs from that of U-1. There are fewer three- and four-generation households, but there is still a fairly large number of collateral relatives. This is due, in part, to the fact that it is a relatively new community—about five years old at the time the data were collected; it is also a government-sponsored project, with dwellings that are affordable to young people in relatively good-paying jobs.

TABLE 7
POPULATION OF SAMPLE HOUSEHOLDS CLASSIFIED ACCORDING TO HOUSEHOLD HEAD AND SEX OF HEAD

CATEGORIES OF KIN	U-1 Male Head No.	%	U-1 Fem. Head No.	%	U-2 Male Head No.	%	U-2 Fem. Head No.	%
Household Head	34	18.4	14	14.7	32	15.0	8	28.6
HH's mates	31	16.8	—	—	29	13.6	—	—
HH's sons	38	20.5	12	12.6	44	20.6	8	28.6
HH's daughters	51	27.6	34	35.8	64	29.9	8	28.6
HH's sons by others	—	—	—	—	—	—	—	—
HH's daughters by others	—	—	—	—	—	—	—	—
Total HH's children	*89*	*48.1*	*46*	*48.4*	*108*	*50.5*	*16*	*57.1*
HH's mates' sons by others	—	—	—	—	11	5.1	—	—
HH's mates' daughters by others	—	—	—	—	16	7.5	—	—
Total Children of Couple	*89*	*—*	*46*	*—*	*135*	*—*	*116*	*—*
HH's sons' sons	—	—	—	—	—	—	1	3.6
HH's sons' daughters	1	0.5	—	—	—	—	—	—
HH's daughters' daughters	4	2.2	8	8.4	3	1.4	—	—
HH's mates' sons' sons	12	6.5	5	5.3	1	0.4	3	10.7
HH's mates' sons' daughters	—	—	—	—	—	—	—	—
HH's mates' daughters' daughters	—	—	—	—	—	—	—	—
Total Grandchildren	*17*	*9.2*	*13*	*13.7*	*4*	*1.9*	*4*	*14.3*
HH's brothers	2	1.1	2	2.1	—	—	—	—
HH's sisters	—	—	2	2.1	—	—	—	—
HH's brother issue	—	—	—	—	2	0.9	—	—
HH's sister issue	—	—	—	—	2	0.9	—	—
HH's mate's brother	—	—	—	—	2	0.9	—	—
HH's mate's sister	—	—	—	—	1	0.4	—	—
HH's mates' bros.' children	3	1.6	—	—	2	0.9	—	—
HH's mates' sisters' children	—	—	—	—	—	—	—	—
HH's mother	5	2.7	5	5.3	1	0.4	—	—
HH's father	—	—	2	2.1	1	0.4	—	—
HH's mates' mother	—	—	—	—	—	—	—	—
HH's mates' father	2	1.1	—	—	—	—	—	—
HH's & mate's grandparents	—	—	3	3.2	—	—	—	—
HH's son's mate	—	—	—	—	—	—	—	—
HH's daughter's mate	—	—	2	2.1	—	—	—	—
HH's parents' siblings	—	—	3	3.2	—	—	—	—
Other kin of HH & mate	2	1.1	3	3.2	3	1.4	—	—
TOTALS	185		95		214		28	

U-3				R-1				R-2			
Male Head		Fem. Head		Male Head		Fem. Head		Male Head		Fem. Head	
No.	%	No.	%	No.	%	No.	%	No.	%	No.	%
33	20.6	9	30.0	37	21.8	10	43.4	32	24.2	8	25.0
31	19.4	—	—	28	16.5	—	—	25	18.9	—	—
34	21.3	4	13.3	38	22.4	6	26.1	31	23.5	5	15.6
24	15.0	4	13.3	35	20.6	—	—	29	19.7	12	37.5
—	—	—	—	—	—	—	—	—	—	—	—
58	36.3	8	26.7	73	42.7	6	26.1	60	45.5	17	53.1
4	2.5	—	—	10	5.9	—	—	4	3.0	—	—
18	11.3	—	—	5	2.9	—	—	2	1.5	—	—
80	—	8	—	88	—	6	—	66	—	17	—
—	—	—	—	1	0.6	—	—	1	0.8	—	—
—	—	—	—	1	0.6	—	—	1	0.8	—	—
4	2.5	—	—	2	1.2	3	13.0	1	0.8	2	6.3
3	1.9	4	13.3	—	—	—	—	—	—	—	—
4	2.5	—	—	—	—	—	—	—	—	—	—
11	6.9	4	13.3	4	2.4	3	13.0	3	2.3	2	6.3
1	0.6	—	—	—	—	—	—	—	—	1	3.1
1	0.6	—	—	1	0.6	—	—	—	—	—	—
—	—	—	—	—	—	—	—	—	—	—	—
—	—	8	26.7	—	—	—	—	—	—	—	—
1	0.6	—	—	—	—	—	—	1	0.8	—	—
1	0.6	—	—	—	—	—	—	—	—	—	—
—	—	—	—	—	—	—	—	1	0.8	—	—
—	—	—	—	—	—	—	—	—	—	—	—
1	0.6	—	—	3	1.8	1	4.3	—	—	—	—
—	—	—	—	2	1.2	1	4.3	—	—	—	—
—	—	—	—	1	0.6	—	—	—	—	—	—
—	—	—	—	—	—	—	—	—	—	—	—
—	—	—	—	—	—	—	—	—	—	—	—
—	—	—	—	—	—	—	—	—	—	—	—
—	—	—	—	—	—	—	—	—	—	—	—
—	—	1	3.3	4	2.4	1	4.3	3	2.3	2	6.3
160		30		168		22		131		30	

HH = Household Head

Total Sample = 1069

TABLE 8
OCCUPATIONAL BREAKDOWN BY COMMUNITY
(RESPONDENTS IN PERCENT)

	U-1	U-2	U-3	R-1	R-2
Professions/inc. teaching	12.4	—	3.4	4.4	—
Clerical	29.2	8.6	6.9	2.2	—
Commercial	4.2	8.6	3.4	6.7	2.5
Crafts	25.0	37.1	17.2	8.9	5.0
Unskilled Labor	16.7	37.1	50.0	—	5.0
Farming (2–10 hectares)	8.3	5.7	10.3	55.6	82.5
Farming (>10 hectares)	—	—	—	13.3	—
Service/Domestic	4.2	2.9	13.8	8.9	5.0

Many individuals engage in more than one occupation, so that they have a primary and a secondary occupation. Secondary occupations are: small farming, small groceries run from the front room or verandah of the residence, and "chance," the local clandestine lottery. Only primary occupations are taken into account in this table.

TABLE 9
Household Composition and Size
According to Ranked Sample Communities

RANKED COMMUNI-TIES	MEAN SIZE	STANDARD DEVIATION	PERCENT-AGE GRAND-PARENTS IN COMMU-NITY	PERCENT-AGE GRAND-CHILDREN IN COMMU-NITY	PERCENT-AGE H[a] MEMBERS NOT HH LINEAL ISSUE
U-1 (N=28)	5.2	2.71	6.1	9.6	12.9
U-2 (N=37)	5.4	2.27	<1.0	3.3	5.8
U-3 (N=32)	4.1	2.44	<1.0	7.9	7.4
R-1 (N=47)	4.3	2.86	4.1	4.1	7.3
R-2 (N=40)	4.3	2.48	<1.0	4.3	5.5

[a] H = Household; HH = Household Head

Consequently, there are many households with young couples and children who are still of school age and younger. Conversely, there are few grandparents and grandchildren in the community.

On the whole, however, there is a high percentage of grandchildren in urban households irrespective of the socioeconomic level. Young women leave their children with their parents or grandparents in order to work or to further their education in some other locale. In other cases, a woman may leave her children with her mother, at least initially, when she establishes a conjugal union with a man other than their father. Some households—of low as well as high socioeconomic level—include four generations. (I visited one Black upper middle-class household in San José with five generations.)

The inescapable conclusion is that migration, usually an aspect of social mobility, plays a significant part in household size and composition. I do not have migration figures for all of the communities, but figures for R-2 show that 84 percent of all the people born there between 1936 and 1962 had left the village when the figures were compiled in 1976. Of these an estimated 65 percent went to Puerto Limón.

The kinship linkages between better-off and poorer households arise from and facilitate this type of movement. The heads of such households are obliged to open their doors to relatives, and occasionally even friends, who are in search of jobs. So far this dynamic has softened class boundaries among Blacks, but as class relations begin to crystallize, it may become less important to maintain kinship relations. Community U-2, for example, with its relatively small number of household members outside the nuclear family, may represent the beginning of a shift from the more open structure characteristic of the region to a more nuclear household. This trend may be seen in terms of a move from intrinsic social organizational characteristics (open or extended structure) to extrinsic, class-coerced ones (closed or nuclear structure).

Family, Values, and Social Mobility

It is now a basic social science principle that the socioeconomic position of the family affects the opportunities and upward mobility of the offspring. Besides strictly material conditions, however, the value orientation of the parents is pivotal in determining whether or not children advance and how far. And inasmuch as values condition the choice of means to advancement, they also exert influence on the form that family relations take.

There is little in the literature about the ties between values and domestic organization. With respect to the West Indies, it has been said that the ideal family form is middle class, but that economic conditions do not permit most to achieve that ideal; poor West Indians therefore "stretch" middle-class values to fit their own family organization (see, for example, Rodman 1971). To some extent this is true, but it is not the whole story. The same values that prompt individuals to try to achieve family forms typical of the middle class may also contribute to division in the family. And the very path to social mobility can contribute to instability. The case presented here illustrates some of these points. This is an exceptional case in many ways, and so I do not argue that these are dominant patterns or trends: I merely suggest that the relationship between class, family organization, and mobility is complex and does not always lend itself to facile generalizations. On the one hand, efforts to achieve an ideal family form by adherence to codes of respectability may produce the opposite. But on the other hand, as this case demonstrates, even in the face of what some social scientists regard as instability, the determination of a single parent can produce the type of result that makes social scientists rethink their assertions about the "ideal" family structure in today's world.

THE HAMILTON FAMILY

Mr. Hamilton arrived in Costa Rica about 1900 at the age of twenty-nine, leaving a wife of eight years and three sons in Jamaica. His wife arrived two years later, followed by his sons. Mr. Hamilton's first job in Costa Rica was as a *mandador* (foreman) for an independent English farmer in the Siquirres area. By the time the Reventazon River overflowed its banks some years later, devastating the farm on which he worked, he was able to establish his own small farm and homestead on the Estrella line, south of Puerto Limón. There he resided with his wife, Martha, his sons, John, Joseph, and Lenny, and his daughter, Lurlina.

His ambition was to teach and pursue his religious commitments (he arrived in Costa Rica a trained primary school teacher). He became acquainted with a United Fruit Company superintendent and through him successfully prevailed upon the company to subsidize a school and church building, which was erected near New Sligoville. Here he was to farm, teach, and preach for the rest of his very distinguished life.

The school, the only one within miles, was the first in the region to be subsidized by the Company. But the subsidy only provided school supplies. Consequently, Mr. Hamilton had to support himself and his family from the proceeds of his farm. Officially, he was supposed to collect a fee from his pupils, but instead, he accepted donations of food and other gifts from parents and often redistributed them to his poorer neighbors—his farm was very fruitful, so he did not need gifts of agricultural produce. The elderly today remember Mr. Hamilton not only as the best teacher they ever had but also as a man brimming with magnanimity. As one woman put it: "Any bag that went into his yard was sure to come out with something in it."

He controlled about fifty acres of land and grew bananas, which he sold to United Fruit. In addition, he was employed by Mr. Bennett, a white American in Bananito, as a tutor for his children. Mr. Hamilton's school activities occupied most of his time. He worked in his fields only in the mornings and on Fridays and Saturdays; on Sundays he was a full-time lay preacher in the Anglican church.

Described as "cross" or tough[6]—the "Englishman type" as one grand-daughter put it—Mr. Hamilton believed in the supremacy of education and rigorous moral comportment as the road to success. This meant not only success in material terms, but as a foundation for the development of the "respectable human being." His aim, therefore, was to have all his children schooled in the best tradition known to Jamaicans at that time, and that meant sending them back to Jamaica—he himself had no intention of returning. He managed to send Lenny to high school in Jamaica, an act that became the basis of a chronic family conflict after his return. A short time later, Alice, the female member of a pair of "outside" children (see Figure 5), was also sent to a high school in Jamaica.

Mr. Hamilton was a man of few words; he spoke only when necessary, and his two enemies were "laziness and lies," particularly when his own children were involved. He never "mixed," and he never allowed his children to play with other children in the community for fear of corruption. In fact, he railed even against religious mixing; he regarded his church, the Anglican church, as unquestionably the highest church, and therefore even the use of a Baptist hymnal in the service was regarded as contemptuous. Nor did he countenance such organizations as lodges—still popular among Blacks in Limón—or UNIA. Yet he seems to have been a very popular man, well-known and widely respected throughout the province, as his children are today.

Lenny, his eldest son, who had studied in Jamaica, took a job as a foreman with the United Fruit Company upon his return to Costa Rica. A sister's daughter describes him at length:

Lenny went to Jamaica an' study an' had a good job an' good education. You know the company wanted people like that for foremen. He married this woman an' had a big farm. They were a selfish family; she got Lenny not to pay any attention to his family [meaning relatives], not even my mother.

Now, in those days my mother was the Cinderella of the family, though she didn't have much education and had all of them children, an' they [Lenny and his wife] were married, Mr. and Mrs., an' since my mother wasn't, you know, they don't want people like that in the family. Sometimes on Sundays we have nothing to eat and we go there an' they would set the table and eat right before us; they would never offer us some. Lenny was there an' he would not say give those children some food.

Apart from that Uncle Lenny had a farm, and right beside it Uncle Joseph had his farm, an' Lenny was always trying to have problem with Uncle Joseph, always fussing over something. When Lenny got sick he had about sixty thousand colones on him and he would not give it up. He got unconscious in the hospital an' somebody took it.

He was always well-dressed and speak very nicely. He was always to himself and he brought all his children up that way. That is why we know very little about his children; Maria and Doris we know almost nothing about, Laura we know 'cause she is a famous nurse in San José, even today. Mario takes care of the farm and now he comes to us. Roy [another son] is married to a Spanish nurse from San José, and Roberto married to one of the Brambels' divorced wife. His first wife went to the United States and send for him but after a while they divorced. Both of these boys are excellent in basketball and they both had good schooling. They all in San José now, leave Limón many years ago. Roy is a university graduate.

As one outsider who has known the family for some fifty years confided:

It is not that Lenny was selfish; he was a man of pride and believed in a respectful life. He didn't think that Lurlina with all them children an' not married was living the right life. You have to understand that he was schooled in the British fashion an' could not be expected to lower himself as some people would like. You have to live at a high level an' don't let others pull you down; when you climb a tree never hang you' leg down to pull someone up until you are in the crutch (of the tree).

Little is known about Mr. Hamilton's second son, Terry, who migrated to Jamaica and never returned. John, another son, went to the United States as a seaman and stayed there. He is said to be ill, in a nursing home. His sister's daughter volunteered that "he came back here once an' we watch him leave right there at the dock, although we told him not to go back to the U.S. You see, he himself say when he was young all he thought about was the almighty dollar. Now see what happen to him."

A fourth son, Joseph, is viewed as the antithesis of Lenny. He is regarded as a warm and caring man, well-respected by all those who know him and loved by members of the family, but he never had the benefit of a Jamaican

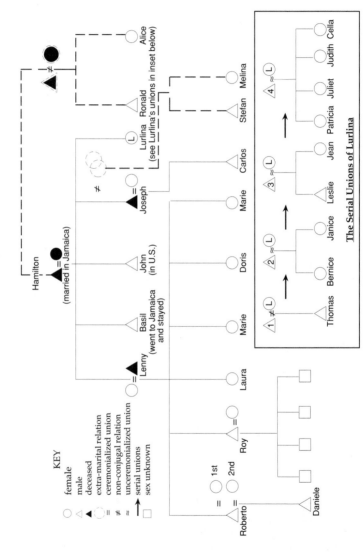

FIGURE 5
THE HAMILTON FAMILY TREE

KEY

○ female
◁ male
▲ deceased
◌ extra-marital relation
= ceremonialized union
≠ non-conjugal relation
≈ unceremonialized union
↑ serial unions
☐ sex unknown

The Serial Unions of Lurlina

Note: The category "non-conjugal sex relation" is distinguished from "extra-marital relation" in that neither partners in a "non-conjugal sex relation" is in an enduring "union" of any sort at the time of the sex relation.

education as his brother had. Yet he was more helpful to the family than most of the other children. His niece observed:

We take him as a father. He is the uncle that was always beside Mamma, and he always had a few colones for everyone. He was a foreman for the Company an' every month he would give something to my family. When Tommy [a sister's daughter's son] was giving trouble we send him to Uncle Joseph an' he was the only one who could take care of him.

While the relationship between Joseph—a beloved man who missed out on a prestigious education—and Lurlina was one of warmth and respect, that between Lurlina and Lenny, the educated snob, was one of coldness and brittle respect. The primary reason for this was that Lurlina was seen as the antithesis of what was expected of a girl from a "decent" family. Circumstances made her an outcast, but having assimilated the social values of her own decent family, she spent all her life struggling to redeem herself through her children.

LURLINA'S FAMILY

By the age of eight, Lurlina was playing the organ in the Anglican church where her father was the lay preacher. She rode a horse to school, even when she was so small she had to be tied to the horse to prevent her from falling off. She was the princess of the family. But by her midteens, misfortune sneaked in: She became pregnant. The indignation of her parents—particularly the moral fury of her father—drove her out of the home. Some say that she was not forced to leave but instead used her pregnancy as an excuse to set out on her own. In any case, she was unwelcome at home, and she was very frightened; she had an aversion to babies because "the baby bedding always smell so bad."

A son, Thomas, was born. Not long afterward, she met a young farmer with whom she established a conjugal union that produced a daughter, Bernice. Soon she became pregnant with a second daughter, Janice, and at about this time she observed that her partner was shying away from his responsibilities. In fact, he was planning to leave her. She took the psychological high ground; she left him, leaving the children behind until she found a place to live.

Hoping to find a stable father for her children, she established a union with another man in 28-Miles, a nearby community. The union produced more children: Leslie and Jean. But again she found this union intolerable; her partner discriminated against her children in favor of his own offspring from a previous union. Once again she decided that a bad union was worse than no union; she left, taking all the children with her except Leslie, returning for him later.

Now without a man, Lurlina had to find work quickly. She temporarily entrusted her first daughter to a godmother and her first son to her half-sister, Alice. The other children were still too young to live with others for long periods, but Lurlina planned to leave them with someone during her working hours. In Puerto Limón she found work as a housemaid, while Leslie's godmother took care of the children during the day.

As her life began to settle somewhat, she renewed her long-severed allegiance to the church. Still searching for a father for her children, she established a consensual union with a United Fruit Company timekeeper within two years. (This timekeeper had obtained his job through the auspices of Lurlina's brother Joseph.) He treated her well, but he soon lost his job and therefore had some difficulty supporting the family. Lurlina found work as a washwoman and continued working until the very day before her fourth daughter, Patricia, was born. A fifth daughter, Juliet, followed soon.

Hardships increased, and her eldest son, Thomas, tried to help support the family: He ran a small lottery whenever possible, and the proceeds helped to purchase food for his mother and siblings. At times, food arrived in the house only late at night after the day's hustle. Whenever this occurred she would let the children sit on the floor and eat without utensils. The idea was to avoid alerting the neighbors to the disgrace of their late meal. Judith and Celia, the last two daughters, were born in equally hard times, their father doing the best he could without a steady job while Lurlina earned a few colones washing clothes and doing other domestic chores.

"But no matter how tough things get we always had to go to church," Patricia reflected. She went on:

All of us grew on the choir an' you had to wear a white dress. That means we had only one white dress each an' we never had dressing shoes. My mother said that I had a tendency to be fat. So she said I had a belly like when kid mumma dead an' him eat grass too soon. So, she put me in a skirt an' blouse to gird my belly. By the time I graduate [from elementary school] she wanted to send us to *colegio* [high school] but she was gaining [earning] only ninety colones a month working at the rectory . . . . She decide to try and matriculate us . . . . When March coming an'a she have to buy shoes an' everything and she don't know where to turn, she ask the priest to give her a hundred colones advance pay. She was looking for a better time an' she say the children going to be my treasure.

Lurlina was an austere and exacting mother; ironically, she took after her father. The children were not allowed to speak "broken English" (Jamaican Creole) around the house. They were not allowed to go to dances and clubs, and if they did they were likely to be removed physically by their mother. In Lurlina's mind, this discipline was necessary in bringing up children properly. For poor though they were, they were convinced that the proper behavior, discipline, and hard work would be rewarded with respect from the community, high achievement in school, and a good life afterwards. "My mother was always saying," said Patricia, "that if we didn't have anything we always had principle."

The principles paid off in the long run. Leslie, the youngest son, was sent to San José where he worked as a helper in a dry goods store. His sister said that "he went to San José because my mother didn't want us to stay in Limón. Every chance she got she would try to push us out." Having done well in San José, Leslie was later dispatched to Limón as manager of a local subsidiary. "We thought that he would employ us," his sister commented, "but he din't pay us any mind for about a year." He staffed the store with nonrelatives, apparently being careful not to attract the ire of his employer. However, with the prompting of an old friend of the family, "in a few weeks he said that all of us should come out to work—five of us." Bernice, the eldest sister, protested, for although she knew the family needed money, she thought that the exposure would spoil her younger sisters.

As soon as they went to work in the store, life began to change for the entire family. Their mother stopped working, and the family moved to a bigger house. In referring to the improved conditions, Patricia commented:

An' you know my mother have this thing about her: everybody should have their own bed, their own night clothes and nice sheet; your skin should not touch the mattress. You should have your own grip [suitcase] and since we could sew we should have a sewing machine. One day Leslie gave Mama the piece of land there in Barrio that him buy cheap from a man who was going to Jamaica. And he borrow the money from the bank to build the house. We pay back that money already, though.

Today, Miss Lurlina owns a spacious three-bedroom house, one of the largest in her barrio.

The daughters continued to work in the store managed by Leslie. They all finished high school, and Patricia went to college in Mexico. With pooled help from home and the money she earned working in the store each holiday, she managed to complete degrees in theology and journalism simultaneously. Celia continued to work in the store to help Judith financially with her studies at the University of Costa Rica. Judith later emigrated to the United States and in turn helped Celia to get a university education at home. Celia has since studied in the United States and Holland, and she is now a university professor in Costa Rica. Juliet eventually left the store to assume a more advanced position in a national semiautonomous entity. Bernice, the eldest daughter, eventually emigrated to the United States, where she is today, and Janice studied nursing in Costa Rica and remained there. Jean, the third-oldest daughter, has also remained in Costa Rica and is now employed in a stable white-collar position. Almost all of the daughters eventually got married.

THE PERSISTENCE OF FAMILY/SOCIAL VALUES

Several points of interest regarding social values and upward mobility of the Hamilton family may be extracted here:

1. Mr. Hamilton achieved a fairly high level of education and a relatively high standard of living.

2. His value orientation centered on the following: an uncritical belief in the efficacy of formal education; strict adherence to Christian principles and the insistence that his children be immersed in these principles. He believed in proper behavior, that is, adherence to strict codes of speech, attire, etiquette, social network, and ambition. To him extramarital sex and consensual unions were sinful—although, interestingly, he himself had a couple of "outside children" from relationships he considered minor indiscretions. In general, he conformed to a set of values that were generally associated with the more prosperous families of the time.

3. Although the family was, by local standards, materially able, Lurlina, with whom I am most concerned here, was cast into poverty and social instability because she violated (and therefore negated) the moral code of her father. I say the father—as opposed to the parents—because it was the male authority that prevailed; Lurlina's mother made entreaties to her husband on Lurlina's behalf but was rejected.

4. Despite her single-handed struggle with nine children, four of whom were for all practical purposes fatherless, none of them received less than a high school education. Four of the nine eventually received a university education.

5. Throughout the struggle to raise her children—in spite of actions that would suggest contravention of the moral codes inherited from her father, and except for not being able to establish a permanent conjugal union—Lurlina ironically conformed rigidly to the same principles by which her father lived, and which were partly responsible for her own difficulties.

Examination of the value orientation of Lurlina's father suggests a man who had an unquestioning belief in the ability of the social system to reward his determination. He saw value in conformity, reward in trying to adapt to rather than change his surroundings. These traits were transmitted to his daughter. The unswerving belief in the certainty of social reward for respectful behavior and hard work was no doubt her source of inner energy—not, of course, to belittle the incomparable satisfaction she must have gotten from raising nine good children.

Lurlina was alienated from her parental family simply because she violated the codes of respectability that her father adopted. And guided by values similar to his father's, her brother Lenny, who was educated in Jamaica and led a respectful and economically stable family life, treated her as an outcast instead of offering a helping hand. In effect, then, both of these male kin contributed to a division in the family primarily because of the dictates of their social values, particularly the prohibition against premarital sex. The aspect of gender is also important here, for had a son sired a child before marriage his fate would not likely have been the same. Avoidance of premarital sex for females is an ideal among African-Americans not often achieved, but the estrangement of pregnant unmarried daughters is not typically practiced.[7]

Mr. Hamilton was exercising extrinsic rather than intrinsic values. In contrast, Lurlina was accepted and aided by other members of the family, such as Joseph, who were less financially able but who showed no pretensions to the high-toned values of someone like Lenny. Had Lurlina's father and brother helped economically, she might have been able to avoid some of the less than fortunate conjugal unions. Furthermore, these unions must be seen as ramifying from the values of her father. The irony is that some of these same values were ingredients in her successful struggle; she has kneaded her values into a life principle—essentially the same principle as her father's—and stuck to it.

According to Peter Wilson (1973, 7–10) the values of respectability are associated with women and older established men. The implication is that such values are transmitted largely through women, and to a much lesser extent, through these few established males. It might very well be, however, that transmission has less to do with gender than with dominance—dominance at two related structural levels: at the level of the community and at the level of the family. And because men tend to assume dominance at both levels (despite the reality of matrifocality), it could be argued that respectability—the values emanating from the dominant sector of society—is to a great extent imposed on women. Women are participants, but it may very well be that they are more inclined to balance intrinsic values. But the full exercise of intrinsic values is compromised by the psychological need to associate with dominant values—by both male and female. Family unity, therefore, becomes a casualty of values transaction.

As Lurlina's life became a casualty of value conflicts, so did that of her daughter. At the time of this study, one daughter's marriage was on the verge of disintegration because, among other things, she and her husband did not share social or economic values, in spite of their similar class backgrounds. The union persists, but the conflict runs deep; the wife shares many of the social values and expectations passed on from her grandfather through her mother, but the husband does not. In a word, the wife is oriented toward success and respectability, the husband toward conviviality and popularity. Indeed this is a classic example of the Peter Wilson (1973) duality.

How Much Does Structure Count?

The foregoing represents two aspects of social mobility related to household and family organization. In the first case, the larger household size in the urban upper economic-level community is attributable to the fact that better-off individuals open their doors to relatives who move in search of economic opportunities. In addition, their economic position allows them to assist grandchildren and grandparents who are too young or too old to work. The evidence suggests that the larger size of households in the rural areas is attributable to the stability and quality of the economic base of the particular community. To be sure, this is a case where economic conditions facilitate kinship cohesion.

In the second case, values of respectability associated with social class clearly affect the form that Lurlina's family took. It is commonly assumed that individuals who accept what may be loosely called middle-class values and who have achieved a stable economic position, will opt for ceremonialized unions and the nuclear family. The assumption is questionable (see R. T. Smith 1988); however, it is not commonly expected that this same set of values can contribute to the persistence of the very form of family which they seek to avoid. As a male-dominated society denies, with assumed propriety, the basic rights and privileges of women, Lurlina's father, supremely confident in the sanctity of his ideals and values, denied her support when she needed it most.

Lurlina's struggles of the 1940s and 1950s are multiplied many fold, in many countries, in the 1980s and 1990s. The difference is, however, that today many women, particularly in the industrial world but increasingly in the nonindustrial countries, lack not only the supporting community but the simple, dogged principles of a Lurlina.

For the social scientist, the two aspects of family organization discussed in this chapter question the notion, popular in the Caribbean since the 1940s

(Simey 1946), that the structure of a family in itself determines how well the offspring fit into the society. It also raises questions about the current view of single-parent families as a primary social problem in many countries today—a view that ignores factors such as low wages, a work regimen that constrains parental care, and the absence of kinship and community ties that could contribute to the care of offspring.

Nothing here suggests that structure is unimportant. What this case and many others like it among African-Americans suggest is that contrary to the dire declaration of the 1960s by wrong-headed social scientists like Daniel Patrick Moynihan (1965), we need worry much less about the structural deterioration of the Black family than about the faulty and even destructive remedies for deterioration, remedies often based on an epistemology that ignores local cultural definitions in favor of standards based on Eurocentric thinking at a particular moment.

Clearly Lurlina was a victim of values that, on the one hand, prohibited premarital sex in the interest of a stable family, and on the other hand, dismissed her, a young girl in a moment of need, from her parental home with no provision for her soon-to-arrive infant. One aspect of this situation that stands out is the shame her parents—particularly her father, a prominent churchman—felt on account of their young, pregnant, unmarried daughter.

It was a relatively common practice among West Indians at home and abroad to send a daughter away who become pregnant "before her time." She might "spend time" with relatives in a distant town or village until after the child was born. Often the child was "given away," placed in the care of distant relatives. If the child returned to its mother's original home, it would be described as adopted to anyone naive enough to inquire. The issue was clearly one of avoiding the loss of face and status in the eyes of the community.

The preoccupation with status rests less on the incidence of children traditionally born within wedlock than on an imposed religious (Christian) cum social ideal regarding respectability. To this extent, both Lurlina and her father, victims of the ideal though they were, would readily agree that the nuclear family, forged in a Christian ritual, is the desirable and respectable goal—in effect, agreeing with social scientists who see the middle-class nuclear family as the norm. Issues relating to the source of that ideal, to its place in the structure of class and cultural relations, or to the lives that are bruised in the rough conflict between societal status demands and the reality that produces premarital pregnancy—these are left to the social scientist. Lurlina, after all her struggles, did not reject the system of constraints she faced. She confronted them, became part of them, and transcended them in the success—through liberal education—of her own children.

OVERVIEW:
THE BLACK EXPERIENCE IN COSTA RICA

Whether for naked survival or out of desire for advancement, Black West Indians have had to adjust to cultures and values that simultaneously restrict their access to a livelihood and belittle their African heritage. It has been no different for West Indians in Costa Rica. Their adjustment is observable on two levels.

On one level, value transaction took place on a day-to-day basis in response to historically imposed social and economic constraints. When Blacks and Hispanics competed for jobs on the United Fruit Company's plantation, Blacks saw advantage in portraying themselves as culturally superior to Hispanics. They used their British-derived culture and values as a banner of legitimacy, particularly such aspects as language, education, and political attachment to Great Britain, aspects they held in common with their North American employers. Not surprisingly, they were favored—as employees—even while they were subjected to North American castelike discrimination and blatant exploitation of their immigrant status. Hispanics, who had nothing in common with North Americans but skin color, were regarded by West Indians as culturally inferior. The North Americans, in characteristic fashion, missed no opportunity to fan the flames of racial, cultural, and national divisions where doing so meant a cheaper labor force.

West Indians, burdened with the accumulated insecurity of generations of servitude and cultural inferiority, grabbed the opportunity to nurture the cultural/values division in the interest of job security and self-esteem. The division was strong enough to be a formidable obstacle in efforts to unionize labor in the 1930s and to fuel arguments against Black integration. In the long run, laborers—both Black and white—were the losers, as profits were reaped by the North Americans who then relocated when conditions were no longer to their liking, leaving their Black employees stranded in a foreign land.

The second level of adjustment took place in response to broader economic and political changes: the transfer of all plantation activities to the western coast of Costa Rica and the eventual control of the eastern coast by the state. With the relocation of the plantation, most West Indians lost their livelihood. There were few choices available: They could seek employment in another country (including the West Indies); remain as a cultural minority on whatever land was still available to them on the Atlantic coast; or brave racial and cultural prejudice to become integrated into the wider society. Some could not find the fare to return home; others could not find the will. A few resigned themselves to small-scale cultivation. Most, spoiled by the proletarian culture of the plantation, wanted employment, and this meant as before that they would now have to adjust to a different society, a different culture, and a different set of values, this time Hispanic rather than Anglo. When the new regime brought about by the 1948 civil war offered Afro-Costa Ricans political enfranchisement, partly in compensation for shedding their blood in the war, they readily accepted. It was a cruel joke of history, for this was the society at whose culture they once thumbed their noses.

With this new dependency—or rather shift in dependency—came the day-to-day struggle of trying once again to be what they were not, what they were too existentially fatigued to be. The difficulty, however, was not the cultural change that was implicitly demanded; generations of slavery and postslavery adjustment had made this somewhat routine. It was the racial and cultural subordination entailed that was difficult. Blacks found themselves submerging their language, their folklore, their religion, their attire, their cuisine, and even their names as the price of acceptance. And what they did not readily submerge—such as cooperative labor and active extended kin ties—would gradually erode under the new political and economic conditions.

Some scholars (Peter Worsley 1984, 250, for example) have implied that changing ethnic identity is not necessarily the soul-wrenching thing it is made out to be. True, for white ethnics, it is straightforward adjustment. For Black ethnics in Costa Rica, as elsewhere in the Americas, however, adjustment gets a little more twisted. Blacks carry the stigma of generations of enslavement and the resultant deliberate disfigurement of their identity. Their saving grace is the flexibility so ably enacted through value transaction; it allows them not only to survive but to advance, in a creative response to this disfigurement.

Two basic historical conditions determine the emergence of transactional strategies. They are (1) the removal of viable economic and social alternatives from imported slaves (deprivation), and (2) the redefinition of their social world (the imposition of new culture and values by those who control the conditions of deprivation).

Caribbean societies began as the first experiment in capitalism in the

Americas based on private property and unfree, propertyless labor. As a condition for the retention of enslaved labor, alternative economic sustenance for Black labor was (except in cases of marronage) limited to what their owners permitted. This allowed owners direct control over the value of labor; not only physical value with respect to labor time but cultural value, in terms of the degree of cultural conformity to the requirements of the productive system. In fact, where some economic freedom was permitted—as with *palengues* or "garden plots" in places such as Jamaica, Haiti, and Guyana—we find a streak of independent spirit developing, and therefore imposed values had to struggle for dominance against a highly resistant substratum of African ideas (see Mintz and Price 1976, Abrahams and Szwed 1983).

Ultimately, however, the productive system imposed a set of values that defined the world in terms of standards based on emergent commodity fetishism, the totalizing market ethos. Over generations, the enslaved Africans' individual and collective self-esteem came to be defined in relation to a world market they did not control and a culture arrogantly rationalized as universal and superior.

Emancipation brought legal modifications rather than real radical structural transformation, with the result that the economic and social conditions that sought to recast Black identity in the dominant culture's own (supremely self-interested) image not only persisted but followed Blacks wherever they went in the Americas. This latter phase of West Indian adjustment in Costa Rica was not new. The real difficulty they have faced since the beginning of their political integration in the early 1950s is not social or cultural adjustment, but gaining recognition as full citizens with the right to participate fully in the determination of their own life circumstances.

The New Black Consciousness

This necessary pragmatic flexibility[1] of West Indians has had and continues to have its drawbacks. Set in the context of the democratic socialist ideology of Costa Rica and the historical events that ushered in the incorporation of West Indians, this pragmatism meant that, on the one hand, Afro-Costa Ricans would make demands on the political system but, on the other hand, they would have to follow the ideological pied piper. Blacks had no special regard for any particular political ideology. They would, therefore, willingly follow any political figure or party that had the courage to facilitate their adjustment. They did so not for ideological reasons, but for the purpose of achieving material and social benefits.

As it turned out, the historical events of the 1940s and early 1950s matched benefits with an attractive political ideology, the social democratic idea of equality and universal opportunity. But this ideology, planted in a social atmosphere of superficial tolerance, denial of racial bias, and cultural superiority, à la the Iberian variant, could not and would not confront the reality of color prejudice. The social democratic ideal would, therefore, lull Afro-Costa Ricans into complacency and conformity, only to be frustrated later by the denigration of their cultural dignity and by the lack of economic advancement.

It is worth reiterating that the incorporation of West Indians into Costa Rican society came about because they were abandoned at a time when Costa Rica was itself experiencing a political crisis, a crisis that Blacks helped to resolve. As with the role of Blacks in Cuban independence, Blacks in Costa Rica contributed their blood for social democracy; they fought on the side of José Figueres in the 1948 civil war, even though at the time most were merely resident immigrants. Their later enfranchisement was, therefore, partly a reward, but some of the social benefits they enjoyed were co-opted demands of the Calderonista-Communist-Catholic coalition that influenced the Tomàs Guardia government.

The Figueres regime, the new darling of Blacks, moved to encourage the election of Black officials and to establish social programs—particularly in health and education—that benefited minorities and the poor in general. The political climate was just right; despite Costa Rica's pride in its "homogeneous Europeanness," a deep-seated social tolerance as well as an abhorrence of being seen as racist made this move acceptable. To be sure, Blacks were aware of racial and cultural prejudice, but up until the 1970s, the ideology of equality was foremost in their minds. Like their Hispanic counterparts, they lulled themselves into believing that if most Blacks were still at the bottom, it was because of individual social inadequacies rather than racial discrimination.

By the late 1970s, however, Blacks began to develop a strong racial and cultural consciousness, as the stench of racial discrimination filtered through the screen of denial and the ideology of equal opportunity. Besides the general climate of discrimination, several factors gave rise to this. First, the subtle but efficient system of state clientelism, which helped to cushion class conflict and stabilize the Figueres regime in the 1960s and 1970s, did not reach deep enough into the Black population. Afro-Costa Ricans were too far removed socially, politically, and geographically from the center of power. Second, the token Black elite encountered real limits to advancement—and acceptance. Also, they were themselves a step removed from the Black masses partly by reason of class values. Access to power is limited not so much by lack of qualification as by the historically insidious attitude among Hispanics that one group only is inherently fit to manage the affairs of the collectivity. Third, instead of turning to the land, many second-generation Blacks—partly because of pressure for land from incoming Hispanics—chose to improve their life chances through the labor market and education, where the Costa Rican ethos of cultural superiority makes the path to advancement more slippery than it need be.

In spite of their willingness to accommodate and conform, Blacks came to realize, not a moment too soon, that political enfranchisement and cultural acceptance—indeed equality—would not come with citizenship and cultural adjustment; it had to be won. The first concrete collective step came in the form of a 1978 national conference on the situation of Blacks in Costa Rica, an event that not only commanded the attention of the nation, but attracted participation from the highest level of the state apparatus.

Apart from the general aim of consciousness raising, the 1978 conference hoped to spur the government to respond with specific affirmative steps. Government response has been slow, but one concrete step so far is important, if symbolic. Through the effort of a few Black educators (under the leadership of Guillermo Joseph) and the Sindicato de Educadores Costaricense (Union of Costa Rican Educators), the government made August 31 part of the educational calendar by declaring it Black Costa Rican Day. August 31 is the day Marcus Garvey declared International Negro Day. Later the government changed the celebration to August 30, to coincide with the celebration of the founding of the republic (see Joseph 1982).

In terms of ethnic process (particularly nationalism), this gesture is of more than passing significance, for the "celebration of difference" is an essential "action aspect" of group self-definition, perpetuation, and general collective psychic strength (Nash 1989, 15). The government has also acknowledged the integrity of Afro-Costa Ricans by declaring that Black history should be included in the curriculum of public schools. Today Black history courses are available even at the university level. Beyond the obvious significance of giving Blacks access to their history through the education system, perhaps the most important contribution of this response is that it reduces white control of knowledge about Blacks and therefore dulls the tools of political control.

Rank and file Blacks eventually, though hesitantly, responded affirmatively to the new consciousness spearheaded by intellectuals. Groups were formed in San José and Limón to discuss and act on the question of racism on an ongoing basis. These groups did not last as functional wholes, but they left the mark of racial/cultural consciousness on those whose lives they touched.

There is the uneasy feeling, however, particularly among some prominent Black women, that the new consciousness resides more among men than women, and that this is a function of persistent and pervasive sexual inequality as well as traditional role differentiation. Women, to a great extent, spend much of their time isolated from other women in the performance of domestic chores. Some must even hold full-time outside jobs while still working as full-time housewives. They are left with little time for political discourse and action. Men, on the other hand, discuss and share information as they congregate at work and at bars and other locations after work. The information and ideas they obtain are not usually filtered into the home. To the extent that this is the case, the new consciousness has not become part of the enculturation of children; by and large, women and not men are most active in bringing up offspring.[2] The emerging generation, therefore, is at risk of losing out on the benefits of this new consciousness.

Progress has been made in other areas, too. Perhaps most importantly, in terms of collective action, Blacks are making greater, though still inadequate, use of the educational system. In the political sphere, Black representation in the national Congress has increased, with signs of even further increase to come. In 1986, for the first time in the history of Costa Rica, two Black diputados were elected in the same general election. Before 1986 Blacks were usually placed in secondary positions on the election ticket for Limón and used, as Guillermo Joseph (1982, 60) and others have argued, as a "trampoline" for white candidates—at times non-Limónese. The 1986 campaign broke that tradition: The main opposition party, La Unidad, placed a Black candidate, Marcelle Taylor, in first position. This prompted the incumbent party, the Partido Liberación Nacional (PLN)—the party traditionally supported by Blacks—to place a Black candidate, Clinton Cruickshand, in first position on its Limón ticket. This maneuver resulted in splitting the traditional PLN Black support between the two dominant parties, but in the process it contributed to the election of two Black representatives.

A DISMAL ECONOMIC PROSPECT

Clearly, an increase in representation alone does not mean that the economic life of Afro-Costa Ricans will improve. In the United States, for example, Blacks have made giant strides in representation, but the gap between Black and white wealth grows despite an increasing Black middle class (U.S. Census Bureau 1986). One drawback is that, for various reasons, national political representatives often feel they must play the political games of the mainstream power brokers if they are to be successful. Even in cases where such feelings do not encumber elected officials, changing entrenched policies and structures in the interest of equality is a Herculean task. Representation without appropriate consciousness and structural adjustment can, therefore, become an empty symbol that obscures the material reality and thereby retards advances.

How the new consciousness will be affected in the 1980s and 1990s will be determined not only at the national but certainly at the international level. The 1980s was a critical transitional moment in Costa Rica's political economy. The Rodrigo Carazo government (1978–1982) attempted to perpetuate an expanding public sector, responsible for comprehensive social services and employing 20 percent of the labor force, by printing money and relying increasingly on commercial bank loans. This policy, following on the failure of industrialization through import substitution and the increased pressure caused by skyrocketing oil prices in 1973, led to massive inflation and devaluation by 1983. From 1977 to 1981, Costa Rica's external debt tripled (Chomsky 1989, 267).

In the political climate created by economic failure, Carazo's successor, the National Liberation Party's Alberto Monge, had little choice but to seek an agreement with the International Monetary Fund (IMF). Recovery ensued, due not only—and perhaps not even primarily—to the IMF's remedy of restructuring. Under the Reagan administration's policy objective to "support U.S. economic, political and security interests and to advance foreign policy objectives" in the region (Edelman and Kenen 1989, 189), assistance to Costa Rica in the form of U.S. Agency for International Development (USAID) economic support funds and the Caribbean Basin Initiative amounted to 35.7 percent of government expenditures between 1983 and 1985. At one point, Costa Rica was the second highest per capita recipient of U.S. aid after Israel (Edelman and Kenen 1989, 189).

But the U.S.-IMF assistance came with strings attached, strings that squeezed Blacks and other disenfrancished groups disproportionately. The IMF demanded, among other things, austerity measures that included reductions of the minimum wage and government spending. Social welfare programs, which traditionally contained ethnic and class conflict, were curtailed. In addition, the USAID channeled funds directly to private groups and withheld funds at critical moments in order to coerce legislative approval of economic restructuring. The United States has used its economic leverage to extract reluctant accommodation to its Nicaragua policy from the liberal government of Oscar Arias (see Chomsky 1989, 266–69).

The effect is that U.S. aid has been used to maintain the illusion of democracy and the illusion of prosperity, while the economy is being radically transformed in the image of the Reagan-Bush notion of free market. The result has been high unemployment, reduced real wages, and a more regressive distribution of income and construction of social welfare. The 1990s, therefore, are likely to be characterized by what one economist and former minister of planning and economic policy under the Albert

Monge government calls a less "socially acceptable" distributive pattern (Villasuso Etomba 1989).

There is little doubt that this new political-economic regime will mean hardship for increasing numbers of people on the Atlantic coast, where Blacks and a large proportion of poor Hispanics and native Americans are concentrated. Since the decline of banana operations there, the Atlantic coast has suffered some of the highest unemployment and underemployment in Central America. The 1985 decision by the major banana companies to shift some of their operations elsewhere was a big blow to the entire economy, given that bananas accounted for about 25 percent of export earnings in recent years, and the industry has long been a major employer (Edelman and Kenen 1989, 191).

Nature contributed to this bleak socioeconomic prospect with the recent earthquake that devastated Puerto Limón. The government has responded conscientiously, but with the already tight national economic condition, and with changing regional politics dictating reduction in U.S. assistance, the quake is likely to leave its mark on the social, political, and economic dynamics of the region. The transformations of the 1980s and 1990s can only deepen the consciousness of Blacks as a group apart.

What Lies Ahead?

There is no inevitability here. Rather than contributing to ethnic divisions, class could be the basis for an alliance across ethnic boundaries, under the stress of hard times. In the United States, however, where similar political economic ideas prevail, and where the principal proponents of those ideas engage in explicit manipulation of race for social, economic, and political benefit, the stress of hard times has intensified ethnic conflict. The historical, social, and political conditions influencing ethnic relations in Costa Rica are evidently very different. Yet the long history of U.S. involvement in the political economy of the country, the high rate of migration between Costa Rica and the United States (involving Costa Ricans as well as North Americans), and Costa Rica's well-known pro-gringo ideology (see Chomsky 1989, 263–69) have likely brought about some degree of convergence in the modality of race relations.

There is little doubt that, as with the Black Power ideology of the 1960s and 1970s, the new ideologies of multiculturalism and Afrocentrism will find their way into Afro-Costa Rican thinking. Where the growing consciousness will lead is difficult to say. Four years after the conference on the situation of Blacks, Guillermo Joseph, himself a Limónese, wrote that Blacks are still linked to forms of thinking that are culturally alienating (1982, 7). At the same time, some whites who join the debate do so with the intention of ideologically "socializing and incorporating" Blacks into the dominant social sector (Joseph 1982, 5).

In a conversation with the author, Joseph Powell, a College of Charleston student who surveyed ethnic consciousness among Black university students in 1991, reported a high level of awareness of their ethnic socioeconomic subordination. Still, Blacks have found no effective organization as a vehicle for making cultural and material demands on the society; they continue to be relatively marginal—culturally, economically, and politically.

Indeed, this raises a crucial issue: Given the process of value transaction, which Blacks have found a necessary adjustment tool, is cultural autonomy possible (or even necessary), as long as Blacks must continually compromise their own view of the world in the interest of pragmatism? The foregoing chapters would indicate that as long as Blacks seek advancement within a competitive political economy whose culture and values deprecate their own, the best they can hope for in the forseeable future is a process of unequal accommodation, regardless of incremental increases in political empowerment.

For Blacks in white-dominated societies, the situation is bleaker than for those in Caribbean countries where Blacks predominate. In predominantly Black societies, the opportunity exists for Blacks to activate their own ideas in political and economic practice, stemming the tide of cultural imperialism (see Nettleford 1986). For Blacks in white-dominated societies such as Costa Rica, incorporation and cultural autonomy seem contradictory. The question is whether Blacks, or any other non-white minorities, can make choices regarding their lives without being fettered by the factor of race and culture. This question centers not so much on whether whites will recognize the dignity of non-white culture and race, or whether they will remove historical barriers to self-determination; it centers on whether whites will cease to create new and ever more subtle barriers to the realization of the cultural and racial dignity of non-whites.

NOTES

1. See Table 10 in Palmer (1976, 29), showing the number of slaves and annual demand for various territories in the Americas, including Panama, Guatemala, Honduras, Mexico, and others, about 1645. See also Melendez (1977).

2. The Black Caribs, referred to as the Garifuna, are products of cultural and biological mixture of African slaves and Caribs, with perhaps a sprinkling of Europeans. Their physical appearance is decidedly African (Wilk and Chapin 1990, 24). The Carifuna is the name of their language. They call themselves Garinagu, and some members of the group have been seeking public usage of that name (Wilk and Chapin 1990, 40, note 3).

3. The term Hispanics has wisely been discarded as a descriptive term for persons of Spanish but also Indian and other racial heritage, living elsewhere. However, here and throughout this work, I am referring to persons who are Caucasian or White by racial heritage and cultural identification.

4. Due largely to the application of theoretical and epistemological schemes that do not fit local conditions, social scientists have ended up using mating patterns—in a few cases insightfully, if not always convincingly—to explain everything from social turmoil (Simey, among others) to variants in race relations (Hoetink, among others).

5. Some outstanding critiques of plural society theory are Braithwaite (1960), Bryce-Laporte (1967), Cross (1977), R. T. Smith (1970), Van den Berghe (1973), Mintz (1966), Leons and Leons (1977), and Austin (1983, 1984). See also Trouillot (1992).

6. The labels I use throughout the book are those commonly used in Limón. For the most part, I use Black instead of *moreno* (meaning brown-skinned), because I regard moreno as a patronizing term—even though many Blacks prefer it. In cases where I think it contributes to clarity, I make a distinction between Blacks—dark-skinned migrants—and Coloreds—those with Black blood but light skin and curly or straight hair. Similarly, where their roots in the West Indies are significant, I use the term West Indians. Where neither distinction is important, I use Blacks or Afro-Costa Ricans.

7. The dark side of blanqueamiento is that it also represents a degree of submission, for it is a dimension of the nationalist ideology of *mestizaje*, which expresses a condescending Spanish racial and cultural hegemony (Whitten and Torres 1992).

8. The notion of duality of value orientation (or double consciousness) has also been attributed to Blacks in the United States. Perhaps the earliest mention—certainly the most often quoted—is the work of W.E.B. Du Bois ([1903] 1969, 45).

9. I use value (or values) to mean a preference—or in Firth's terms "the recognition of preference qualities" (Firth 1964, 221, quoted in Paine 1974)—based on knowledge of a system of cultural/moral principles, the source of the criteria or judgment. Values may be spontaneously generated within a culture or may be imposed or imported. There is, therefore, no actual or theoretical requirement for a consensus of values within a society. A culture is a moral order in the Durkheimian sense; a society need not be. The distinction can, therefore, legitimately be made between values that are social ends in themselves and those that are strategies.

10. Barth (1966) bases his case for the utility of transaction on the assumption that the major task of social anthropology is to understand the relationship between social forms and constraints and the incentives influencing those social activities that give rise to the forms. For this, he insists, one needs a model that can generate the social forms from social activity. The model is *transaction*. The model is illustrated thus:

$$A_x \longrightarrow B \qquad A \longleftarrow_y B$$

where prestation x offered by A is reciprocated with prestation y offered by B. Barth notes that each party consistently tries to ensure that the value gained is greater than the value lost. Thus the thresholds: for A, $x>y$, and for B, $x<y$. The outcome of each transaction is a process of choices, exercised under the influence of certain constraints and incentives. If the value of prestation cannot be judged by the same canons, some overarching value principle between those two disparate canons must be constructed. This constitutes a step in creating consistency of values.

Chapter Two. From Plantation Colony to National Enclave:

1. It has been said that there were never more than about two hundred slaves in Costa Rica at any one time. Following the emancipation decree in 1824, only eighty-nine persons were freed. The reason for the small number of slaves is that Costa Rica lacked mines and large-scale agriculture during the colonial period. It was only in the latter part of the seventeenth century that slaves were used for other than personal chores. Another reason is that the slaves frequently escaped to join the Zambo Moskitos —a group consisting of interbred Amerindians and Blacks who occupied the Atlantic coast of Central America. For further information on the slave population, see Melendez and Duncan

([1974]1977), Olien (1967, 1977), and Melendez (1977).

2. The labor migration to Costa Rica must be viewed in the context of a massive labor movement worldwide. The expansion and intensification of capitalism in the nineteenth and early twentieth centuries triggered progressive segmentation or differentiation of the world labor market. Capitalism carried one wave of labor toward the industrial centers, such as Great Britain; a second wave carried Europeans overseas; and yet a third sent casual and contract laborers of diverse origins—many ex-slaves—toward the mines and plantations of the tropics. This latter group included laborers for the South African mines and for the "new-style" Asian plantations, as well as Asian laborers for West Indian plantations. It also sent Italian labor to the coffee plantations of Brazil, and Chinese, Italian, and West Indian labor to transportation projects and plantations in various parts of South America (see Wolf 1982, 362–79).

3. By 1908, banana exports totaled more than $5 million. At the peak, about 1913, almost 11 million bunches of bananas were being exported from a total of nearly 48,000 acres under cultivation. In 1930 the United Fruit Company's total assets were $242,398,164, while lands, cultivation, buildings, ships, and other fixed assets were valued at $171,154,589. Between 1900 and 1930 their assets were multiplied fourteen times.

4. For a description of the monopolistic practices of the United Fruit Company, see Kepner and Soothill (1935, 64–76, 235–37) and Kepner (1936, 42–51).

5. One cannot but wonder if the presence of such a large block of workers, hostile to Hispanic labor activism and the Communist party that was in the vanguard of this activism, was of any particular political interest to the U.S. Department of State at that time. The United States, which through the Monroe Doctrine and later the (Woodrow) Wilson Corollary insisted on keeping foreign influence—including Communism—out of the region, was fully aware of the role of the Communist party (then called *Bloque de Obreros*) in the 1934 strike. Fourteen years after the strike, the State Department regarded Costa Rican labor as one of the most fertile grounds for Communism in the region (La Feber 1983, 79–99). It is worth raising the question therefore—a point for later research—as to whether the anti-Communist position of Blacks may have been used in the interest of U.S. policy in the region. Consciously or not, it did serve that interest.

CHAPTER THREE. TRANSFORMATION OF THE PRODUCTIVE SYSTEM AND RACIAL HIERARCHY

1. In 1978, the Junta Administrativa Portuaria y de Desarrollo de la Vertiente Atlantica (JAPDEVA), as the port and railway operation is called (until recently

dubbed BLACKDEVA because of the predominance of Blacks), now has a Black-Hispanic ratio of 1:2.7 with a corresponding salary ratio of 1.8:2.

2. Some informants noted that the prohibition against Blacks entering the Mesata Central was not fully enforced, for there were occasional excursion trips to the capital. The claim that Blacks were not permitted outside of the Atlantic zone has been disputed by Jeffrey Casey (1979) in his recent book, *Limón: 1880–1940*. Oral accounts, however, still support my position.

3. I use the word *incorporation* instead of *integration* or *assimilation*. Blacks still have not been fully integrated, and although assimilation is part of the general process of incorporation it does not dominate the process. The word *incorporation*, with its legalistic connotation, best describes what in my mind is a political and legal process with ethnic ramifications.

Chapter Four. Space and Social Inequality in Limón

1. The term *obeah* is used in Jamaica and other areas of the Caribbean to refer in general to shamanistic practices and more specifically to the practice of casting "evil spells." The practitioner, usually but not always a male, is referred to as *obeahman*, a term that may be contrasted with *myalman*, a spiritual healer. The word *obeah* was derived from the Twi word *obayi*, which means "witchcraft" (see Allayne 1989, Christaller 1964).

2. One sure measure of a person's social value is whether or not he or she has personal contacts in banks or the various government offices that dispense services. Such contacts permit the individual to bypass normal channels when seeking services. The higher the social worth of the individual, the less likely it is that he or she will have to go through regular channels. The relationship between clerks (and administrative personnel) and such individuals is kept alive by an occasional drink, a gift, or reciprocal service where possible. Through such favoritism the enterprising clerk may develop a broad and productive socioeconomic network.

3. In considering status and prestige, a distinction is made between the larger-scale farmer (20 hectares and upwards), some of whom are rural dwellers, and the small-scale farmer whose holdings average around 5 hectares. Many of these larger-scale farmers possess their own means of transportation and may have other business interests such as *pulperias* (small grocery stores) or cacao purchasing depots. Small-scale farmers and peasant cultivators, however, tend to form a homogeneous category.

4. The category of the Black *peon* is almost empty; it is only in extremely rare cases that one finds a Black rural dweller who does not have access to some land, whether it is his own bought land or land inherited from close kin. Most unskilled agricultural jobs are therefore filled by Hispanics.

CHAPTER FIVE. FROM SOLIDARITY TO EQUALITY:
WEST INDIANS JOIN THE MAINSTREAM

1. While the social democratic ideology has been imposed consciously on the Costa Rican polity, the ideology of solidarity has not, at least not as a coherent body of ideas that inform social life. Much of what I present here as a principle, therefore, is deduced from activity unreflected upon by the actors. The presentation of equality, on the contrary, is informed less by actual social practices—which would require a thorough study of the functioning of the entire Costa Rican polity—than by an intellectualized understanding of the role of equality as a social principle.

2. Thanks to Dr. R. S. Bryce-Laporte, who conducted fieldwork in New Sligoville in 1962, for clarifying the idea of a hierarchy of acceptance.

3. A similar idea is expressed in Eleanor Smith Bowen's (1964) *Return to Laughter*, where Yako, once discovered to be a witch, must "sit alone"—and it is bad for a man to "sit alone."

4. Attendance at one's funeral is the most accurate barometer of how one has lived. A wedding can potentially serve the same purpose, but even a well-respected person may choose to limit attendance at his or her wedding, though at the risk of losing popularity.

5. Villagers frequently referred to all government officials— and particularly the police—as "government."

6. There is a tremendous personal pride in being able to "take your liquor," that is, to drink all that is available without showing obvious signs of intoxication. Consequently, a group of friends who enter a bar to have one or two drinks may find themselves spending hours as new friends join them, each insisting on buying drinks for the others.

CHAPTER SIX. PATTERNS OF SOCIAL MOBILITY IN LIMÓN

1. For a description of *puk-kumina* religious practices, see George Eaton Simpson (1950), Donald Hogg (1960), Martha Beckwith (1923), Cheryl Ryman (1979), and Edward Brathwaite (1979). Unfortunately, most ethnographers of Caribbean societies have emphasized the more exotic religious practices while giving little attention to the Judeo-Christian groups. Some notable exceptions are Mintz (1956, 1960, 1974) for Puerto Rico, Conway (1978) for Haiti, Fischer (1974) and Austin (1984) for Jamaica. Absence of adequate treatment is understandable only when studies are viewed against the history of choices of subject matter in anthropology; the exotic has been and continues to be more attractive to many anthropologists.

2. The Company did subsidize some of the veranda schools but this was not evidence of any real commitment to the social welfare of the worker beyond

what served its own interest. When the Company came under criticism, both in Costa Rica and elsewhere, it used information about its expenditures on education as an instrument of public relations to disarm its critics.

3. I have no figures concerning the relation of student population to school capacity or on the ratio of students to teachers. The general impression, however, is that school capacity has not been a serious problem. The only problem seems to be the long distance that rural children usually have to travel to get to school, combined with the inadequacy of transportation services in some areas.

CHAPTER SEVEN. THE INEQUALITY OF LANGUAGE IN SOCIAL PRACTICE

1. My analysis of language in Limón owes much to the work of Diana Woollard (1978 and 1979) and my frequent discussions with her during the latter stage of my fieldwork.

2. That is, if one accepts that Limón Creole, as described by Wright-Murray (1974) and Herzfeld (1978), is a separate language. In positing three languages, I am obviously accepting their classification, since at the moment I see no grounds on which to question it. Nevertheless, there is no clear break between the various zones of production of Creole speech and Standard Limonese English itself.

3. The distinction between Standard English and Standard Limón English or Standard Jamaican English is made for analytical purposes only. In all cases, although there are differences in pronunciation, the structure is similar. I use Limón Creole here for simplicity. However, it would be more accurate to use Jamaican Creole, because it was not until after the 1948 civil war, when Blacks began to be absorbed into the mainstream society, that the inevitable influence of Spanish caused significant phonological, lexical, and syntactical changes in the original Creole (that is, Jamaican Creole). Strictly speaking—in linguistic and political terms—we really cannot make reference to a Limón Creole until the inception of this period of massive social transformation.

4. The use of the infinitive form of the Spanish verb—*hablar* in this case— instead of the appropriate conjugated form frequently occurs among Afro-Costa Ricans whose competence in Spanish is not well developed.

CHAPTER EIGHT. COLOR AS SOCIOECONOMIC VALUE

1. The color categorizations used in Jamaica to classify individuals and allocate honor and prestige were apparently transplanted to Costa Rica during the plantation epoch. In that usage, the term *colored* refers to fair-skinned Jamaicans variously called "brown-man," "red-man," "high-colored," or even "red-niega." For more on this and its role in stratification see Brathwaite (1971),

Henriques (1953), and M. G. Smith (1965a).

In Costa Rica today, Blacks, especially those of the first- and second-generation, refer to themselves as Coloreds. Most third-generation individuals, certainly those of the fourth- generation, and some of the second, prefer to be called Blacks. When speaking Spanish, however, Blacks use the term *negro* for people of dark complexion, and *moreno* (meaning brown-skinned) for those of lighter skin. Occasionally Blacks refer to themselves as Antillanos or Jamaicanos, both fairly neutral terms also used by Hispanics.

Some Hispanics, on the other hand, use *moreno* to refer to Blacks in general, as they believe *negro* is offensive. Other Hispanics continue to use the term *negro*, which today carries the connotation of being darker and of lower social status. There is a small minority of Blacks who prefer to refer to themselves publicly as "Spanish." It is an expression of nationalism.

Both Hispanics and Blacks use the term *mulatto* to refer to individuals of mixed Hispanic-Black parentage. The term *mestizo* is used in its usual sense to refer to people of mixed Native American and Hispanic descent. Mestizo is rarely used among Blacks; they simply refer to this group in the same way they refer to Hispanics, as *los blancos* (whites), Spanish, Spaniard, or *latinos*.

2. With respect to the relationship between color and social inequality, the literature, though not always based on sound scientific footing, is abundant. Some notable works on the Caribbean are Henriques (1953), Hoetink (1967), M. G. Smith (1965 a & b, 1969, 1984), R. T. Smith (1970), Braithwaite (1960), Harris (1964), Brathwaite (1971), and Nettleford (1978).

3. Such statements do not refer to Black skin in particular but to both skin and culture. All such statements I have heard were by "clear-skinned" individuals, although the little boy who made the statement about Blacks being ugly has a jet-black sister and mother. Spanish is mostly spoken at home, so there it is perhaps through the language that children seem to identify themselves with Hispanics rather than Blacks.

CHAPTER NINE. KINSHIP, VALUES, AND SOCIAL MOBILITY

1. The literature on West Indian family structure has been reviewed in several places. The most comprehensive of them is Price's (1970) review. Some of the other relevant works that include reviews are Davenport (1961), Kunstadter (1963), M. G. Smith (1973), Staples (1971), Gonzales (1969), Marks (1976), and R. T. Smith (1988).

2. The information here is based mainly on oral accounts gathered in the field and from discussions with Kathleen Sawyers-Royal, an Afro-Costa Rican linguist. Some information on initial arrivals came from Melendez and Duncan (1977). In a very general way the passage is also informed by other written historical sources mentioned in Chapter 2.

3. No figures are available on the sex ratio of workers in the United Fruit Company plantations.

4. According to the Spanish naming system in Costa Rica, the father's family name follows the child's name, and this is followed by the mother's maiden name. If the mother is not married, or for some other reason does not want to use the father's name (or cannot), only her maiden name follows the child's name. The catch is that her maiden name is doubled; for example, if she has a son whom she names Juan, and her maiden name is Bennett, she would have to register that son as Juan Bennett Bennett—at least that is how the clerks at the registrar's office would register the birth. Consequently, an "illegitimate" child is easily spotted.

5. The use of household as a unit of analysis here is not intended as a suggestion that it alone can explain the significant aspects of kinship relations. It is used only to support the point that certain aspects of adjustment are reflected in the form the household takes. Also, I am no longer comfortable with the category *Household Head*, because it implies a hierarchy that does not always exist. It does, however, reflect in a very general way the situation I describe.

6. The term *cross*, pronounced "crass," is used by Jamaicans and descendants of Jamaican migrants in Costa Rica to refer to individuals who are tough, outspoken, chafing, single-minded disciplinarians. Since blind obedience and discipline were highly valued in the plantation system, today these qualities are usually found among those who are highly respected in the community. As such, the term connotes aggressive refinement. As used by Jamaicans, the term carries a mere shade of the British usage, meaning angry.

7. My colleague, Dr. Monica Gordon, related a number of instances in Jamaica and in New York where autocratic fathers have attempted to "put out" pregnant daughters but were prevented by the mother. In one instance a mother asked "where do you expect her to go," and in another the mother threatened to pay for a place for the pregnant daughter if she were expelled.

CHAPTER TEN. OVERVIEW: THE BLACK EXPERIENCE IN COSTA RICA

1. The concept of "pragmatic flexibility" is credited to Charles Carnegie (1983), who developed the idea from his research on informal marketing strategies in the West Indies.

2. This information and analysis came, for the most part, from a discussion with Señora Joyce Sawyers-Royal, a teacher and community leader in Puerto Limón. The view was corroborated by other individuals.

REFERENCES

Abrahams, Roger, and John Szwed, eds. 1983. *After Africa*. New Haven: Yale University Press.

Allen, Sheila, and Christopher Smith. 1974. Race and ethnicity in class formation: A comparison of Asian and West Indian workers. In *The social analysis of class structure*, edited by Frank Parkin, 39–53. London: Tavistock.

Alleyne, Mervyn. 1984. The worldview of Jamaicans. *Jamaica Journal* 17(1):2–8

———. 1989. *Roots of Jamaican culture*. London: Pluto Press.

Augelli, John P. 1962. The rimland-mainland concept of culture areas in Middle America. *Annals of the Association of American Geographers* 52(2).

Austin, Diane J. 1983. Culture and ideology in the English-speaking Caribbean: A view from Jamaica. *American Ethnologist* 10(2):223–40.

———. 1984. *Urban life in Kingston, Jamaica: The culture and class ideology of two neighborhoods*. New York: Gordon and Breach.

Barth, Fredrik. 1966. Models of social organization. Royal Anthropological Institute of Great Britain and Ireland, Occasional Paper 23.

Beckford, George. 1972. *Persistent poverty: Underdevelopment in plantation economies of the Third World*. New York: Oxford University Press.

Beckwith, Martha. 1923. Some religious cults in Jamaica. *American Journal of Psychology* 34(1):32–45.

Bell, John Patrick. 1971. *Crisis in Costa Rica: The 1940 revolution*. Austin: Institute of Latin American Studies, University of Texas Press.

Bendix, Reinhard. 1970. Tradition and modernity reconsidered. In *Essays in comparative social stratification*, edited by L. Plotnicov and A. Tuden, 273–338. Pittsburgh: University of Pittsburgh Press.

Berry, Brian J.L., and William L. Garrison. 1958. Recent developments of central place theory. *Regional Science Association* 43:380–402.

Best, Lloyd. 1968. Outlines of model of pure plantation economy. *Social and Economic Studies* 17(3):283–326.

Biesanz, John, and Mavis Biesanz. 1945. *Costa Rican life*. New York: Columbia University Press.

Biesanz, Richard, K. Z. Biesanz, and M. H. Biesanz. 1982. *The Costa Ricans*. Englewood Cliffs, NJ: Prentice Hall.

Blau, P. M. 1964. *Exchange and power in social life*. New York: Wiley.

Bloch, Maurice. 1977. *Political language and oratory in traditional society*. London: Academic Press.

Blom, Frans. 1935. Commerce trade and monetary units of the Maya. In *Annual Report of the Board of Regents of the Smithsonian Institution*.Washington, D.C.: U.S. Government Printing Office.

Bourgois, Philippe I. 1985. *Ethnic diversity on a corporate plantation: The United Fruit Company in Bocas Del Toro, Panama and Talamaca, Costa Rica*. Ann Arbor: University Microfilms.

Bourdieu, Pierre. 1977. *Outline of a theory of practice*. New York and London: Cambridge University Press.

Bourdieu, Pierre, and Jean-Claude Passeron. 1977. *Production: In education, society and culture*. Sage studies in social and educational change, no. 5. Beverly Hills, CA: Sage.

Bourgois, Phillippe I. 1989. *Ethnicity at work: Divided Labor on a Central American banana plantation*. Baltimore: The Johns Hopkins University Press.

Bourguignon, Erika. 1952. Class structure and acculturation in Haiti. *The Ohio Journal of Science* 52:317–20.

Bowen, Elenore Smith. 1964. *Return to laughter: An anthropological novel*. New York: The Museum of Natural History and Doubleday.

Bozolli de Wille, Maria E. 1972. Resumen de la obra de Roy Simon Bryce-Laporte, Social Relations. . . In *El Negro in Costa Rica*, edited by Carlos Melendez and Quince Dunncan, 215–31. San José: Editorial Costa Rica.

Braithwaite, Lloyd. 1953. Social stratification in Trinidad. *Social and Economic Studies* 2:5–175.

———. 1960. Social stratification and cultural pluralism. In *Social and cultural pluralism in the Caribbean*, edited by V. Rubin. *Annals of the New York Academy of Sciences* 83:816–31.

Brathwaite, Edward. 1971. *The development of Creole society in Jamaica, 1770–1820*. Oxford: Clarendon Press.

———. 1979. Kumina—The spirit of African survival. *Jamaica Journal* 42:44–63.

Brush, John E. 1953. The hierarchy of central places in Southwestern Wisconsin. *The American Geographical Society* 43:380–402.

Bryce-Laporte, Roy S. 1962. Social relations and cultural persistence (or change) among Jamaicans in a rural area of Costa Rica. Thesis for advanced certificate in Caribbean Studies, University of Puerto Rico.

———. 1967. M. G. Smith's version of pluralism—the questions it raises. *Comparative Studies in Society and History* 10:114–20.

———. 1973. Family, household, and intergenerational relations in a "Jamican" village in Limón, Costa Rica. In *The family in the Caribbean*, 65–94. Rio Piedras: Institute of Caribbean Studies, University of Puerto Rico.

———. 1980. *Sourcebook on the new immigration*. New Brunswick, NJ: Transaction Books.

Bryce-Laporte, R.S., and Trevor Purcell. 1982. A lesser-known chapter of the African diaspora: West Indians in Costa Rica, Central America. In *Global dimensions of the African diaspora*, edited by Joseph E. Harris, 219–39. Washington, D.C.: Howard University Press.

Campbell, Mavis C. 1992. The long night of slavery (the NACLA Report). *Report on the Americas* 25(4):38–39.

Cancian, Frank. 1976. Social stratification. *Annual Review of Anthropology* 5:227–58.

Carnegie, Charles V. 1983. Strategic flexibility in the West Indies. *Caribbean Review* 11:11–13.

Casassas Simo, Montserrat, and Rodolfo E. Osorio Ponce. 1977. Projecto "Capacitacion familiar y laboral de la mujer Limonense": Dianostico de Limón. Unpublished mimeo.

Casey, Jeffrey. 1979. Limón: 1880–1940. *Un estudio de la industria bananera en Costa Rica*. San Jose: Editorial Costa Rica.

Christaller, Rev. J.G. 1964[1875]. *A grammar of the Asante and Fante language called Tshi*. London: Greg Press.

Chomsky, Noam. 1989. *Necessary illusions: Thought control in democratic societies*. Boston: South End Press.

Conniff, Michael L. 1985. *Black labor on a white canal: Panama, 1904–1981*. Pittsburgh, University of Pittsburgh Press.

Conway, Fredrick. 1978. Pentecostalism in the context of religion and health practice in Haiti. Ph.D. dissertation, American University, Washington, D. C.

Costa Rica Ministerio de Culture, Juventud y Deportes. 1977. *La Costa Rica del ano 2000*. San José, Costa Rica: Author.

Cross, Malcolm. 1977. On conflict, race relations and the theory of plural society. In *Race, ethnicity and social change*, edited by John Stone. North Scituate, MA: Duxbury Press.

Davenport, William. 1961. The family system of Jamaica. *Social and Economic Studies* 10(4):420–54.

Denton, Charles F. 1971. *Patterns of Costa Rican politics*. Boston: Allyn and Bacon.

Despres, Leo A. 1967. *Cultural pluralism and nationalist politics in British Guyana*. Chicago: Rand McNally.

———. 1968. Anthropological theory, cultural pluralism, and the study of complex societies. *Current Anthropology* 9:3–24.

Direccion General de Estadistica y Censos. 1963. *Censo de poblacion de Costa Rica*. San Jose: Ministerio de 1973 Economia, Industria y Comercio.

DuBois, W.E.B. 1969. *The souls of Black folk* [original work published 1903]. New York: Times-Mirror.

Duncan, Quince. 1972. New Sligoville: 10 años despues. In *El Negro en Costa*

Rica, edited by Carlos Melendez and Quince Duncan. San José: Editorial Costa Rica.

———. 1975. *El Negro en la literatura Costaricense.* San José: Editorial Costa Rica.

Dzidzienyo, Anani, and Lourdes Casal. 1979. *The position of Blacks in Brazilian and Cuban society* (Paper no. 7). London: Minority Rights Group.

Edelman, Marc, and Joanna Kenen. 1989. Editors' introduction. In *The Costa Rican reader,* edited by M. Edelman and J. Kenen, 187–93. New York: Grove Weidenfeld.

El Equipo Cornell-Costa Rica. 1973. *El potencial de los recursos naturales para el desarrolla regional de la provincia de Limon: Un survey preliminar.* Ithaca, NY: Cornell University. Mimeo.

Elster, Jon. 1985. *Making sense of Marx.* New York: Cambridge University Press.

Engels, Frederick. 1976 [1894]. *Anti-Duhring (Herr Eugen Duhring's revolution in science).* Peking: Foreign Languages Press.

Evans, Roberto. 1978. "La iglesia en el desarrollo cultural del Negro." Speech given at the First Conference on the Situation of Blacks in Costa Rica, San Jose.

Facio Brenes, Rodrigo. 1942. *Estudio de economia Costaricense.* San José: Editorial Zurco.

Fallas, Carlos. 1975. *Mamita yunai.* San José: Lehman S.A.

Fernandez, M. E., A. Schmidt, and V. Basauri. 1976. *La poblacion de Costa Rica.* San Jose: Instituto de Investigaciones Sociales de la   Universidad de Costa Rica.

Fischer, Michael M.J. 1974. Value assertions and stratification: Religion and marriage in rural Jamaica. *Caribbean Studies* 14(1).

Foner, Laura, and Eugene D. Genovese, eds. 1969. *Slavery in the New World: A reader in comparative history.* Englewood Cliffs, NJ: Prentice-Hall.

Fontaine, Pierre-Michel. 1985. *Race, class, and power in Brazil.* Los Angeles: UCLA CAAS Publications.

Geertz, Clifford. 1973. Ideology as a cultural system. In *The interpretation of cultures,* edited by Clifford Geertz, 393–433. New York: Basic Books.

Genovese, Eugene D. 1969. Materialism and idealism in the history of Negro slavery in the Americas. In *Slavery in the New World: A reader in comparative history,* edited by Laura Foner and Eugene D. Genevose, 238–55. Englewood Cliffs, NJ: Prentice Hall.

Gledhill, Sabrina. 1988. The Latin model of race relations. In *Castro, the Blacks, and Africa,* by Carlos Moore. Los Angeles: UCLA CAAS Publications.

Gonzalez, Nancie Solien. 1969. *Black Carib household structure: A study of migration and modernization.* Seattle: University of Washington Press.

———. 1988. *Sojourners of the Caribbean: Ethnogenesis and ethnohistory of the*

Garifuna. Urbana: University of Illinois Press.

Gordon, Edmund T. 1987. History, identity, consciousness, and revolution: Afro-Nicaraguans and the Nicaraguan revolution. In *Ethnic groups and the nation state: The case of the Atlantic Coast in Nicaragua*, edited by the CIDCA/Development Study Unit, 1135–70. Stockholm: University of Stockholm.

Gouldner, A. 1960. The norm of reciprocity: A preliminary statement. *American Sociological Review* 25:161–78.

Gray, L. C. 1941. *History of agriculture in the southern United States to 1860*. New York: Smith.

Greaves, Ida. 1968. *Modern production among backward peoples*. New York: Augustus M. Kelly.

Habermas, Jurgen. 1984. *The theory of communicative action. Vol. 1, Reason and the rationalization of society*. Boston: Beacon Press.

Hamilton, Ruth Simms, and Lorein Powell-Bernard. 1990. African identity: Lost or denied? The case of La Mansion, Costa Rica. *Coñexoes* 2(1):1–2.

Harris, Marvin. 1964. *Patterns of race in the Americas*. New York: Walker.

Haviland, John B. 1977. *Gossip, reputation, and knowledge in Zinacantan*. Chicago: University of Chicago Press.

Headley Mullings, Ana Maria. 1983. Algunas caracteristicas de la familia negra en la cuidad de Limón basada en una comparacion con la familia blanca. Master's (Licenciada's) thesis, Facultad de Ciencias Sociales, Universidad de Costa Rica.

Heidegger, Martin. 1962. *Being and time*. New York: Harper and Row.

Helms, Mary W. 1977. Negro or Indian: The changing identity of a frontier population. In *Old roots in new lands: Historical and anthropological perspectives on Black experiences in the Americas*, edited by Ann M. Pescatello, 157–72. Westport, Conn.: Greenwood Press.

Henriques, Fernando. 1953. *Family and color in Jamaica*. London: Eyre and Spottiswoode.

Herskovits, Melville J. 1937. *Life in a Haitian valley*. New York: Alfred A. Knopf.

Herskovits, Melville J., and Frances S. Herskovits. 1947. *Trinidad village*. New York: Alfred A. Knopf.

Herzfeld, Anita. 1978. Tense and aspect in Limón Creole: A sociolinguistic view towards a Creole continuum. Ph.D. dissertation, University of Kansas.

Hill, George. 1964. The agrarian reform in Costa Rica. *Land Economics* 40:41–48.

Hoetink, Harry. 1967. *The two variants in Caribbean race relations*. London: Oxford University Press.

———. 1973. *Slavery and race relations in the Americas: Comparative notes on their nature and nexus.* New York: Harper & Row.

Hogg, Donald William. 1960. The convince cult in Jamaica. In *Papers in Caribbean anthropology,* edited by Sidney W. Mintz. New Haven: Yale University Publications in Anthropology.

Inter-American Development Bank. 1978. *Economic and social pogress in Latin America.* Washington, D.C.

International Bureau of American Republics. 1909. *Report.* Washington, D.C.

Jain, Ravindra. 1970. *South Indians on the plantation frontier in Malaya.* New Haven: Yale University Press.

Jayawardena, Chandra. 1963. *Conflict and solidarity in a Guianaese plantation.* London: Athlone Press.

———. 1968. Ideology and conflict in lower class communities. *Comparative Studies in Society and History* 10:413–46.

Jimenez, Luis Barahona. 1979. *El pensamiento politico en Costa Rica.* San José: Editorial Fernandez Arce.

Jones, Chester Lloyd. 1935. *Costa Rica and colonization in the Caribbean.* Madison: University of Wisconsin Press.

Joseph, Guillermo. 1982. Area de extension sobre la problematica del Negro en Costa Rica: Temas para un debate y un analisis historico-cultural. Mimeo.

Keesing, Roger. 1979. Linguistic knowledge and cultural knowledge: Some doubts and speculations. *American Anthropologist* 81(March):1–28.

Keita, L. 1979. The African philosophical tradition. In *African philosophy: An introduction,* edited by Richard Wright. Washington, D.C.: University Press of America.

Kepner, Charles D. 1936. *Social aspects of the banana empire.* New York: Columbia University Press.

Kepner, Charles D., and Jay H. Soothill. 1935. *The banana empire: A case study of economic imperialism.* New York: Vanguard Press.

Kerr, Madeline. 1963 [1952]. *Personality and conflict in Jamaica.* London: Collins; Jamaica: Angster's Book Stores.

Knight, Franklin W. 1970. *Slave society in Cuba during the nineteenth century.* Madison: University of Wisconsin Press.

———. 1974. *The African dimension in Latin American societies.* New York: Macmillan.

Koch, C. W. 1977. Jamaican Blacks and the descendants in Costa Rica. Unpublished paper, University of Omaha.

Kunstadter, Peter. 1963. A survey of the consanguine or matrifocal family. *American Anthropologist* 65:56–66.

Kuper, Leo. 1970. Stratification in plural societies: Focus on white settler societies in Africa. In *Essays in comparative social stratification,* edited by Leonard Plotnicov and Arthur Tuden, 77–93. Pittsburgh: University of

Pittsburgh Press.

LaFeber, Walter. 1983. *Inevitable revolutions: The United States in Central America*. New York: W. W. Norton.

Leons, Madeline Barabara, and William. 1977. The utility of pluralism: M. G. Smith and plural theory. *American Ethnologist* 4:559–75.

Levi-Strauss, Claude. 1985. *The view from afar*, translated by Joachim Neugroschel and Phoebe Hoss. New York: Basic Books.

Lowenthal, David. 1961. Caribbean views of Caribbean land. *Canadian Geographer* 5(2):1–8.

———. 1972. *West Indian societies*. New York: Oxford University Press.

Marks, A. F. 1976. *Males and females and the Afro-Curacaoan household*. The Hague: Nijhoff.

Marx, Karl, and Frederick Engels. 1970. *The German ideology*. New York: International Publishers.

Mbiti, John S. 1970. *African religions and philosophy*. Garden City, NY: Doubleday.

McCann, Thomas. 1976. *An American company: The tragedy of United Fruit*. New York: Crown.

Melendez, Carlos. 1977. *Costa Rica: Tierra y poblamienta en la colonia*. San José: Editorial Costa Rica.

Melendez, Carlos, and Quince Duncan. 1977 [1974]. *El Negro en Costa Rica*. San José: Editorial Costa Rica.

Mergener, John W. 1965. A study of the political patterns of behavior of the Chinese, White and Negro in Puerto Limón, Costa Rica. Associated Colleges of the Midwest Central American Field Program. Mimeo.

Mintz, Sidney. 1956. Canamelar: The sub-culture of a rural sugar plantation proletariat. In *The people of Puerto Rico*, edited by J. H. Steward et al., 314–417. Urbana: University of Illinois Press.

———. 1959. The plantation as a socio-cultural type. In *Plantation systems in the New World*. Washington: Pan American Union Social Science. Monograph.

———. 1960. *Worker in the cane*. New Haven: Yale University Press.

———. 1966. Review of the plural society in the British West Indies M. G. Smith. *American Anthropologist* 68:1045–47.

———. 1971. Groups, group boundaries and the perception of "race." *Comparative Studies in Society and History* 13(4):437–50.

———. 1974. *Caribbean transformations*. Chicago: Aldine.

Mintz, Sidney W., and Richard Price. 1976. *An anthropological approach to the Afro-American past: A Caribbean perspective*. Philadelphia: Institute for the Study of Human Issues, Occasional Papers in Social Change, no. 2.

Mintz, Sidney W., and Eric R. Wolf. 1950. An anlaysis of ritual co-parenthood (compadrazgo). *Southwestern Journal of Anthropology* 6(4):341–68.

Moore, Carlos. 1988. *Castro, the Blacks, and Africa*. Los Angeles: UCLA CAAS Publications.

Moynihan, Daniel P. 1965. *The Negro family: The case for national action*. Washington, D.C.: Office of Policy Planning and Research, U.S. Department of Labor.

Naipaul, V. S. 1969. *A flag on the island*. Harmondsworth, England: Penguin.

Nash, Manning. 1989. *The cauldron of ethnicity in the modern world*. Chicago: University of Chicago Press.

Nettleford, Rex M. 1973. National identity and attitudes to race in Jamaica. In *Consequences of class and color: West Indian perspectives*, edited by David Lowenthal and Lambros Comitas, 35–56. New York, Anchor Books.

———. 1978. *Caribbean cultural identity: The case of Jamaica*. Los Angeles: UCLA CAAS Publications.

———. 1986. Definition and development: The need for Caribbean creativity. *Caribbean Review* 14(3):7–10.

OFIPLAN (Officina de Planificacion). 1977. Diagnostica poblacion de la region Atlantica. San Jose: Author. Mimeo.

Olien, Michael. 1967 [1976]. The Negro in Costa Rica: The ethnohistory of an ethnic minority in a complex society. Ph.D. dissertation, University of Oregon.

———. 1977. The adaptation of West Indian Blacks to North America and Hispanic culture in Costa Rica. In *Old roots in new lands*, edited by Ann Pescatello, 132–56. Westport, CT: Greenwood.

Ossowski, Stanislaw. 1963. *Class structure in the social consciousness*. New York: Free Press.

Paine, Robert. 1974. *Second thoughts about Barth's models* (Occasional Paper no. 23). London: Royal Anthropological Institute of Great Britain and Ireland.

Palmer, Colin. 1976. *Slaves of the white god: Blacks in Mexico, 1570–1650*. Cambridge, Mass.: Harvard University Press.

Palmer, Paula. 1977. *What happen; a folk-history of Costa Rica's Talamanca coast*. San Jose: Ecodesarrollos.

Parkin, Frank. 1979. *Marxism and class theory: A bourgeois critique*. New York: Columbia University Press.

Parsons, James. 1954. English-speaking settlements of the Western Caribbean. *Yearbook of the Association of Pacific Coast Geographers* 16:3–13.

Price, Richard. 1970. Saramaka emigration and marriage: A case study of social change. *Southwestern Journal of Anthropology* 26:157–89.

———. 1975. *Saramak social structure: Analysis of a maroon society in Surinam*. Rio Piedras: University of Puerto Rico.

Purcell, Trevor. 1988. Modern maroons: Economy and cultural survival in a Jamaican peasant village in Costa Rica. In *Afro-American villages in historical perspective*, edited by Charles Carnegie, 45–62. Kingston: Institute of Jamaica.

Purcell, Trevor, and Kathleen Sawyers. 1993. Democracy and ethnic conflict: Blacks in Costa Rica. *Ethnic and Racial Studies*, vol. 16, no. 2.

Reisman, Karl. 1970. Cultural and linguistic ambiguity in a West Indian village. In *Afro-American anthropology: Contemporary perspectives*, edited by Norman E. Whitten and John Szwed, 129–44. New York: Free Press.

Rodman, Hyman. 1971. *Lower class families: The culture of poverty in Negro Trinidad*. New York: Oxford University Press.

Rout, Leslie B. 1976. *The African experience in Spanish America, 1502 to present day*. New York: Cambridge University Press.

Ryman, Cheryl. 1979. The Jamaica heritage in dance. *Jamaica Journal* 44:2–13.

Sawyers Royal, Kathleen. 1972. Participacion politica del Negro Limonense. In *El Negro en Costa Rica*, edited by Carlos Melendez and Quince Duncan. San José: Editorial Costa Rica.

———. 1977. Participacion politica del Negro Limonense: Un esbozo historico. In *El Negro en Costa Rica*, edited by Carlos Melendez and Quince Duncan, 218–28. San José: Editorial Costa Rica.

Silverman, Marilyn. 1979. Dependency, mediation and class formation in rural Guyana. *American Ethnologist* 6(3):466–90.

Silverman, Sydel F. 1966. An ethnographic approach to social stratification: Prestige in an Italian community. *American Anthropologist* 68:899–921.

Simey, T. S. 1946. *Welfare and planning in the West Indies*. Oxford: Clarendon Press.

Simpson, George Eaton. 1950. The acculturative in Jamaican revivalism. In *Men and cultures: Selected papers of the Fifth International Congress of Anthropological and Ethnological Sciences*, edited by Anthony F.C. Wallace, 332–41. Philadelphia: University of Pennsylvania Press.

Smith, M. G. 1953. Some aspects of social structure in the British Caribbean about 1820. *Social and Economic Studies* 1(4):57–79.

———. 1960. Education and occupational choice in rural Jamaica. *Social and Economic Studies* 9(3):332–54.

———. 1962. *West Indian family structure*. Seattle: University of Washington Press.

———. 1965a. *The plural society in the British West Indies*. Berkeley: University of California Press.

———. 1965b. *Social stratification in Grenada*. Berkeley: University of California Press.

———. 1969. Institutional and political conditions of pluralism. In *Pluralism in Africa*, edited by L. Kuper and M. G. Smith, 27–65. Berkeley: University of California Press.

———. 1973. A survey of West Indian family studies. In *Work and family life*, edited by David Lowenthal and Lambros Comitas. New York: Doubleday Anchor.

———. 1984. *Culture, race, and class in the Commonwealth Caribbean.* Mona, Jamaica: Department of Extra-Mural Studies, University of the West Indies.

Smith, R. T. 1956. *The Negro family in British Guiana: Family structure and social status in the villages.* London: Routledge and Kegan Paul.

———. 1970. Social stratification in the Caribbean. In *Essays in comparative social stratification*, edited by L. Plotnicov and A. Tuden, 43–76. Pittsburgh: University of Pittsburgh Press.

———. 1973. The matrifocal family. In *The character of kinship*, edited by Jack Goody, 121–44. England: Cambridge University Press.

———. 1982. Family, social change and social policy in the West Indies. *Nieuwe West-Indische Gids* 56(3&4):111–42.

———. 1988. *Kinship and class in the West Indies: A genealogical study of Guyana and Jamaica.* New York: Cambridge University Press.

Sojo, Ana. 1984. *Estado empresario y lucha politica en Costa Rica.* San José: Editorial Universitaria Centroamericana.

Staples, Robert. 1971. Towards a sociology of the Black family: A theoretical and methodological assessment. *Journal of Marriage and the Family* 33:119–38

Stewart, Watt. 1964. *Keith and Costa Rica.* Albuquerque: University of New Mexico Press.

Stone, S. 1975. *La dinastia de los conquistadores: La crisis del poder en La Costa Rica contemporanea.* San José: Editorial Universitaria Centroamericana.

Trouillot, Michel-Rolph. 1984. Caribbean peasantries and world capitalism: An approach to micro-level studies. *Nieuwe West-Indische Gids* 58 (142):37–59.

———. 1992. The Caribbean region: An open frontier in anthropological theory. *Annual Review of Anthropology* 21:19–42.

U.S. Census Bureau. 1986. Household wealth and asset ownership: 1984. Washington, D.C.

Van Den Berghe, Pierre L. 1973. Pluralism. In *Handbook of social and cultural anthropology*, edited by John Honigman, 959–72. Chicago: Rand McNally.

Villasuso Etomba, Juan Manuel. 1989. The impact of the economic crisis on income distribution. In *The Costa Rican reader*, edited by Marc Edelman and Joanne Kenen, 197–204. New York: Grove Weidenfeld.

Wallerstein, Emmanuel. 1979. *The capitalist world-economy.* London and New York, Cambridge University Press.

Weber, Max. 1978. *Economy and society*, Vol. 1., edited by Guenther Roth and Claus Wittich. Berkeley: University of California Press.

Whitten, Norman E., Jr., and Arlene Torres. 1992. Blackness in the Americas (the NACLA Report). *Report on the Americas* 25(4):16–22.

Wilk, Richard, and Mac Chapin. 1990. Ethnic minorities in Beleze: Mopan, Kekchi and Garifuna. In *SPEAR Reports* I. Mexico: Cubola Productions.

Wilson, Peter. 1969. Reputation and respectability: A suggestion for Caribbean ethnology. *Man* 4:70–84.

———. 1973. *Crab antics: The social anthropology of English-speaking Negro societies of the Caribbean.* New Haven and London, Yale University Press.

Wolf, Eric R. 1957. Closed corporate communities in Meso-America and Central Java. *Southern Journal of Anthropology* 13(1):1–8.

———. 1975. Review of Horizon Trajets Marxistes en Anthropologie, by Maurice Godelier. *Dialectical Anthropology* 1:99–108.

———. 1982. *Europe and the people without history.* Berkeley: University of California Press.

Wolf, Eric, and Sidney W. Mintz. 1957. Haciendas and plantations in Middle America and the Antilles. *Social and Economic Studies* 6:380–412.

Woollard, Diana. 1978. Background to the learning of English in St. Mark's School, Limón, Costa Rica. Unpublished paper, University of York.

———. 1979. Approaches to language in Limón, Costa Rica: With particular regard to the teaching of English to Limón Creole speakers, especially at primary level. Unpublished paper, University of York.

Worsley, Peter. 1984. *The three worlds: Culture and world development.* Chicago: University of Chicago Press.

Wright-Murray, F. 1974. Limón Creole: A syntactic analysis. Ph.D. thesis, La Universidad de Costa Rica.

INDEX

ABOUT THE AUTHOR

Trevor W. Purcell is currently an assistant professor in the African Studies and Anthropology Departments of the University of South Florida, Tampa, where he teaches courses in economic anthropology, African-American studies, and Caribbean studies. He earned his Ph.D. in social anthropology from The Johns Hopkins University in 1982. Currently he is completing research on the potential role of Caribbean indigenous knowledge in socioeconomic development and is a regular contributor to such journals as *Caribbean Quarterly*. His most recent article on democracy and ethnic conflict in Costa Rica was published by Ethnic and Racial Studies, London School of Economics.